Best in the Game

The Turbulent Story of the Pittsburgh Penguins'
Rise to Stanley Cup Champions

Dave Molinari

Foreword by Kevin Stevens

SAGAMORE PUBLISHING
Champaign, Illinois 61820

©1993 Sagamore Publishing

Production supervision
  and book design: Susan M. Williams
Cover and photo insert design: Michelle R. Dressen
All photos: Bruce Bennett Studios
Proofreaders: Brian J. Moore, Phyllis L. Bannon

Library of Congress Catalog Card Number:92-82548
ISBN: 0-915611-66-x

Printed in the United States of America.

To Debbie, whose love, patience, and understanding mean so very much. And whose own work in progress as this book was being written turned out to be an absolute masterpiece. And to that masterpiece, Kelsey Lynn.

CONTENTS

ACKNOWLEDGMENTS

This book would not have been possible without the efforts of countless people, to whom the author is deeply indebted. They include:

The staff and players of the Pittsburgh Penguins, for putting together two triumphant and memorable seasons that will live in hockey history long after these pages have yellowed. They've done something many people in Pittsburgh and around the hockey world thought would never happen. And they've done it twice.

The good folks at Sagamore Publishing, for giving me the opportunity to write this book. And particular thanks go to Peter Bannon and Michelle Dressen, for their courageous service on the front lines of my long and often ugly battle to become computer literate. Their efforts made it possible for me to survive a whole series of Mac Attacks.

My editors at the *Pittsburgh Press*, for giving their permission to take on this project. And my co-workers, especially Bill Modoono, whose assistance has been so invaluable during my years on the hockey beat.

My colleagues, past and present, in the hockey writing profession, some of the most dedicated and intrepid people in the newspaper industry. I have learned so much from so many.

Kevin Stevens and Mike Lange, for their outstanding contributions to this work. Both have been widely recognized for the exceptional way they do their jobs and, while it's true they are world-class professionals, both rate even higher as people.

Finally, and most importantly, my family. Words cannot convey my gratitude to my brothers, Ralph and Donald, for always being there when I've needed them. To my late father, Milan, for setting standards of dignity and manhood I will spend a lifetime trying to reach. And especially to my mother, Ethel, who brought me into the world and has been there with love, support, and guidance every step of the way since.

FOREWORD

Our team might have experienced as many highs and lows during the 1991-92 season as any group of athletes in the history of professional sports. We won our second Stanley Cup in a row, but we had to overcome some incredible adversity along the way.

The most difficult setback to deal with was the death of our coach, Bob Johnson. He made our first Stanley Cup possible by teaching us how to win, how to stick together through good times and bad. He was only with us for one year, but it seemed like 10. Whenever you lose a friend like Badger Bob, it's tough, and Bob Johnson was a friend to everybody. Any other problem, you can get by, you can work it out, but you can't bring back a man who has passed away. And Bob was a man none of us will ever forget.

We also had to cope with the sale of our franchise, with speculation that the new owners would sell off some of our teammates, with the big trade that took away two players from the core of our team, Mark Recchi and Paul Coffey. But through the whole thing, our team stayed pretty focused, even though there were times in the middle of the season when we were losing games and weren't playing that well. In the middle of the year, we'd win one game, lose two, win one, lose two. We were losing a lot more than we wanted to, and there were times when I'd be driving home with my wife, Suzanne, after a game, and I didn't really know if we could win the championship again.

Still, we stuck together and hung in there. We always felt we were going to get that little lift that would put us on a good run. Losing to Hartford 8-4 at home in late February was the low point of the season for us. We definitely hit rock-bottom then, in fourth place with the New York Islanders just a point behind us. Everybody kept their cool and we all pulled together, but it wasn't easy. When you're not winning, nothing is easy.

The guys had a team meeting around that time, and we talked about how embarrassing it would be to win the Stanley

Cup one year, then not make the playoffs the next. After that, we lifted our game to another level, and the next thing we knew, we were 10 or 11 points ahead of New York.

There wasn't any one individual who helped to guide us through those difficult times. We had four or five real strong individuals, like Bryan Trottier, and Mario Lemieux, and Ron Francis, and everybody kind of learned from them.

Everybody says you can't turn it on and off, but I knew our team could play well and beat anybody when we were on our game. I said at the beginning of the year that we could beat anybody in a seven-game series; we just had to get into the playoffs. Players of the caliber that we have are the kind who want to play well in the playoffs, whose quality of play rises when the stakes get higher. That's when we want to shine, and that's what we've been able to do.

When we got into the playoffs, I felt Washington was going to be our toughest competition. After we fell behind 3-1 in the series, and then came back to win it, I was sure we could win another Cup.

When we played the New York Rangers during the next round, it was just incredible the way our team pulled together, with different guys stepping up to carry the load after Mario and Joey Mullen were hurt in the second game. Looking back, it's hard to believe we were able to do what we did against that team.

Getting through the playoffs this time was even tougher than in 1991. The Patrick Division is by far the best in hockey, and we had to clear a lot of hurdles to win that second Cup. There's no guarantee we'll ever win a third Cup, because you need luck to win championships, but we have some great players and should be contenders as long as management keeps our team together. We'll be contenders for the next five years, maybe more.

Having this book written about us is great for the players, because you don't get a book written about you unless you've really done something special. And our team has done something very special after getting through some trying situations. Very few pro teams ever win back-to-back championships the way we have.

If anybody can tell the story of the Pittsburgh Penguins, it's Dave Molinari. He spends as much time with us as the players spend together, and he understands what we go through every day. He's been there with us through the good times and the bad times, and realizes what we had to overcome to do what we did.

But the story of our team doesn't necessarily end with winning our second Stanley Cup in Chicago Stadium. We all would like to add a few more chapters during the coming seasons.

— Kevin Stevens

CHAPTER ONE

The Top of the Mountain

May 28, 1991 was a steamy day in the Golden Triangle. The only thing higher than the temperature was the humidity. Unless you count the decibel level in Point State Park, hard by the confluence of the Monongahela and Allegheny rivers on the edge of downtown Pittsburgh.

For this was a hockey day in Pittsburgh, a day like no other in the history of the Pittsburgh Penguins. It was a day for civic celebration, a day to revel in the accomplishments of a team that had achieved so little during most of its existence. A day when the dismal past of the franchise seemed more distant than most fans ever thought it would. A day to cherish an impossible dream come true.

For 23 years, the Penguins had rewarded their followers with little more than heartbreak and frustration. They had never won a championship of any type, had made front-office moves that suggested a drunken monkey had been put in charge of the operation, and had consistently sat out the playoffs in a league in which postseason play is a given for most teams.

It was telling that, for more than two decades, the more memorable moments in franchise history had come in defeat. For example, in 1975, when the Penguins became only the second team in NHL history to lose a seven-game playoff series after winning the first three. Or in 1981, when the Penguins took St.

Louis to double-overtime in the final game of another playoff series before losing. Or in 1982, when they came within minutes of upsetting the defending Stanley Cup champion New York Islanders during the first round, only to lose the deciding game in overtime. Or in 1990, when they lost a playoff berth to the Islanders by giving up a goal in overtime of the final regular-season game against Buffalo.

But all those failures were forgotten on this afternoon, all the disappointments buried beneath an avalanche of affection for the Stanley Cup champions, the Penguins. Finally, the franchise could talk about being the best in the game, without fear that someone would giggle. Or laugh out loud. The team that had never won anything, the Pittsburgh Penguins, had claimed hockey's ultimate prize, the Stanley Cup, three days earlier with a final-round victory against the Minnesota North Stars.

The North Stars had been having a Cinderella playoff run of their own in the spring of 1991. By the time the Stanley Cup final rolled around, they were being widely described as a team of destiny, and they probably were. Except it turned out that their destiny was to have a Stephen King finale to their fairy-tale season. The Penguins proved to be Minnesota's worst nightmare, and the North Stars' dream of a championship was vaporized at the Met Center on May 25. Pittsburgh left the arena that night with an 8-0 victory and exclusive property rights to what coach Bob Johnson called "the top of the mountain."

How many people turned out for the victory rally in Point State Park might never be known. Some initial estimates were as high as 80,000, although others put the attendance at about half that.

What counts is that thousands of people stood elbow-to-elbow for more than an hour, cheering everyone on the stage, and relishing a triumph few ever believed they would experience. It was a day to be grateful, a day to be giddy. A day when there were enough Kodak moments to create a feature-length film.

The crowd obliged defenseman Larry Murphy, when he pulled out a camera and asked the fans to raise their index fingers en masse so he could have a photographic record of the day. They showed affection for every player, no matter how minor his role had been, and sent thunderous waves of adulation to their favorites. Like Mario Lemieux, the most valuable player in the playoffs and the cornerstone of this championship team, and Jaromir Jagr, the teen-aged rookie with a limited command of English, but hockey potential limited only by the imagination.

There was special fondness for players who had survived the darkest days of this franchise. For Bob Errey and Troy Loney and Phil Bourque, the guys who had endured the 38-point season in 1983-84, who had been at the bottom with the Penguins and were still around to reach the top. They had known the despair of losing ad nauseum, experienced too many seasons that were doomed to failure even before they began. Yet those players lasted long enough to enjoy the heady, intoxicating high produced by reaching the absolute peak of their profession.

Cup celebrations were nothing new to center Bryan Trottier — he had won four consecutive championships as a member of the New York Islanders in the early 1980s — but no one seemed to savor the moment more. Trottier hoisted the Cup over his head and, addressing the vibrant throng before him, howled, "Enjoy it, Pittsburgh. Enjoy it, baby."

Not that his impromptu spasm of exuberance surprised any of his teammates. Trottier's enthusiasm was as much a part of his game as the knowledge he had accrued over so many winters in the NHL. "He's more like a kid than anybody I've ever seen," Loney said. "He was more excited about this than almost anybody."

Most of what was said that day was quickly forgotten — how could the emotions of such a time be captured by mere words? — but Bourque summed up the prevailing sentiment quite nicely.

"What say we take this Cup down to the river," he said, "and party all summer." The crowd roared back its approval, which wasn't surprising because this party had been a long time coming. But it would be over sooner than anyone could have imagined.

CHAPTER TWO

A Terrible Day for Hockey

Bob Johnson thought he was having tooth trouble. Nothing unusual about that. It sometimes seemed he spent as much time at the dentist's office as he did at the Civic Arena during the 1990-91 season.

So when he didn't feel well during the flight from Saskatoon to Pittsburgh in late August, he figured his teeth were acting up again. After the plane landed, Johnson made a hasty visit to his dentist. The dentist could find nothing wrong, however, and advised Johnson that an extensive physical examination was in order. Johnson, at the dentist's behest, went to Mercy Hospital in Pittsburgh, made arrangements to undergo a thorough check-up the next day, then went to dinner with his wife, Martha.

If this was not the best of times for Bob Johnson, it was close. He was the coach of the defending Stanley Cup champions and had finally made it to the top of the mountain. And in less than two days, he would be coaching Team USA in its Canada Cup tournament opener against Sweden at the Civic Arena. That was a challenge that excited Johnson like few others, because he regarded the Canada Cup as "the finest pure hockey tournament in the world." Hockey, you see, was an addiction for Bob Johnson, and there was no fix like watching the greatest players in the world perform.

Hockey in the United States has had few champions like Bob Johnson, and Team USA was regarded as a legitimate contender for the tournament championship. A gold medal in the Canada Cup would be a satisfying addition to a resume that already included a Stanley Cup and three NCAA titles at the University of Wisconsin.

But the Canada Cup exhibition game Johnson coached in Saskatoon August 28 would be the final footnote of his extraordinary career. A few hours after leaving Mercy, Johnson was rushed back after apparently suffering a stroke during dinner.

Frightening as the early speculation about his ailment was, the reality was infinitely worse. Tests showed Johnson had developed multiple brain tumors, and the early evidence was that they were malignant. Paul Martha, the Penguins' general counsel, offered few specifics about the nature of Johnson's disease during a midday press conference August 30, but said flatly that "The prognosis is not good."

The news of Johnson's illness blindsided the North American hockey community. Johnson was only 60 years old, and was more vigorous and vital than men half his age. He radiated energy and enthusiasm, and his passion for the game — and life — was boundless. Johnson was grateful for every breath he drew, and determined to squeeze the most out of every waking second. And he usually succeeded.

The thought of him stricken by such an insidious disease conflicted with every image the hockey world had of Bob Johnson. "I saw him about a week and a half ago," Pittsburgh center Mario Lemieux said. "He was the same old Badger everybody knows. It's scary. Really sad."

Pittsburgh general manager Craig Patrick, Johnson's longtime friend and the man who had hired him little more than 14 months earlier, struggled vainly to choke back tears and described himself as "devastated" by the severity of Johnson's illness. Patrick's shock and despair were echoed by nearly all who knew Johnson.

Word of Johnson's ailment had a profound impact inside the locker room of Team USA, where Yale coach Tim Taylor had been named to fill in for Johnson. Losing its coach in such a way was a horrifying and high-impact distraction, but Taylor vowed the team would not lose focus on its primary objective. "One of Bob's favorite expressions is, 'If you want to reap a harvest, you have to plow,' " he said. "So we're going to keep plowing. I think we're subdued, but I think it's going to give us a strength and resolve to play our best."

"We know Badger would want us to go out and have it be a great day for hockey," Team USA forward Ed Olczyk said. "We've got to carry this thing as far as we can. We want to do it for him. It's difficult, but we've got to use it as he would want us to use it — in a positive way." In truth, that wasn't just the way Johnson would have wanted his team to deal with his illness; it was the only way he would have known to have them handle it. From Johnson's perspective, there were two ways to approach a situation: The positive way, and the wrong way.

Winning the Stanley Cup had not established Johnson as a significant figure in the hockey world; it simply enhanced his reputation as a coach who could look at a hopeless situation and see nothing less than a great opportunity. And that meant the Penguins represented an opportunity like few others. A franchise so firmly rooted in failure and frustration would be the ultimate test for Johnson's unwavering optimism.

When Patrick introduced Johnson as the Penguins' coach and Scott Bowman as their director of player development and recruitment on June 12, 1990, he proclaimed that Pittsburgh had assembled "the best management team in the National Hockey League." It was a stunning statement, considering Patrick's disdain for superlatives and the quality of some front offices in other cities. But his sentiment was not out of line. No less an authority than Edmonton Oilers general manager Glen Sather, who had put together a team that won five Stanley Cups in the previous seven years, told reporters "that's a pretty impressive front-end team they've put together in Pittsburgh."

People familiar with Johnson's work during a five-year stint with the Calgary Flames didn't dispute Sather's assessment. Johnson had a history of working with hockey teams the way an artist works with clay, patiently molding and manipulating until he had sculpted a masterpiece. "He'll make their good players better, and he'll turn the ones who aren't very good players into good players," said Al MacNeil, Calgary's vice president of hockey operations. "He's got the best chance of anybody to make that club win."

Bringing high-profile people like Johnson and Bowman into the organization struck some as a calculated risk by Patrick. Some observers theorized he effectively had made himself expendable, that if owner Edward J. DeBartolo ever decided he needed a new GM, he could find two qualified replacements already on his payroll. Courtesy of the guy whose nameplate was already on the GM's office door.

Patrick, however, shrugged off such thinking. "I've always been taught to surround yourself with great people," he said. "Why not get the best? I think we're going to be a perfect fit because I understand what we all want to accomplish. We all have the same goal." The goal was to scrape away the years of tarnish that had built up on the franchise, to make the Penguins sweater a source of pride to the men who wore it. And to someday bring a championship to Pittsburgh, preferably before any players on the current roster qualified for Social Security benefits.

Bowman would play a major, albeit low-profile, role in Pittsburgh's 1990-91 season. He assessed talent on other teams and made suggestions on possible personnel moves. He convinced Patrick to acquire defenseman Gord Roberts, who was languishing with the St. Louis Blues' farm team in Peoria, Illinois, and endorsed the deal that brought Ron Francis, Ulf Samuelsson, and Grant Jennings from Hartford in perhaps the most significant trade in franchise history.

Bowman had been general manager of the Buffalo Sabres before becoming a Hockey Night in Canada commentator, but had no interest in coping with the day-to-day details, complications, and negotiations that are an integral part of the GM's job. "My job will be to get out and watch hockey games," he said. "It's never been a burden for me to go out and watch a game. I'm not interested in functions of certain kinds. The part I like is going and watching games . . . My job is not an office job, not a paper job."

But while Bowman primarily was operating behind the scenes, Bob Johnson was back in the spotlight. Finally. He had spent the previous three years as executive director of USA Hockey, which governs the game on an amateur level in the United States. His tenure was, by all accounts, a success, for Johnson was an accomplished fund-raiser and there could be no better salesman for the game.

But he was most comfortable behind a bench, not a desk. He preferred going over X's and O's with players to discussing tax write-offs with prospective sponsors. Coaching wasn't just a way of life for him; it was, in many ways, a reason for living. Maybe he wouldn't coach for free, but the paycheck never was Johnson's biggest reward for doing his job.

"He's the best person for our particular situation," Patrick said in annoucing Johnson's hiring. "He's a great teacher, great communicator. He's very enthusiastic, a person who encourages performance as opposed to demanding it. I feel that (style) will work best in our scenario. Every time I analyzed our needs, it always came down to Bob Johnson as the bottom line.

"If I was told I had to have a coach the day I got here (December 5, 1989), I would have pursued Bob Johnson. He's got a great knowledge of the game, every aspect of the game. He's got a great knowledge of the National Hockey League and a great knowledge for people."

Johnson described himself as "a guy who enjoys going to the rink," but his passion for hockey ran much deeper than that. He didn't just enjoy going to the rink, he loved it. Loved everything about it. Loved to teach the game and to learn about it. Loved to motivate players and to be inspired by what they did. And mostly, he just loved the game. Loved the pucks and sticks. Loved the ice. Loved the camaraderie and the challenges of hockey.

"He has a very, very high energy level," said Bob Murdoch, who had been one of Johnson's assistant coaches during his five-year stint with the Calgary Flames. "His enthusiasm spills over onto his players and anyone who's around him."

Johnson, the son of a Swedish immigrant who had changed his surname from Olars to Johnson when he passed through Ellis Island, was raised on the south side of Minneapolis. He was good enough at baseball to earn a contract from the Chicago White Sox, but his baseball career was interrupted by a military stint during the Korean War.

After leaving the service, Johnson was preparing to leave for a summer of minor-league baseball when he made a momentous decision: It was time to get on with his life's work, and that meant coaching hockey. "I was going to Oklahoma (to play baseball)," Johnson said. "I sent my wife down with her folks and was going to take the train down. I finally said, 'This is stupid. I'm married and have got a couple of kids. I'll go back to school.' "

And so, in 1956, he took a job at Warroad High School in rural Minnesota. Subsequent winters would take him to Colorado College, the University of Wisconsin — where he became known as "Badger Bob" — and ultimately, the Calgary Flames of the NHL.

But although his address changed occasionally, Johnson's atittude did not. Overwhelming adversity was nothing more than an intriguing challenge. His outlook ran counter to nearly everything that had happened during the Penguins' first 23 seasons in the NHL, and was, in many ways, the perfect antidote for more than two decades of almost non-stop despair.

He didn't care that the Penguins had missed the Stanley Cup playoffs seven of the previous eight years, or that the franchise had declared bankruptcy in 1975, when the Internal Revenue Service slapped padlocks on the doors. He wasn't disturbed when a live mascot that had once waddled around the Civic Arena ice surface before games had died after contracting pneumonia, a vile omen that Penguins and winter were not a good mix.

Anyone who had watched the franchise for an extended period of time was convinced that the worst-case scenario actually was a script that dictated the course of events around the Civic Arena, that the franchise was governed by the strictest possible interpretation of Murphy's Law. Even if it had been for a lot of years, Johnson never doubted he would get that repealed. He always looked for the best in people, and had a rare gift for bringing it out in them.

"I don't like to be around negative people," Johnson said midway through training camp in 1990. "You enjoy life more if you're being positive." Not that he knew any other way to do it. And there was a sincerity and contagious quality about Johnson's upbeat approach that affected all who came in contact with him.

"He has kind of an infectious quality about him," said Jamie Macoun, who played for Johnson in Calgary. "He can drive you nuts, but you really like what he's trying to get across. Before you know it, you're mimicking what he says. Everybody talks just like him, and that's exactly what he wants."

What people liked to imitate most about Johnson was his habit of rubbing his face, brow to chin, with his hand. He did it frequently, often in mid-sentence, and that idiosyncrasy became something of a trademark. But people who were around Johnson enough to get a chuckle from his mannerisms also couldn't help but absorb his message about the power of positive thinking.

"I remember when he first came here, the first little while, saying to myself, 'Nobody can be like this. Nobody can be this positive. Up every day,' " Penguins defenseman Paul Coffey said. "But he was like that for eight months."

"I never thought I'd see a coach who could bring players up, spirit-wise, but that's the way it was," goalie Wendell Young said. "I never met a guy more positive than Badger. He was always upbeat, always found something positive in everything. We could lose 8-0, and he never went with the negatives. He always found something good in a bad situation."

"He was the happiest guy I ever saw," said right winger Mark Recchi. "Happy to wake up, happy to come to the rink. He was just full of life."

Johnson insisted on nothing less than a total effort at all times from his players, but realized the folly of expecting his personnel to give more than they were capable of. That explained the sign that hung on his office door for months. It read: "Never try to teach a pig to sing. It wastes your time, and it annoys the pig."

Long before he arrived in Pittsburgh, Johnson had taken a simple phrase, "It's a great day for hockey," and turned it into a way of life. He cherished the game at every level, and had traveled around the world to watch, study, and coach it. When he mentioned that, for example, Jaromir Jagr's hometown of Kladno, Czechoslovakia was "a great hockey community," you knew that he had been there. And that he meant it.

Johnson's upbeat attitude occasionally carried him outside the bounds of credibility. Like when he was coaching the Flames, and chided reporters covering the team about dwelling so much on "our so-called slump." Never mind that the Flames had lost 11 games in a row at the time. And while there was nothing contrived about Johnson's optimism, even his players were taken aback sometimes.

"Can every day be a great day for hockey?" Pittsburgh left winger Troy Loney had wondered aloud a few months before Johnson was stricken. "I mean, every day? Isn't there ever a day that isn't a great day for hockey?"

It turned out that there was. August 29, 1991 wasn't a very

good day for hockey. In fact, it was a terrible one. For the day Bob Johnson was felled by brain cancer will be remembered as the day hockey was robbed of one of its leading evangelists, a man who spread the gospel of the game wherever he went. A man who turned cynics into converts. A man who could energize others simply by walking into a room.

"He makes you feel like you're 15, 16 years old," Pittsburgh equipment manager Steve Latin said. "If he told me to move that wall, I'd try to move that wall for him. I wouldn't even ask a question."

"What he's done for this city and this hockey club in one year is pretty incredible," Mario Lemieux said. "Nobody thought we'd win the Cup, but with Bob Johnson, anything was possible." And if it wasn't, well, that was a detail Johnson wouldn't waste time dwelling on. He'd simply go about accomplishing whatever it was that others said couldn't be done.

Doctors theorized that Johnson's ailment was related to skin cancer he had been diagnosed with a few years earlier. And in the days that followed the discovery of the tumors in his brain, the most frequently-asked question was "Why?" There was, of course, no answer.

Before long, the question became "When?" It was agonizingly clear that nothing less than a medical miracle would save Johnson's life, and even experimental treatments had no more than modest success in slowing the grim assault of his disease.

The cancer and treatments conspired to rob Johnson of his voice, but his interest in hockey and his teams never waned. He offered Tim Taylor a lineup for the Sweden game, and a few tactical pointers on how to deal with Sweden's forechecking system. Taylor used the lineup, followed the advice, and guided Team USA to a 6-3 victory.

"I visited him this morning (before the game) and he asked if the team was ready," Taylor said. "I told the players that here's a guy battling for his life, and he's still talking about beating Sweden. He gave us the thumbs-up. I think he's going to be very, very happy with this game." Steve Latin took a videotape of it to Johnson's hospital room that evening, before Team USA went on the road for its next game.

Johnson's left side was paralyzed by the surgery he underwent after being rushed to the hospital, but Craig Patrick said, "His mind is as sharp as ever, and it's always going. Because he can't speak, he gets frustrated, and has difficulty communicating with us, but he does write down his thoughts."

Johnson did just that when he learned an arbitrator had awarded St. Louis defenseman Scott Stevens to the New Jersey Devils as compensation after St. Louis had signed Devils forward Brendan Shanahan, a free agent. Johnson scribbled a note to Patrick that read, "Uh-oh. New Jersey's got a great defense."

Shortly after Johnson was hospitalized, it became apparent he would not be able to return to coaching anytime soon, if ever. Patrick, however, opted against naming a replacement immediately, and said the Penguins would stick to the arrangement made several months earlier for training camp. Because of Johnson's commitment to the Canada Cup, it was decided in late June that assistant coaches Rick Paterson, Rick Kehoe and Barry Smith would oversee camp, with help from Muskegon Lumberjacks coach Phil Russell and direction from Scott Bowman.

"I've thought about it, but the way I see it now, there's no need to rush into any decisions," Patrick said. "We have a fine staff that can handle things for the time being until we know the extent of Bob's situation. Right now, there's no urgency to make a decision."

Patrick said he anticipated that camp would go along pretty much as scheduled because "we've got things organized and responsibilities delegated." Barry Smith said there was "a hard job in front of all of us," but that it would be counterproductive to dwell on Johnson's absence. "I don't think you try to make a big thing about Bob not being there," he said. "You just try to get the job done. Let's not try (to mimic Johnson), but let's try to put on a real good training camp we can get a lot out of. We'll run a practice Bob Johnson would be proud of."

On September 11, Johnson underwent a relatively rare surgical procedure known as "gamma knife" at Presbyterian-University Hospital in Pittsburgh. In that procedure, the patient is fitted into what looks like an oversized skullcap, then subjected to cross-fired beams of radioactive cobalt-60. Patrick reported that the treatment, which was employed to neutralize a tumor that had not been targeted during Johnson's initial surgery, apparently was successful, but described Johnson's prognosis as "not a good situation to be in."

Johnson was flown to his home in Colorado Springs on

September 12, still fully believing that he would return to Pittsburgh, and to coaching the game that meant so much to him. In a statement released by his son-in-law, Tim McConnell, Johnson said, "The fire of coaching still burns inside of me — I will be back. When I return, it will be my greatest day in coaching."

"Bob affects all of our lives on a daily basis with his attitude about living," Patrick said. "The enthusiasm with which he approaches each day . . . that hasn't changed throughout this whole process."

But Johnson would never return to Pittsburgh, and he watched the Penguins play in person for the final time when they had an exhibition game against the Flames at McNichols Arena in Denver on September 19. He was in a private box on a gurney with members of his family. He visited with players and staff from both teams before the game, and several players who were not in the lineup stopped by his box during the evening. "He was really excited to be here," Patrick said. "Excited to be at the game, to see his players."

One side of Johnson's head had been shaved, and radiation treatments were sapping his strength, but he communicated with the players through notes. Mark Recchi said "his mind was still sharp," and Johnson clearly enjoyed the chance to interact with his players again. "You could just tell that he wants to be here," goalie Frank Pietrangelo said. "It was good for him to get a chance to see the guys."

A few days later, most of the team bused from Denver to Colorado Springs to visit Johnson. It meant giving up an afternoon off, but that seemed a minor sacrifice compared to all that Johnson had given them. And it proved to be the last time they were together. The Penguins delayed raising their championship banners, hoping that Johnson could attend the ceremony, but his condition continued to deteriorate, and he was forced to watch the proceedings via satellite dish.

After the banners were pulled into place before a game against the New York Rangers October 19, public address announcer John Barbero read a message from Johnson to the capacity crowd of 16,164 at the Civic Arena. It said, in part, "I walked in the arena one year ago and noticed that there were no championship banners here. Well, tonight it is great to have these championship banners raised for the fans of Pittsburgh, signifying that we have reached the top of the mountain."

Johnson had led the Penguins there, but would not get the chance to take them there again. He died early in the morning of November 26 in Colorado Springs, and Patrick informed the players of his passing when they came off the ice after practice that day. They had known for weeks that death would be the inevitable outcome of Johnson's illness, but still sat in stunned silence for more than 15 minutes when they received word that he was gone.

"There was just silence," Paul Coffey said. "Everybody was out in space, remembering their own memories of Bob Johnson. I don't think Bob's impact on any player he coached is ever going to be over. I just feel lucky I had a chance to play for him."

Mark Recchi said, "It's a shock, no matter how much you expect it," and that sentiment was expressed repeatedly. "You hear he's struggling and so on, yet even though you somewhat expect this to happen, it still hits you over the head like a hammer," Ron Francis said.

After learning of Johnson's death, Bowman said, "a big part of us is gone now," and Patrick said Johnson's impact on the Penguins had gone far beyond that of a typical coach. "He created an atmosphere around our organization that was very family-like," he said. "He was really like the father of our organization."

When word of Johnson's death reached Calgary, the Flames taped black armbands to their practice sweaters. "We were just paying tribute to him in a small way," Calgary defenseman Gary Suter said. "That's how he'd best like to be remembered, on the ice. He would have liked to have been out there stickhandling with us."

The reaction was much the same in all corners of the continent. Wherever hockey was played, and wherever Johnson had friends — which were pretty much one and the same — acquaintances reminisced about Johnson. About how, while running a summer hockey school at Wisconsin, Johnson came across a player who wore a golden helmet and called himself "The Golden Hawk." And how Johnson promptly painted a helmet of his own gold and came to be known to his friends as "The Hawk," a name that stuck for the rest of his days.

But mostly, people who knew Johnson reflected on his upbeat attitude toward hockey and life, and how it affected everyone who knew him.

Barry Pederson, who played for Johnson in 1990-91, said, "He'd come into a room for a practice and he'd say, 'Hey, why are you down? We have our health, and this is just a game we're playing. Let's have fun, and away we go.' I think we all tend to dwell on the negative, but he'd never let you do that."

Ron Wilson, who played for Johnson on two United States national teams, remembered: "We'd be about 4,000 miles from home in some communist country, and we'd be staying in some old, drafty hotel and he'd still say, 'Great day for hockey.' You'd hear it once or twice, and you'd figure, 'Hey, who is this guy kidding?' Then when you'd hear it day after day, you knew he meant it."

Minnesota North Stars owner Norm Green, whose team was beaten by the Penguins in the 1991 Stanley Cup final, said: "I felt someone 'upstairs' was looking out for us in the playoffs. I think the same guy up there smiled on Bob. It doesn't always work out so the good guy gets the ultimate reward, but it worked that way for Bob Johnson."

Johnson's passing obviously had a profound impact on his players and friends, but the Penguins' schedule allowed little time for grieving. The New Jersey Devils would be at the Civic Arena the next night for a significant meeting between the Patrick Division contenders. Focusing on a mere hockey game might have been difficult, but the Penguins were convinced Johnson would have had it no other way. "Bob would have wanted us to play our hardest and win," defenseman Peter Taglianetti said.

The Penguins did play hard and won 8-4, but it was what happened before the game, not during it, that made this night memorable. The Penguins, wearing patches emblazoned "Badger," formed a circle at center ice before the opening faceoff. The phrase that will forever be associated with Johnson — "It's a great day for hockey" — was painted on the ice outside each blue line. And with the Civic Arena lights lowered, the fans held battery-powered candles while a soloist sang "The Lord's Prayer." It was a short, simple, and touching tribute to a friend who had been lost all too soon. Bowman said later that Johnson's widow, Martha, told him she "loved every second" of the ceremony.

Memorial services for Johnson were held simultaneously December 2 in Pittsburgh, Colorado Springs, Madison, Wisconsin, and Minneapolis. Management chartered a plane that took the players and many of the team's office workers to the service at the First Presbyterian Church in Colorado Springs. Before the plane left Greater Pittsburgh International Airport, Ron Francis peeled back his suit coat to reveal a wad of tissue. Bob Johnson no doubt would have approved; he liked his players to be prepared.

The service in Pittsburgh, which attracted about 200 hockey fans and friends of Johnson, featured a video of Johnson, and the Rev. Bruce Wheeler Thielemann spoke of his visits with Johnson after he was hospitalized.

"The last thing I said to him, before our final prayer, was this: 'I have lived in this city for 53 of my 60 years, and I have never known a single person to claim the heart of this city as quickly and completely as you have done,' " he said. "We will always remember this as the year we won the Stanley Cup. We will always remember this as the year in which Coach Johnson died."

The Colorado Springs service was as much a celebration of Johnson's life as a chance to mourn his passing. On the church altar, there was a photo of the Badger, smiling broadly, with his arm around the Stanley Cup. Before the service began, the song "Climb Every Mountain" was performed. There could have been no more fitting tribute to a man who had done just that during his coaching career.

Johnson's pall bearers were a cross section of the hockey community. They included his sons, Mark and Peter; Craig Patrick, Toronto Maple Leafs GM Cliff Fletcher; and Dave Peterson, who would coach the 1992 U.S. Olympics team. The crowd was sprinkled with players and management members from other teams, people whose careers had intersected with Johnson's at one point or another.

The Los Angeles Kings, for example, had a three-man contingent at the funeral: center Randy Gilhen, who had played for the Penguins the year Johnson coached; winger Tony Granato, a member of several U.S. national teams coached by Johnson; and broadcaster Bob Miller, who had done play-by-play at Wisconsin during Johnson's tenure there.

Dr. John H. Stevens, the pastor of First Presbyterian, said the overflow crowd that attended the service was "testimony to the quality of his life and the enormous impact he has had on so many of us," and that Johnson's death "left an empty place in our world and the hearts of many."

During the service, friends and family members reflected on the good times they had enjoyed with Johnson. Dr. Conrad Andringa, a friend from Madison, Wisconsin, talked about Johnson's "unbelievable ability" to make people feel close to him. "He made you feel good, made you feel important," Andringa said. "He knew how to make you feel better than you were. He had the ability to be a friend with so many people at all different levels."

Harley Hotchkiss, one of the Calgary Flames' owners, remembered that Johnson "never had any pretenses and always had time for people," qualities that enabled Johnson to have "a strong impact on our city." Hotchkiss said, "Bob climbed a lot of mountains, and took a lot of people with him. And he took them a lot higher than they ever would have gotten on their own."

Tim McConnell, Johnson's son-in-law, told the crowd that Johnson "was able to achieve every goal he ever set, and how many of us can say that?" McConnell then spoke directly to the Penguins players. "As much as you loved and respected him," McConnell said, "he loved and respected you more."

But the players' respect and affection for Johnson knew virtually no bounds. Johnson, like every other coach, had been the target of random gripes and grumblings over the course of the season. There's never enough ice time to keep 20-plus players happy; that's one of hockey's unwavering truths.

That did not mean, however, that his work was held in anything less than the highest of esteem.

He coached the Penguins for only one season, but it was a season that no one would ever forget.

"Nothing gave him greater pleasure than being behind the bench and seeing us play well under his leadership," Tom Barrasso said. "Bob pushed all of us to be the best people we could be, as well as the best players."

"I remember some days I came in here and didn't want to be here, and then you'd see him," Kevin Stevens said. "He'd make you feel that much better. It's hard to say a coach does that—you never really feel that way about a coach — but he was the type of coach who brought out the best in you as a hockey player and as a person. He made you realize what life was really all about.

"We know there's a place where he can see us . . . you can see him on that bench looking down on us, instructing us. That's a good feeling. We should maybe pull together and do it for Bob, because we know he's watching out for us. Hopefully, we can do the same for him."

And the Penguins did just that. A little over six months after Johnson died, they won their second Stanley Cup. He wasn't behind the bench for this one, but he was in their thoughts. His presence helped to make them champions — "Bob was a great teacher," Mario Lemieux said, "and more than anything else, he taught us how to win"—and his absence taught them to appreciate the chance for greatness that was before them. They embraced the final lesson Johnson imparted.

"When Bob passed away, all the players . . . realized what we have here," Barrasso said. "Realized that this may not be here forever, this team we have and the talent we have, and the opportunities that are in front of us."

When the Penguins' four-game sweep of the Chicago Blackhawks in the Stanley Cup final was complete, defenseman Ulf Samuelsson dedicated the championship to Johnson, and to Samuelsson's father, Bo, who had died early in the season. "I didn't think it was going to be as nice a feeling as it is," Samuelsson said. "But thinking of my dad when I was holding the silver (Cup) out there, and Bob, made it even more important for me."

Other players offered tributes to Johnson. "Everybody on this team realizes how important Bob Johnson was to this Cup," defenseman Larry Murphy said. "Bob was always on our minds this year," Lemieux said. "He certainly was the reason we won last year."

And the man who filled in for him after Johnson was stricken invoked his memory during a civic celebration at Three Rivers Stadium. "Thanks to Bob Johnson's vision, all of this is possible," Scott Bowman said. "The coach of the Pittsburgh Penguins will always be Bob Johnson."

Bob Johnson will be remembered as the man who made every day a great day for hockey. And the man who played such an important role in making the greatest days in the Penguins' first 24 years possible.

CHAPTER THREE

Starting Over

The shock of Bob Johnson's illness still was terrible and fresh when the Penguins opened training camp September 6 at the Civic Arena. He was such a commanding presence that it was impossible to overlook his absence. By all rights, he should have been striding down the runway to the ice at any moment, tugging on his cap, rubbing his face and telling anyone who would listen that it was another great day for hockey.

But Johnson wasn't the only familiar face missing on that Friday afternoon. Eleven of the 20 players who dressed for the Cup-clinching victory in Game 6 against Minnesota a few months earlier were not around. Randy Gilhen had been lost to the North Stars in the expansion draft less than a week after the finals ended. Ulf Samuelsson, Larry Murphy, Paul Coffey, Joe Mullen and Jaromir Jagr were competing in the Canada Cup. And five players did not have contracts.

Defensemen Gord Roberts and Jim Paek wrapped up their negotiations in the early days of camp, but three players who had been integral parts of the Penguins' championship team — Kevin Stevens, Mark Recchi and Ron Francis — did not. All had contributed mightily during the playoffs, but none had been able to reach a contract settlement with Craig Patrick during the offseason. And there was no indication that any of them would be showing up in the foreseeable future.

"It's going to take a lot of time (to reach agreements), especially at their (salary) level," Mario Lemieux said. "Everything that they can get, they deserve. I hope they're doing the right thing... by not coming to training camp. Hopefully, they'll all sign for what they're worth and everything will be all right."

Stevens and Francis were Group II free agents, which meant the Penguins had the right to match any offer they received from another team. Consequently, the chances of either leaving Pittsburgh were nominal unless some team was willing to pay a thoroughly outrageous salary. Recchi, however, was a Group I free agent; the National Hockey League's collective bargaining agreement with its Players Association did not permit the Penguins to retain him simply by matching the contract another team would give him.

Recchi was coming off a 40-goal, 113-point season and, at age 23, had established himself as one of the premier right wingers in the NHL. He was neither tall nor large, but played with a controlled fury that earned him the nickname, "Wrecking Ball." There clearly was a market for a player of such caliber, even though a team signing him would be forced to compensate the Penguins with players, money, or draft choices. The prevailing wisdom was that Recchi would be particularly attractive to Philadelphia. Flyers assistant Ken Hitchcock had been his junior coach in Kamloops, British Columbia, and the two were so close that they were partners in a racehorse.

Recchi repeatedly expressed his desire to remain in Pittsburgh, but on the eve of training camp said he was "very disappointed" that a deal hadn't been reached and said, "I can't take much more of this." The snag was obviously monetary, but Recchi's frustration was compounded by being kept away from the game he loved. Few people go about their jobs with an exuberance such as his.

But Recchi's anguish didn't translate into action by the Penguins. By mid-September, Recchi's agent, Rick Curran, was into intense negotiations with the Flyers. Recchi's departure seemed almost inevitable, when in Curran's words, "Pittsburgh decided it had better come forward with something." In this case, a contract proposal worth about $3.6 million over four years. That would more than cover any increases in the cost of living for a guy who made $105,000 the previous season.

Nonetheless, Recchi had underscored his wish to stay with the Penguins by accepting their offer, even though the Flyers were prepared to put a more lucrative package on the table. "There came a time in his life when he had to make a decision," Patrick said. "I'm sure it was a difficult one."

"I could say that, although our negotiations with the other team were not complete, a deal with them would have been for more money," Curran said. "Mark felt that his happiness was worth more than the difference in dollars. I told him he shouldn't feel bad about taking a little loss in exchange for his happiness."

Hearing that Recchi was about to rejoin the team was a major morale boost for the Penguins, who had been bombarded with bad news for weeks. Troy Loney said it was "probably the first good, big thing that's happened to us since we won the Cup," and Frank Pietrangelo agreed. "Mark Recchi is a very important part of this team," he said. "All of us want to repeat as Stanley Cup champions, and I don't think there's any way we could do it without Mark Recchi and Kevin Stevens in the lineup."

Stevens was biding his time in Boston when he learned Recchi's deal had been finalized, and said it was "great for Recchs and great for our team" that the negotiations were finally fruitful. But Stevens was growing increasingly bitter that he could not get what he deemed to be a fair contract offer from the Penguins. He had earned $150,000 the previous year, but figured he deserved to move up a few tax brackets after scoring 40 times during the regular season and adding 17 more goals— just two shy of the league record— during the playoffs.

As the team prepared to open training camp, Stevens vowed he would not sign with the Penguins for "as long as it takes me to get the market (value), what I'm worth. The offer that he (Patrick) has made now is not fair. All we're asking for is fair market, not $2 million or $1.5 million. He seems to think it's less than we think it is."

He went on to express a thought that more than a few fans had put forth in light of the large, across-the-board ticket increases the team had announced earlier in the summer. "Why isn't anybody getting signed?" Stevens said. "What are they doing with all the money they made in the playoffs? Why did they raise ticket prices?"

Patrick's talks with Stevens and his agent, Jay Grossman, went almost nowhere during the first two weeks of camp and might have dragged on indefinitely if the Boston Bruins hadn't intervened. Stevens had been a dominant force during Pittsburgh's third-round playoff series against the Bruins in May, and his performance likely influenced Boston's decision to offer him a five-year deal worth $5.375 million.

Stevens signed the Bruins' offer sheet on September 19, and Patrick had a week to decide whether to match the offer or accept a package of five first-round draft choices as compensation from the Bruins. Pittsburgh's gamble to let Stevens explore free agency was shaping up as a costly mistake. The Penguins had the choice of surrendering either an outstanding player or a hefty chunk of owner Edward DeBartolo's bank account, and neither option was particularly appealing.

"They let us go out and test it (the open market) and it finally worked," Stevens said. "It's in their hands now. It's a great contract, but I don't think it's outrageously high. I don't think it's way out of line . . . I hope they do it (match the offer) before seven days, but I know how (slowly) they move."

Patrick declined to discuss Boston's proposal until he saw a copy of the offer sheet. He rarely acts in haste, and used most of the week to "weigh all of our options" about whether to match the offer. But inside the Penguins' locker room, the consensus was that there wasn't all that much to think about. Either the Penguins were willing to spend the money needed to keep a player who was about to blossom into the premier power forward in the NHL or they weren't.

"I guess in the next week or so, we're going to find out if the Penguins want to win another Stanley Cup," Mario Lemieux said. "If they do, they have to sign him."

Patrick must have agreed, because on September 25, he matched the offer. But he also attached an asterisk: Patrick said the Penguins were "still going to consider all of our options," the inference being that Stevens might be traded to reduce a payroll that was swelling rapidly. "We felt that the five first-round picks weren't as attractive as some of the other (trade) offers we've received," Patrick said. "All this means is that he's not going to be playing in Boston."

Free-agency rules dictated that a Group II free agent who signs with another team cannot be traded to that team if his original team elects to match the offer, which is why sending Stevens to the Bruins was not an option. And the Bruins didn't seem surprised to find out that Stevens wouldn't be playing in his hometown. "There's no real shock," Coach Rick Bowness told the *Boston Globe*. "Just disappointment."

There was some disappointment in the Stevens household, as well. He had bought a bottle of champagne a year earlier with the intent of sharing it with his wife, Suzanne, when he got a new contract. But the lingering uncertainty about where he would be playing, even after Pittsburgh matched Boston's offer, left Stevens feeling more than a little flat.

Sure, he had a contract that exceeded his most outlandish expectations, but Stevens' ordeal didn't end when he signed the agreement; it just moved into a new phase. He had enough money to build a mansion, but no guarantee that he'd be in Pittsburgh long enough to see it built.

"I was hoping he (Patrick) would come out and say, 'We're happy to sign Kevin, and we want to keep him and have him help our team for five years,'" Stevens said. "But that's business, I guess."

At least one other guy understood how Stevens felt. Francis, who was spending early autumn at his home in suburban Hartford, said he'd been keeping a bottle of champagne ready for two years. Another month dragged by before he got a chance to open it; Francis did not reach a settlement with the Penguins on a five-year, $4.1 million contract until October 25, three weeks after the regular season had begun.

There were numerous times before the deal was struck when it appeared Francis' career with the Penguins would go down as a three-month fling. He was courted heavily by the fledgling Continental Hockey League and received an offer to play for the Canadian Olympic team in late September. On the day Pittsburgh decided to match Boston's offer to Stevens, the chances of Francis returning to the Penguins seemed slim.

Francis said Pittsburgh had just pulled a long-term offer off the table and replaced it with a proposal for one year and an option. "We faxed them and said that wasn't acceptable," he said. "It wasn't even a consideration. I don't want to break the bank or be ridiculous. I've been in the league for 10 years now. The numbers (statistics) are there, the consistency is there." But an agreement on what all that was worth in raw currency wouldn't come about for several more weeks.

Contract negotiations dominated the headlines during training camp, but the Penguins still had to go about the business of getting ready for the regular season, regardless of which players would or would not be back by that time. Every facet of the preseason, however, seemed to be overshadowed not only by the absence of some big-name players, but of Bob Johnson.

He had been a larger-than-life presence before he was stricken by brain cancer, and loomed over the franchise even after being hospitalized. Assistant coach Barry Smith even left a spot open for Johnson behind the bench during Pittsburgh's first exhibition game. "I think Barry and I were both a little choked up when we walked out on the ice the first time," assistant Rick Paterson said. "We were used to Bob leading us out."

The assistant coaches stuck to the technical systems Johnson had put into place a year earlier, but there was an intangible quality only Johnson could bring to the bench. "The void is definitely there, and we're trying to work around it," Smith said. "We're not going to try to hide that fact. We all miss the man. Just his personality alone kept us going. We're never going to replace him. But we can do our work, as a coaching staff, to get the team playing well."

Johnson's absence was even more noticeable when training camp shifted to Vail, Colorado for a few days. He had a deep love for that area, and had been responsible for the Penguins spending time there during the preseason for two years running. His players had snickered when, in 1991, Johnson took command of the public-address system at Dobson Arena and narrated a practice for the crowd, but everything in Vail reminded the Penguins of how badly they missed their coach. "Colorado is where he really got excited to play," Paul Stanton said.

As the exhibition season wound down, and it became increasingly evident that Johnson would not coach again, the Penguins grew concerned that steps had not been taken to name a replacement. Patrick did not rule out the possibility that the coaching-by-committee approach employed during the preseason would continue, and said only that a decision would be made before the season-opener. His players had been hoping for something a bit more conclusive.

"The coaching is a little unsettled," Gord Roberts said. "There's no doubt about that. They've got to come in and let us know . . . who is in charge and give that person (control) so we stop talking and worrying about it and just move on."

But even with all the confusion and chaos that disrupted training camp, the Penguins prepared for the regular season fully believing that another Cup was within reach. "We have three or four of the top players in the game," Roberts said. "It's nice to build from that. It brings the other players' level of play up. If we can get everybody healthy and signed and get rolling from where we were last year, we've definitely got an opportunity to repeat."

An exceptional nucleus of talent wasn't all the Penguins felt they had in their favor. A unique bond had been formed between the players during the previous season. The petty jealousies and personal conflicts that can destroy the delicate fabric of a team were nowhere to be found in the Pittsburgh locker room.

That might have carried over from the year they spent with Bob Johnson, or perhaps it was a by-product of their success in the playoffs. In any case, it was an asset that could not be overlooked, even if it couldn't be quantified, either. It's always nice to have an edge, tangible or otherwise.

"We do have an abundance of talent, but we have that chemistry," Phil Bourque said. "Not only on the ice, but off it. This is the first time I've been with a Penguin team where the guys have gotten together not only in the winter, but in the summer. On the ice, off the ice. When the season ended before, everybody just went their separate ways.

"Last summer—maybe it was just because we won the Cup, I don't know — but guys were constantly in touch with each other. We just had that chemistry. When you have that, you want to win for each other. You're not winning just for another 'W' in the win column or to make the coach happy. You're doing it for the guys in the room with you."

"You don't really have a lot of grumbling, where guys on the fourth line think they should be on the first line," Roberts said. "There's really good chemistry. Guys get along real well. There's no jealousy on this team, by any means."

Of course, players getting along didn't ensure a successful season, let alone another championship. The playoffs can be four rounds of Russian Roulette, and one spasm of misfortune can end a team's season in a heartbeat. "With four series, you have to have a lucky bounce here, a big save there," said Bryan Trottier, who played for the New York Islanders when they won four Cups in a row in 1980-83. "When we were going through it on the Island, there was always a big play by a key individual, a lucky bounce for our team or a mis-hit for the other team. The next thing you know, you're sliding along. And with that, your confidence seems to grow and grow."

The coaching uncertainty finally ended on October 1, when Patrick revealed that Scott Bowman would take the job on an interim basis. "Under the circumstances, we're very grateful he's willing to carry the ball for us," Patrick said. "This gives us the best opportunity to continue our successes." At the same time, Patrick announced that Pierre McGuire would shift from a scouting job to being an assistant coach, and that Rick Paterson would get a new assignment in pro scouting.

Bowman brought impeccable credentials to the job — he was the winningest coach in NHL history and had just been inducted to the Hall of Fame a week or so earlier — but had a style that was in striking contrast to the methods employed by Johnson. Badger was able to become his players' buddy; there was no question Bowman would be their boss. "There's a lot of difference in their personalities, but very little difference in their knowledge of the game," Patrick would say later. "Any time there's a coaching change, the players have to adapt to the personality (of the new coach)."

But many of the Penguins never had played for a coach who had Bowman's approach to the job. That's because few coaches, at least in contemporary times, were as inflexible as Bowman was reputed to be. He was willing to push his players to the brink of rebellion by showing a total disregard for anything except the bottom line, which was wins and losses.

"He (Bowman) is a tough loser, a real tough loser," said Danny Gare, who had been captain in Buffalo during Bowman's coaching tenure there. "You never knew what he would do behind the bench. He kept you on your toes by being intense. That way, you didn't get too close. He was very distant. That was Scotty's way. I wish there could have been more communication sometimes. Maybe he's mellowed. I don't know."

That was always a possibility, of course, although no one really believed Bowman had become laid-back during his years away from coaching. The idea of a warm and fuzzy Scott Bowman just didn't jibe with his track record. He insisted on nothing less than perfection — every game, every shift — and anyone who didn't meet that standard should not expect their failure to go unnoticed. Or unmentioned. At high volume.

"It's going to be a new experience for a lot of guys," said goalie Tom Barrasso, who also had played for Bowman in Buffalo. "He has a different kind of intensity from Bob. If you don't show up every night, it won't be rah-rah stuff that will be used to get you going. It will be yelling and screaming."

Shortly after Bowman was named interim coach, a story from Gare circulated around the locker room. He said that once during Bowman's tenure in Buffalo, defenseman Richie Dunn was struggling with a drill during practice. Bowman, making no attempt to conceal his anger, began to tap Dunn on the helmet with the taped knob of his stick. As he rapped on the helmet, Bowman said, "Am I loosening any logs in there? Am I? That's you, logjam, logjam, logjam." Suffice to say, that didn't qualify as communication in the classic Bob Johnson style.

Ken Dryden, the Hall of Fame goaltender who played in Montreal when Bowman coached the Canadiens, offered some keen insights on Bowman in his acclaimed book, *The Game*. Dryden wrote "Scotty Bowman is not someone who is easy to like . . . He doesn't call anyone by his nickname . . . He is complex, confusing, misunderstood, unclear in every way but one. He is a brilliant coach, the best of his time."

Dryden also mentioned Bowman's coaching style, and how he was an honors graduate from the old school of management techniques. "He has no coach's con about him," Dryden wrote. "He does not slap backs, punch arms or grab elbows. He doesn't search eyes, spew out ingratiating blarney, or disarm with faint, enervating praise. He is shy and not very friendly. All the time you talk, one foot on the brake, the other on the accelerator, he lurches away, inch by inch."

For his part, Bowman suggested that he had softened somewhat since leaving the bench in Buffalo, that his coaching style had lost some of its autocratic edge. "As you grow older, and you've been around Bob for a year, maybe his style kind of spills off on everybody," he said.

Regardless, no one expected Bowman to be transformed into the Badger. There could only be one Bob Johnson, and Bowman would be doing an injustice to all concerned if he tried to imitate him. Besides, it was pretty tough to question Bowman's qualifications for the job. You don't get the best record of any coach in history by accident. "It's not like he was just dragged off the street," Paul Coffey said. "Bob was a winner wherever he went and Scotty's no different."

Bowman was a winner in his first night with the Penguins, too. They fell behind the Buffalo Sabres, 3-1, during the second period of the opener October 4, but had no trouble ignoring the scoreboard or the problems inherent in playing on the under-sized ice surface at The Aud. They never lost their composure, which is probably why they didn't lose the game. "They didn't get flustered," Bowman said. "I've been here with visiting teams before — great teams in Montreal — and it's not an easy rink to come back in."

Of course, having an imposing collection of goal-scorers at your disposal the way Bowman did in this game does terrific things for a team's confidence. Pittsburgh could send out waves of menacing forwards, including Mario Lemieux, Mark Recchi, Jaromir Jagr, and Kevin Stevens, guys who can wipe out a seemingly comfortable lead in a shift or two. It's never a bad idea to have some electricians on call when Pittsburgh is in town, because there's always a chance the scoreboard will get short-circuited. "We've got five or six of the best offensive players in the game on this team," Barrasso said. "We're never out of the game, and that's how we played."

The Penguins also had developed a knack for getting timely offense from unlikely sources, and on this night defenseman Gord Roberts, who had turned 34 two days earlier, provided it. At 13:08 of the third period, he lashed a slapshot past Sabres goalie Daren Puppa for the game-winning goal. "It was kind of like a flashback to the 70s, when I could shoot the puck," Roberts said, laughing.

But there was nothing even remotely familiar about their next game, because there never had been one like it in franchise history. For the first time ever, the Penguins would appear at the Civic Arena as Stanley Cup champions.

They postponed their banner-raising ceremony hoping Bob Johnson would be well enough to attend at some time in the near future, but the Stanley Cup was positioned at center ice before the opening faceoff, and each player was introduced to the capacity crowd of 16,164. So was Fred Rogers, the Mr. Rogers of public television fame, who was serving as the Penguins' honorary captain as part of the NHL's 75th anniversary celebration.

Mr. Rogers got off a crowd-pleasing line — "It is a beautiful day in this neighborhood" — but Mike Lange, the Penguins' longtime play-by-play announcer and master of ceremonies for the pregame program, unleashed an even better one.

Lange has earned a national following with his unique goal calls ("Lemieux beat Hextall like a rented mule" and "Beaupre didn't know whether to cry or wind his watch," among many others), but his spontaneous remark to Rogers might have been one of his best. "Only a few years ago, Mr. Rogers," Lange said, "you might have been able to play for this team." He apparently didn't consider the possibility that even Mr. Rogers might have been too feisty and competitive to play hockey in Pittsburgh for a lot of seasons.

The home-opener gave the Penguins their first look at a Patrick Division opponent, and they couldn't have liked what they saw. The Philadelphia Flyers, who had finished fifth in the Patrick the previous season, charged into the Civic Arena and came out a few hours later with a 2-2 tie, thanks mainly to a 33-save performance by goalie Ron Hextall. It was an early indication of the caliber of play the Penguins would face in the Patrick all season.

The Penguins had two significant, albeit short-lived, concerns after the game. One was their power play, which had failed to score on eight opportunities. "I should have scored three times on the stupid thing," Stevens said. The other was the condition of Mario Lemieux's lower lip, which had been ripped open by Hextall's stick. The blow also cost Lemieux a tooth.

Hextall has long been regarded as one of hockey's most aggressive goalies and seems to enjoy being cast as a villain on the road, but televised replays exonerated him of any guilt for Lemieux's injury. It seems Hextall had his stick up after clearing the puck, and simply clipped Lemieux on his follow-through. For years, the book on Hextall had been that he was perfectly willing to maim opponents with his stick, and he would rather use it on someone's shins than the puck, but the charges just wouldn't stick this time. "I didn't even know I hit him," Hextall said. "Honest, I didn't."

Even though it violated every instinct they had developed during years of playing against Hextall, the Penguins agreed there had been no malice on the play.

"I just got in the way," Lemieux said. "I don't think he knew I was there." Bowman pointed out, "a lot of people, their reputation precedes them," but he declared Hextall innocent on all counts. "I was just as upset as anybody when Mario got cut," he said, "but Hextall just came out to play the shot."

The Penguins got a taste of life without Ron Francis during the early days of the season, and while his absence was impossible to overlook, veterans Bryan Trottier and Jiri Hrdina were doing a commendable job of filling in for him. Neither could take over Francis's vast array of duties, at least not for an extended period, but both enjoyed the extra playing time and responsibilities they were getting. "We have to rely on more experienced players," said Hrdina, 33. "And at my age, I'm experienced."

Bowman tried to preserve the legs of Trottier and Hrdina by limiting their work on off-days, but Trottier said there was no danger of his energy reserves being depleted. "That (extra duty) has never been a problem for me," he said. "Most players thrive on ice time, and I'm no different. Wearing down is never a problem. Never."

But there was a danger of some of his teammates wearing something out. Specifically, the videotapes of their bid for the Stanley Cup a few months earlier. They had proven to be a better anti-depressant than anything in a pharmacy. "You see a lot of highlight tapes — you've got them in your house — and they're always great to watch," Stevens said. "Whenever you feel down a little bit, you stick one of those tapes in and it gives you a lift, because it's everything any hockey player ever wanted to do."

But four games into the season, the Penguins didn't have much need for such emotional pick-me-ups. There were a few isolated concerns about how Stevens and Mark Recchi were struggling to regain their form of the previous season, but the Penguins were 2-1-1 and fairly satisfied with the caliber of their play.

And they were even more pleased by what they had seen of Bowman's work behind the bench. He wasn't berating players at the slightest provocation, or belittling them when they made mistakes. The players had felt they knew all about Bowman before he took the job, but their experiences were contradicting their expectations. They feared they'd be working under Attila the Coach; what they got was closer to Gandhi in a sports jacket.

"Everybody thought he was going to be a hot-headed guy on the bench, but he's been a good coach," Stevens said. "He hasn't been one of those guys who's been crazy. He's been pretty calm."

Tom Barrasso, whose run-ins with Bowman in Buffalo had been the stuff of local legend, offered a few insights on how Bowman had changed, and why it might have happened. "He's such an intense person, and before he used to take that out in negative ways, always trying to almost badger you into playing well," Barrasso said. "And it worked for a lot of guys but, as time went on, it stopped working. But I think he's lost that from his repertoire. I don't think he feels it's necessary now to hound guys, to yell and scream. He's beyond that.

"He's not behind the bench out of a matter of want. He's there because an unfortunate circumstance put him there. The most important thing is it's not his team that he put together, so he doesn't feel directly responsible for winning and losing. I think he's pretty comfortable with what he's achieved as a coach, and I don't think he feels he has to go out of his way to prove himself working with us. As time went by, I think he really grew to be comfortable with who he was as a person and what he's accomplished as a professional, and that's all anybody could ask for."

Actually, there was one more thing Bowman could have requested: That his players be a little more considerate of his central nervous system. Returning to coaching was tough enough; doing it with a team that had the Penguins' penchant for building and blowing leads had to be infinitely more difficult. When the Penguins are involved in a game, no lead is safe. For either team.

Consider the events of October 15, when they visited Nassau Coliseum on Long Island for the first time during the regular season. They spotted the New York Islanders a 6-2 lead — Derek King scored three of New York's goals in a span of one minute, 18 seconds — and committed some of the most glaring defensive gaffes imaginable while doing it.

For example, giving the Islanders a two-on-zero break. Then yielding a four-on-one break about a minute later. Ignoring assignments all over the ice. It was, for much of the evening, a clinic in bad hockey. "It was embarrassing," Bowman said. "Let's face it, the first period and a half was embarrassing to everybody."

But Mark Recchi scored 29 seconds into the third period to whittle Pittsburgh's deficit to 6-3. Mario Lemieux completed his 27th career hat trick with goals at 9:17 and 10:26. Jaromir Jagr scorched New York defenseman Joe Reekie one-on-one and tied it at 11:43. The juggernaut that is the Pittsburgh offense had started to roll, and New York was powerless to slow it. The issue no longer was who would win the game, but when it would happen. And at 2:30 of overtime, Phil Bourque shoveled a Paul Coffey rebound past New York goalie Glenn Healy for the game-winner.

"As soon as we started to get two, three, four goals, you could see they were just in disarray," Bourque said. "When we get on a roll like that, I don't think anybody can stop us. I thought the best thing they could have done was call a timeout . . . and maybe punt."

So the Penguins finished the night with two points, but a lot of misgivings about how they got them.

"I hate these games," Bourque said. "These are the worst games to play in, so many peaks and valleys. It's not how we played in the playoffs last year, that's for sure. We can't have shootouts like this. This is old Penguin hockey, where you win five of these and lose five of these, and what good is that?"

The lessons delivered during that game on Long Island still were fresh two nights later, when New York came to the Civic Arena. This time, the Penguins vowed they wouldn't fall behind the Islanders, and it worked. They blew out to a 4-1 lead by the middle of the second period. But although getting ahead wasn't much of a problem, staying there was. The Islanders reeled off four unanswered goals in the final 6 1/2 minutes of the second period to seize a 5-4 lead before the Penguins scored four of their own to claim an 8-5 victory. "This is not the kind of hockey we expected to play," Bowman said. "It looked like the last shot was going to win for a while."

But there were at least a couple of bright spots on this night, as Paul Coffey broke two of Denis Potvin's scoring records for NHL defensemen. His assist on Bob Errey's goal at 4:47 of the third period was the 1,053rd point of Coffey's career, one more than Potvin put up during his storied tenure with the Islanders. And the assist he earned on Kevin Stevens' goal at 5:31 was No. 743, one more than Potvin.

It was inevitable that Coffey, the finest skater in recent NHL history, would become the most prolific offensive defenseman of all time, but even a longtime observer like Bowman said Coffey's point total "is hard to believe." For his part, Coffey seemed almost overwhelmed by the magnitude of his feats. "It's kind of hard to believe, coming from a small town (Weston, Ontario) and putting those kinds of numbers up. Passing two great hockey players in Bobby Orr and, of course, Denis Potvin . . . it's a nice feeling."

Statistics aside, Coffey had long been criticized in some quarters for his offense-oriented style of play. He is the antithesis of a classic defenseman, and it has been suggested that he sometimes looks as if he is wearing street shoes when playing in the defensive zone. There are times when he spends so much of the game on his knees around his team's net that running the Zamboni there between periods seems unnecessary.

But his speed and offensive skills add a dimension no other defenseman in the game can provide — Bryan Trottier called him "a classic skater, the purest skater in the league" — which is why his teammates were so alarmed by persistent talk that Coffey's stay in Pittsburgh would not last much longer, that he had taken up residence on the trading block.

"There's only one player like that in the league," Mario Lemieux said. "You can't replace him. The way he skates, the way he moves the puck, the way he shoots it, the way he makes plays, he's probably the best of all-time at his position."

"I don't think you can replace a guy like him," Stevens said. "No question, you can't. He's one of the best offensive defensemen ever to play the game, and he's still playing the way he did when he was 19 or 20." But that didn't mean Coffey wasn't playing on borrowed time, at least in Pittsburgh.

The Penguins raised their 1991 championship banners before a game against the New York Rangers October 19, then promptly were shown how difficult it would be to earn another set. Perhaps it was appropriate that the banners lurched up as Civic Arena workers tugged them into place without mechanized assistance — "I got a sore neck watching them go up," Bob

Errey said — because so few things had ever gone smoothly for the Penguins.

And they certainly didn't on this night, as Pittsburgh spotted New York a two-goal lead, then rallied to tie the game, 4-4, before Rangers center Darren Turcotte got the decisive goal with 70 seconds left in regulation. This time, the Penguins found out what it was like to be on the wrong end of late-game heroics. "It's an exciting way to play," Bowman said. "But it's not practical."

It didn't help that the Penguins played part of the third period without their two best forwards. Stevens got a five-minute penalty, an automatic game misconduct for butt-ending New York's Paul Broten, even though Stevens insisted he struck Broten with his hand, a blow that "wouldn't have hurt my grandmother." Lemieux pulled out of the game after his back began to spasm for the second time in little more than two weeks.

Losing to a bitter division rival like the Rangers took much of the pleasure out of the Penguins' banner-raising ceremony, although the players recognized that a touch of tradition had been added to an arena that had none. That those pieces of cloth hanging from the ceiling might someday give them an edge, because hockey is a game in which intangibles have enormous value and impact.

"This building's been around for a while and I'm sure a lot of visiting teams, when they come in, are going to take a look up there," Phil Bourque said. "I know when I go into the Montreal Forum, the first thing you do is look up at those banners. Same thing in Boston Garden. You look up and you just can't believe how many banners are hanging there. And I guess you've got to start somewhere."

While the banners might have an effect on visiting teams, they didn't seem to do much for the Penguins, who by this time were openly questioning their approach to games. The on-off switch that controlled their intensity was wearing out from overuse, and it was clear that a serious attitude adjustment was needed before a disturbing trend became a nasty habit. "We play hard at times, but we don't do anything at other times, and we've got to put that to an end," Barrasso said. "Over the course of the season, games like we've been playing, we will not win. We will not tie. We will lose. And that's not going to make it."

Barrasso's point was reinforced dramatically in an 8-0 loss on October 29 to Washington at the Civic Arena , the low point in the early part of Pittsburgh's season. It was the first time the Penguins had been shut out at home in four years, and the game was even more lopsided than the final score indicated. Anything bad that could happen, did, on just about every shift. Bowman told reporters "the only people who should escape criticism are the ones who didn't dress for the game," and Mario Lemieux said, "I've never seen a hockey game like this in my whole life. Everybody's embarrassed."

But that most humbling defeat, coupled with the game that followed it two nights later, was a testament to the resilience of this team. The NHL schedule brought Minnesota, which had severely tested the Penguins during the Stanley Cup finals a few months earlier, to the Civic Arena on Halloween. And it proved to be a night more scary than anything the North Stars could have imagined.

The Penguins had gotten over their 60-minute meltdown against Washington, and scorched Minnesota for eight unanswered goals before Minnesota's Derian Hatcher spoiled Frank Pietrangelo's shutout bid by scoring at 17:55 of the third period. Not that the goal mattered much; there was little danger of the North Stars getting the touchdown they needed to salvage a tie. The only repercussion from Hatcher's goal was that Pietrangelo lost his shot at a shutout bonus, a regular-season rarity in Pittsburgh.

The events of their 8-1 victory reaffirmed one of hockey's eternal truths for the Penguins, that it is easier to play when you have a lead. In the previous five games, they had been ahead of their opponents for a total of 50 seconds.

And the Penguins' victory meant more than two points in the Patrick Division standings. It verified that, when motivated, the Penguins could perform at a level few teams can reach. "There was no sense in panicking, but the way we've been playing is pretty atrocious," Kevin Stevens said. "When you get a win like this, it's a lift for the team. Maybe the loss the other night helped. You hate to say a loss helped, but instead of losing 1-0 or 2-0, losing 8-0 opened our eyes."

Losing games, of course, should not be construed as a positive thing. If it were, expansion teams could count on having their names engraved on the Stanley Cup at the conclusion of their first season in the league. But being thrashed so soundly by the Capitals had been shock therapy for the Penguins. It had driven home the idea that winning the Stanley Cup the previous spring would have no tangible impact on the season that followed.

One impressive victory hardly meant the Penguins had turned their season around — especially when they lost defenseman Paul Stanton with a torn ligament in his right knee — but the locker-room sentiment was that Pittsburgh had hit its nadir a few nights earlier, and now was headed in the only direction possible. Up.

"They say you have to hit rock-bottom before you go to the top," Pietrangelo said. "And we hit rock-bottom the other night. Hopefully, we won't go there again."

CHAPTER FOUR

Putting Out the "For Sale" Sign

Edward J. DeBartolo is one of the country's leading shopping-mall magnates and has been involved with the Penguins since 1977, when he purchased a one-third interest in the team. He took over as sole owner April 5, 1978, and little more than 13 years later was telling the throng at Point State Park how winning the Stanley Cup had cost him about $25 million.

There were no signs of people passing the hat to give DeBartolo a little spending money, but perhaps somone should have. He is often named as one of the richest men in the United States, but business deals reportedly had caused crippling cash-flow problems in his organization, and speculation that he was about to sell the Penguins became rampant during the summer of 1991. He said after the Point State Park rally that he was not entertaining offers for the team, but it became apparent in subsequent months that he would be willing, however grudgingly, to part with the franchise and the rights to operate the Civic Arena.

Howard Baldwin and Morris Belzberg, who had jointly purchased the Minnesota North Stars a little over a year earlier, eventually emerged as the men most likely to buy the team, and Spectacor became the front-runner to run the building. Later, it became known that Thomas V. Ruta, a partner in a New York accounting firm, was part of the Baldwin-Belzberg group.

Baldwin, one-time managing general partner of the Hartford Whalers, and Belzberg, a retired executive with Budget

Rent-a-Car, had purchased the North Stars in 1990, but sold out to Norm Green, a close friend of Belzberg's, later that year. Baldwin had been retained by DeBartolo in the summer of 1991 to broker the sale of the franchise. Paul Martha, president of the Civic Arena Corp. and general counsel to the Penguins, spent part of the offseason trying to put together a group of Pittsburgh-based investors after DeBartolo said he wanted to sell the team.

Belzberg confirmed in early October that his group was negotiating with DeBartolo, and a week or so into the season a deal was apparently reached. The Baldwin-Belzberg group reportedly would pay $31 million for the team, and Spectacor would ante up $24 million for the Arena, and there was strong evidence that a local group would purchase a share of the team from Baldwin and Belzberg. "I think our first order of business will be to involve some local people," Belzberg said. "We feel we should have some local ownership."

Local ownership had been a key facet of Baldwin's approach in Hartford, where he got the Aetna and Travelers insurance companies involved with the Whalers when they moved from the World Hockey Association to the NHL in 1979. Baldwin had founded the New England Whalers with a cash investment of $25,000 in 1971, and put in a stint as WHA president before the 1979 merger between the leagues — a merger in which Baldwin played a pivotal role.

The prospective owners, whose deal with DeBartolo was finalized but who still hadn't had the transaction approved by league officials, experienced their first major crisis November 4. One day earlier, a copy of a letter from Baldwin to Paul Martha was leaked to several media outlets. The letter, dated August 23, alluded to the possibility of helping to finance the purchase of the team by selling "certain assets of the hockey team for a net sales price of $7,000,000."

The local reaction, in and out of the locker room, was immediate and almost universal: The prospective owners were obviously intent on removing the numbers from some high-caliber players' uniforms and replacing them with price tags. They would buy the team and have it dismantled before sundown.

That interpretation, Baldwin insisted, was totally inaccurate. He acknowledged writing the letter, but said "absolutely, unequivocally" no deals had been made to trade or sell highly paid players, and that Craig Patrick, not the owners, would be responsible for all personnel moves.

"All we were trying to do when we structured this deal was to structure it in such a way that, economically, we can survive," Baldwin said. "Any reference to the sale of players . . . we have to keep (the) payroll at a certain level. I've got to know we can at least break even. There's no way anybody can buy anything without knowing that. But we would never, never just wholesale players. Never. We won't do that. Let me be very clear on something: We are closing this sale without the sale of any assets. We are closing this deal with our own resources. We are not selling assets."

Baldwin could not have been more emphatic, but skepticism continued to swell. Players wondered if they had any future in Pittsburgh, and fans questioned whether the team they had purchased tickets to see would remain intact for more than a few days. Baldwin acknowledged the speculation about selling players was a major public relations blow to his group, but said, "all we can do is assure everybody that Craig Patrick runs the team. We will do what we think is right for the franchise. I've never done anything to the detriment of a franchise."

Baldwin said leaking the memo could have been construed as an attempt to torpedo the sale, although "I would hope that isn't the case." He also said he was confident the NHL Board of Governors would give the three-quarters approval needed for the sale because it would be a sound business move. "The deal is what it is," Baldwin said. "We hope it will be judged on its merits, not on rumors. I've seen a lot of transactions in this league over the years and this is as good as, if not better than, any of them."

The Board of Governors apparently didn't agree, however; on November 6, it tabled the issue of whether to approve the transaction, citing a need to study it in greater detail. NHL President John Ziegler said the approval process was "held up" because "we have not had the luxury of time" to consider such a complicated transaction. Minnesota owner Norm Green said the governors decided to table the sale because "in a large transaction like that, there are a lot of facets to it, and some of them had questions. The buyers have to get the questions answered. It seems like none of them are very serious."

Baldwin said the governors asked him "head-on" if he planned to sell any of the Penguins' hockey assets to finance the deal, and he told them "Absolutely there is no understanding at all to wholesale assets of the Pittsburgh hockey club." Ziegler said he believed Baldwin and his partners had no intention of selling players because such action would be self-defeating. "If they're doing something damaging to the product, it isn't only the fans who lose," Ziegler said. "The owners' stake in this is substantial."

One snag in getting league approval was a dispute over whether Baldwin's group had agreed to sell 50 percent of the franchise to a local group headed by Martha. Martha contended such an arrangement had been worked out, while Baldwin insisted "we have no obligations to him."

As the Board's next session approached, Baldwin said he was confident a revised version of the transaction would be approved. "I just think they need to evaluate the whole deal," he said. "I don't anticipate any problems. And if there are any, we will fix them to their satisfaction."

Baldwin's group went back before the Board with the restructured proposal November 18, and the governors gave their consent to the sale. Under the revamped plan, DeBartolo retained a limited interest and reportedly agreed to underwrite a portion of the team's losses. Ziegler said the reworked agreement "made the equity side and the investment side stronger. Very simply, we asked them to put up more money and borrow less." Another part of the deal reportedly involved having Martha sign a waiver releasing Baldwin and his partners from any legal obligation to his group of investors, although Baldwin denied that.

Ziegler said the Board felt it was not necessary to have Baldwin, Belzberg, and Ruta put their pledge that high-priced players would not be sold into writing. "We've known Howard Baldwin for a while," he said. "I've gotten to know Morris Belzberg when he joined with Howard to purchase the North Stars. As to both these gentlemen, we believe in their word and their integrity. There is nothing in our relationship with Mr. Baldwin and Mr. Belzberg that would have given us any cause not to take their word."

Not everyone was willing to do that, however. At a press conference the day after the sale was approved by the league,

Baldwin had a verbal sparring match with Beano Cook, a Pittsburgh resident and sports commentator. When Baldwin told the assembled media the new owners "want to be standing here 10 years from now," Cook cut in, and said, "Would you be willing to pay me $20,000 if you are not the owner 10 years from now?"

"Would you be willing to pay me $20,000 if I am?" Baldwin responded.

The wager was refined to $1,000, based on whether Baldwin would still be team president in five years. But the details of the bet were far less significant than the skepticism conveyed by Cook's challenge. The perception among much of the public and press was that Baldwin and his partners were guilty of something — even if nobody knew just what — and would stay that way unless they exonerated themselves.

Baldwin recognized that serious questions had been raised about his group's credibility, valid or not, and again sought to ease concerns that the franchise would be strip-mined of its assets for a quick profit. "We're anxious to prove ourselves as owners," he said. "All we ask is that you just give us a chance."

While he stressed that no deals to unload high-priced talent had been arranged, and that Craig Patrick had the final say on personnel matters, Baldwin did acknowledge concerns about the financial futures of teams like the Penguins, who play in a relatively small market and rely heavily on the ticket-buying public for revenue. "Whatever problems we have here in Pittsburgh, you can bet all the other teams have the same problems," Baldwin said. "And everyone should be addressing them, not just us."

He talked about finding "creative ways" to generate income, about exploring the possibility of pay-per-view television for some games. He also called for the NHL to investigate ways to implement a salary cap and revenue-sharing, much as the National Basketball Association has done. "It works great in the NBA," he said. "If we're prospering, who minds sharing? But if we're going down ..."

Baldwin said the new owners would establish financial guidelines under which Craig Patrick would operate, but that should not be construed as giving Patrick a mandate to hold a clearance sale on highly paid players. "You don't buy a product and dismantle it," he said.

He also shrugged off speculation that the sale was a prelude to the transfer of the franchise, and said he planned to spend considerable time in Pittsburgh, even though his Baldwin Sports and Entertainment business was based in Los Angeles.

"I have spent 20 years in the business of professional hockey," he said. "I'm coming in with a great deal of enthusiasm. We plan to be hands-on owners, but we're not fools . . . we'll support the good people who are already here. This (Pittsburgh) is where we want to be. These have been a difficult and confusing last couple of months. We're anxious to prove ourselves as owners."

It didn't take long for Baldwin to prove at least one of his points, that Patrick would have control over personnel matters. Baldwin had a strong affection for Ulf Samuelsson, whom he knew from Hartford, but said he had no intention of intervening in the negotiations to get Samuelsson a new contract. "I like Ulfie, but it's only fitting and proper that Craig handle that," he said. "I don't want to interject myself in one negotiation and not in another."

Baldwin said all the right things — and said most of them over and over — but uncertainty about the franchise's future still percolated around the Civic Arena. Players who had known Baldwin during his days in Hartford, however, said they believed any fears about how he would run the Penguins were unfounded. "He's gone through a lot of bad publicity in Pittsburgh," Gord Roberts said. "Hopefully, people will give him an opportunity. Howard's a very involved person who will be a positive influence on the Pittsburgh community."

Ron Francis said Baldwin was "very well liked by the players" in Hartford and had been "very good to work for" when they were together with the Whalers. "He was more of a hands-on type guy than what they've had around here in the past," Francis said. "If you'd go on a Western trip, he'd take the team out for a nice dinner, do different things like that."

If nothing else, at least the players finally knew who would be signing their paychecks, who was setting the course the franchise would follow. And that meant one fewer off-ice issue to worry about. "It obviously distracts you somewhat, because you're interested in it, and it can ultimately affect you," Francis said. "But the bottom line is that none of us has that kind of money to buy a club, and we just have to do our job."

Baldwin and his partners got their first look at the team they had purchased two days after the Board of Governors approved the deal. Baldwin, Belzberg, and Ruta, along with dozens of their friends, crammed into the owner's superbox at the Civic Arena and watched a 5-2 victory against Philadelphia.

They enjoyed seeing the Penguins win, and the capacity crowd attending the game. They enjoyed being able to watch the game without hearing a single outburst of the obscene chants that had been directed at them when speculation about the wholesaling of players was at its zenith. "For starters, this was great," Baldwin said.

Of course, the Penguins had more motivation than usual on this night. Not just because the Flyers were a Patrick Division rival, or because their new bosses were at the game. No, there was a post-game party with the owners — attendance was mandatory — and the atmosphere could have been pretty tense if the Penguins had been forced to explain a lopsided loss.

"This makes things a little more hospitable," Tom Barrasso said. "We get paid to perform and these are the people who pay us. It's a nice way to get them into their new organization."

CHAPTER FIVE

The Power and the Glory

The stereotype of the U.S.-born hockey player persisted for years, and it was, for the most part quite accurate, if not flattering. It held, in short, that American players were hard workers who could exchange their sticks for shovels without having their production suffer to any great degree. Guys who were quite willing to sweat, but could offer very little skill. Blue-collar laborers, not craftsmen.

But that image has been eroding for a decade or so, since a pack of supremely gifted Americans made their way to the NHL: Joe Mullen, Jeremy Roenick, Brian Leetch, Pat LaFontaine, Gary Suter, and Craig Janney. And a lot of others who hardly were shortchanged when hockey skills were being handed out.

And if there is a new prototype of the U.S.-born player, it is Kevin Stevens. He has linebacker size (6-3, 220 pounds) complemented by fuel-injected speed and a platinum scoring touch. That is a combination few players from any country can claim, and has enabled Stevens to supplant Boston right winger Cam Neely as the premier power forward in the league. "He's in a class by himself, strictly because he combines so many features," said Ron Francis, Stevens' occasional linemate. "The thing a lot of guys who play like that (a physical game) don't have is his speed. He's like a locomotive when he gets on the tracks. You don't want to step in front of him."

Rick Tocchet, who would finish the season on a line with Stevens and Mario Lemieux after joining the Penguins in a trade with Philadelphia, said he gained an even greater appreciation of Stevens' game when he began to watch him on a daily basis. "I never really respected his speed until I was on this team. He's one of the fastest guys in the league. When you have a guy who can skate like that who's 220, he's a rare commodity."

But while Stevens has been an extraordinary find for the Penguins, success at this level of the game wasn't always a certainty for him. The Los Angeles Kings had taken him in the sixth round of the 1983 entry draft, a few months before he enrolled at Boston College. On September 9 of that year, Eddie Johnston, then general manager of the Penguins, pried his rights away from Los Angeles for journeyman forward Anders Hakansson. The deal was regarded to be so minor that the Penguins didn't announce it to the media. Or bother to tell Stevens. He found out about the deal a week or so later while reading the "For the Record" column in *Sports Illustrated*.

"We were sitting in his room at Boston College," said Suzanne Stevens, who became his wife in 1990. "It was his freshman year. He found his name in the back of the magazine, in real small print. It was like he said, 'Oh,' and I said, 'Oh,' and we didn't talk much about it. I think playing in the National Hockey League was a dream for Kevin, but I don't think he thought it could come true. He didn't make a big deal about seeing his name in *Sports Illustrated* because he didn't think anything would ever come of it."

No, Stevens didn't approach hockey as a potential career during his formative years in the game. During the 1991 playoffs, Suzanne Stevens said, "I think deep down inside he wondered if he could make it." Jay Adams, his roommate at Boston College, echoed that sentiment. "Kevin is a guy who always questions himself, and I think he has always questioned whether he belongs in the NHL," he said. His doubts were somewhat understandable. Outside of size, speed, and skill, Stevens really didn't have *that* much to offer a team.

Stevens spent four seasons at BC, where he made the Hockey East first all-star team in his senior year, then played for the 1988 U.S. Olympic team before joining the Penguins for the final 16 games of the 1987-88 season. He showed considerable promise by scoring five goals, but was exiled to the Penguins' farm team in Muskegon, Michigan, for much of the following year. The management team in power at the time, general manager Tony Esposito and coach Gene Ubriaco, had decided that spending time busing between the backwater towns of the International Hockey League would accelerate Stevens' development.

He was fairly productive in 1989-90, scoring 29 goals in 76 games with the Penguins, but 1990-91 was a breakthrough year. Stevens piled up 40 goals in 80 games, and began to consistently play the style that was a hybrid of finesse and muscle. And it was during the playoffs in the spring of 1991 that Stevens evolved into the conscience of this team.

The Penguins had just lost Game 2 of their Wales Conference final series against Boston, 5-4 in overtime, to fall behind the Bruins 2-0 in the series. The talk around most of Boston Garden that night was of the possibility of a Bruins sweep, but not in the corner of the Penguins' locker room occupied by Kevin Stevens.

He agreed that the outcome of the series was a foregone conclusion, that it was pretty clear which team would be going to the Stanley Cup finals. The thing is, Stevens' way of thinking conflicted with the prevailing sentiment in the Garden that night. He was convinced the Penguins would win the series, and he shared this belief with anybody who would listen. Not that he thought the Penguins had a chance to win the series, or that they might pull it off. That they would win. He guaranteed it. To wave after wave of reporters, and anyone else who bothered to ask.

"We're confident we can beat this team, and we will beat this team," Stevens said that night. "We'll beat this team. I'll say right now, we'll beat them." It was pretty tough to miss his point.

Maybe that wasn't the logical thing to do, to promise that the Penguins would climb out of such a deep hole. Maybe it wasn't prudent. But it was bold. It was gutsy. And it was accurate. The Penguins swept the next four games from the Bruins, with Stevens cast in a leading role. He had backed up the most brash statements of his career with some of his finest hockey. And he had earned a place alongside the likes of Mario Lemieux as a legitimate team leader.

Bryan Trottier, who had been part of the New York Islanders' nucleus during their run of four consecutive Stanley Cups in the early 1980s, likened Stevens' locker room presence to that of Clark Gillies, the mammoth left winger who was a fixture with those great New York teams. "It's so contagious when Kevin says it," Trottier said. "He can convince a lot of people that he's right ... I think it's a gift. He can almost will guys to think his way. Clark Gillies used to have that presence. Big guys have that ability to do things and say things, and when they do, other guys respond."

Stevens said his evolution into a locker room leader "just kind of happened," but it is an honest extension of his personality. He is laid-back off the ice, but his emotional thermostat skyrockets when he puts on a uniform. "Kevin's an intense player," Scott Bowman said. "He's got a lot of Cam Neely in him in that regard. He does get involved in the game ... He's the type of player who, if you're on the other side, you don't want to get him riled up."

Stevens made that point most emphatically at a game in Boston Garden during the 1990-91 regular season. Bruins defenseman Jim Wiemer provoked Stevens into fighting, and, seconds later, left the ice with a broken nose, a long trail of blood marking the path Wiemer followed to the dressing room. Not surprisingly, few opponents have shown much interest in trading punches with Stevens since that night.

But it was not Stevens' prowess as a fighter that finally convinced Craig Patrick to match the $5.375 million offer sheet Boston signed Stevens to during September of 1991. The lure was Stevens' unique package of bulk and ability. Some in the organization whispered that Stevens would never equal his 40-goal output of 1990-91, but any fears in that regard vanished fairly quickly the following season.

Stevens scored two goals in that resounding Halloween victory against Minnesota, and used that game as a springboard to perhaps the most spectacular months in his outstanding season. He was named the NHL Player of the Month for November, when he piled up 15 goals and 13 assists in 13 games.

But while he was particularly productive in November, Stevens was a paragon of consistency for most of the year, and by the end of the 1991-92 season, he was firmly established as the game's consummate power forward. He finished with 54 goals, more than anyone in the league except Brett Hull of St. Louis, and was second to Mario Lemieux in the NHL scoring race with 123 points, most ever by a player born in the United States. Those numbers were irrefutable evidence, if any more was needed by that time, that American-born players could not only survive, but thrive, in the NHL.

Stevens grew up in Pembroke, Massachusetts, and was a member of the Bobby Orr generation, players who took up the game because of their reverence for Orr and his Big, Bad Bruins teammates of the early 1970s.

Stevens was a versatile athlete in high school, and his father, Art, played minor league baseball for the Cincinnati Reds, but when Stevens decided to pursue a career in sports, he chose skates over cleats, as so many New Englanders have done in recent years. "From the beginning, Kevin had a knack for scoring," Art Stevens said. "He had a knack for being in the right position, then putting the puck in the net."

"He's a good example of what Bob Johnson used to talk about: A top athlete," Bowman said. "John Elway, what would he be like if he were a hockey player? Well, Kevin Stevens was a good athlete in football and baseball, and he chose hockey."

The list of Stevens' superlatives from the 1991-92 season is long and impressive. He was the first left winger since the legendary Bobby Hull in 1968-69 to finish as high as second in the scoring race. He broke Michel Goulet's record for most points in a season by an NHL left winger. He became the first player in league history to get more than 100 points and 200 penalty minutes in the same season. He was chosen the Wales Conference's starting left winger for the All-Star Game in voting by the fans, and was named a first-team All-Star when the season was over.

And, until the final days of the regular season, he stayed alongside — and sometimes, in front of — a couple of living legends named Lemieux and Gretzky in the scoring race. "The first month or so, you're up there and people say, 'Oh, he'll drop off, he'll drop off,' " Stevens said. "But I've been lucky to be with some great players and score some goals."

There were lots of skeptics, folks who doubted Stevens' ability to keep up with the pace set by two of the game's all-time greats. For a brief time, even the guy who dressed at Stevens' locker room stall and wore his uniform questioned whether he could do it. "I didn't expect myself to be up there with those guys," he said. "You always want to be confident you can score goals or whatever — I thought I could help the team that way — but I didn't think I'd be right up there."

But Stevens converted the cynics, including himself. He proved it didn't matter that he was a sixth-round draft choice, or that he grew up in Massachusetts instead of Manitoba. He proved that skill and desire meant far more than any biographical details. No one wonders about Stevens' ability anymore, or about the wisdom of signing him to such a lucrative contract; the only question that matters is what level of greatness he will reach in coming seasons. "With his speed and size and strength," Joe Mullen said, "there's no telling what he can do."

CHAPTER SIX

The Ups and Downs of Autumn

The opening faceoff was less than two hours away, and John Cullen was standing on the stage that separates the locker rooms at the Civic Arena, engaged in an animated conversation with Paul Coffey. Nothing new about that. They were close friends and had chatted for countless hours over the previous few years.

But this time they went in different directions when the conversation was over. Coffey headed to the Penguins' locker room, Cullen to the one that houses the visiting team. It was Cullen's first game at the Civic Arena since the March 4 trade that sent him, Zarley Zalapski, and Jeff Parker to the Hartford Whalers for Ron Francis, Ulf Samuelsson, and Grant Jennings.

Cullen spent much of the afternoon of November 2 renewing acquaintances with old friends Kevin Stevens, Mark Recchi, Jay Cufield, and Steve Latin. After all, changing employers doesn't necessarily change the way you feel about old co-workers. "They're all my good friends, and we'll be great friends the rest of our lives," Cullen said. "But when you get on the ice, you're not friends."

Cullen reinforced that point before the evening was over, by getting a goal and an assist in the Whalers' 6-5 victory. So did Rob Brown, another former Penguin. Zalapski chipped in an assist. All things considered, it was quite a homecoming for the Whalers' pack of former Penguins, and they clearly enjoyed being back in familiar surroundings.

There were only two things they didn't recognize about the place: The banners hanging from the Arena ceiling, and the guys who dressed in the home team's locker room. Oh, they knew most of the names and faces, but the Penguins sure didn't look like the defending Stanley Cup champions during the game. They resembled nothing so much as a group of guys who had made other plans for the evening, then were summoned to work on short notice. They were present for the game, but that doesn't mean they showed up for it. "We wanted to win it more than they did, it looked like," Zalapski said.

Indeed, by the time Hartford took its two points and headed for the airport, the Penguins looked like they wanted nothing more than the easy way out. They were on a 1-5-1 skid — their 8-1 thrashing of Minnesota on October 31 being the only victory in that stretch — and were in no danger of triggering a mettle detector. If any of them had a passion for their work, they kept it well concealed. They were performing like a team whose psyches had staged a wildcat walkout, and whose sweat glands were honoring the picket line.

"We're definitely complacent," Bob Errey said. "That's exactly what's happening. We just haven't been into the games from the first period on. We find ourselves down in almost every game. We haven't been ready to play the games, and that comes from nobody but the people in the room (players)."

The numbers made it tough to argue with Errey's conclusion, which is why there was renewed talk that some of those players might not be working out of the Pittsburgh dressing room for much longer. If the Penguins didn't begin to register a pulse soon, there was every reason to believe they would have to undergo an emergency talent transfusion. "That can always happen in your profession," Errey said. "They made some changes (the previous season) and it worked out, so there's no reason why, if we don't snap out of it and get our act together, that they wouldn't make more."

"I guess you start looking from within first, what we're going to do with some of these guys if they don't start playing better," Scott Bowman said. "We've got to get going here. I'm more embarrassed than frustrated. I'm embarrassed that we're giving up so many goals (an average of 4.3 in the first 13 games). I don't even look forward to seeing the league statistics. I've got friends around the league who call me on the phone, and I don't look forward to getting their calls. I don't like it."

Not when the Penguins' leaky team defense was sure to be a prime topic of their conversation. Pittsburgh's greatest strength was its high-powered offense, of course, but Bowman was dismayed by the general lack of interest his players were showing in defense. No one expected the Penguins to win praise, let alone awards, for their defensive prowess, but some of them looked like they couldn't get around their own end of the ice without assistance from the auto club.

"I'm not looking for shutouts or one-goal games," Bowman said. "Shutouts are scarce, and you rarely need them to win. I'm looking for more shutout periods. We've only had eight or nine shutout periods all year. That isn't enough. We shouldn't have to score seven goals to win a game."

Maybe that means things got better in the Penguins' next game, because they could have won it with six. Trouble is, they only got five, which is the same total they allowed Boston to score. And the really distressing part was that the Penguins squandered a 5-2 lead. On home ice. Even more infuriating was that Boston had gotten back into the game because of a series of penalties called against Pittsburgh, including a bench minor against Bowman. The lack of discipline, it seemed, was contagious.

The penalty that referee Dan Marouelli gave to Bowman was the third against Pittsburgh in a span of 70 seconds. "I felt bad I got a penalty," Bowman said. "He (Marouelli) just stood and looked at me and I reminded him of the game he had in Montreal (a 4-1 Canadiens victory October 26) and also what he did to our team last year. But he couldn't wait to call it right away, with the team a couple of men down."

Bowman put Marouelli's performance on a level with his work in Game 2 of the 1991 Wales Conference final, which Bowman characterized as "that fiasco in Boston." In that game, Marouelli had assessed minor penalties to Peter Taglianetti and Gord Roberts in a 17-second span late in the third period, and Boston used the resultant five-on-three power play to tie the game. The Bruins went on to win 5-4 in overtime.

"We've had a real tough run with this guy," Bowman said. "There's not much you can do about it, I guess. They (the players) talked about the referee before the game, and we tried to tell them he's human and everything else. It makes me look like kind of a fool . . . But we'll have him again, so we've got to be careful."

Their problems with Marouelli gave the Penguins a cheap and easy explanation for why they had been unable to preserve their 5-2 lead, but when a team is on a 1-5-2 skid like the Penguins were, it needs points, not excuses. "Anytime you're up by three goals, you should be able to win the game, no matter what happens," Mario Lemieux said. "If you go through a situation where you have to kill a five-on-three, you kill it. But tonight, we didn't do the job."

The quality of their work improved significantly on November 8, when the Penguins squeezed out a 3-1 victory in Winnipeg, and Paul Coffey put his signature in the NHL record book yet again. This time, it was for scoring his 311th career goal, one more than Denis Potvin's standard for defensemen. That meant Coffey could claim a hat trick of scoring records — points, goals, and assists — for players at his position.

Never mind that the goal wouldn't go down as the most artistic of his career, and might not even make the top 300. Coffey's shot from the right-wing boards hit the stick of Jets defenseman Randy Carlyle and caromed past Winnipeg goalie Rick Tabaracci during a power play at 13:45 of the second period. Coffey didn't quibble about the aesthetics of the goal ("It's all right with me. I'll take it any way I can get it."), and his teammates didn't seem to care, either. "He scored 310 before that, and they were not all tip-ins," Mario Lemieux said.

Coffey cautioned that "we're not out of this thing (slump) by any means," but the Penguins sustained their momentum with a come-from-behind, 3-2 victory in Minnesota the next night. Those two points, however, nearly came at an extreme cost. Early in the second period, Phil Bourque was hooked from behind by North Stars center Neal Broten as he charged toward the Minnesota net. Bourque crashed into the boards in the left-wing corner and was prone for several minutes before being taken to the locker room with what was described as a "mild concussion."

That diagnosis was confirmed when Bourque, who at first could remember all details of the incident, later was unable to recall any of them. He then returned to the locker room, took a shower, dried his hair and got dressed. Then remembered that he'd better take a shower, dry his hair and get dressed. Which he did. Twice in a matter of minutes.

Broten, hardly known as one of hockey's leading hit men, knocked Pittsburgh goalie Frank Pietrangelo out of the game seconds after he finished serving his penalty for hooking Bourque. Broten stole the puck from Larry Murphy inside the Minnesota blue line and broke in alone, but lost his balance, slid into the goal crease and bowled over Pietrangelo, who went to the locker room with a lower back injury.

Pietrangelo's problem didn't seem to be serious, but the Penguins were in critical condition after Mike Modano and Bobby Smith had staked Minnesota to a 2-0 lead that carried into the final half of the third period. But Lemieux ignited Pittsburgh's comeback when he steered a Jaromir Jagr pass behind North Stars goalie Jon Casey at 10:06, and Stevens tied the game with a power-play goal at 15:24.

At that point the spotlight shifted to an unlikely figure, Jiri Hrdina. With 2:39 left in regulation, Hrdina blindly threw a backhander at the Minnesota net from the top of the faceoff circle. He was, Hrdina said, "just trying to get it close to the net, get a rebound." Instead, he got a game-winning goal, as the puck sailed past Casey and inside the left post. That gave the Penguins a 3-2 victory and only their second two-game winning streak of the season.

Bourque's concussion forced him to stay home for the next game in Madison Square Garden November 11, which was probably just as well. Seeing what happened that night could have done awful things to his blood pressure.

The Penguins lost 3-1 after giving up one of the most controversial goals of the season. New York Rangers right winger Joey Kocur was credited with it at 15:45 of the third period when, after a lengthy delay, replay official Tim Rappleye ruled the puck Kocur shot had not only entered the net, but had gone through the mesh.

The goal judge did not turn on the goal light after Kocur had shot the puck. Referee Terry Gregson did not signal that a goal had been scored. Players from both teams continued to skate and chase the puck after the puck caromed off the boards behind the Pittsburgh net. Rappelye, however, decided after studying a series of replays that the puck had gone in, and the Rangers had a 2-1 lead.

When the decision was announced, the Madison Square Garden crowd erupted, and so did the Pittsburgh bench. Tom Barrasso charged at Gregson during the next stoppage in play and was ejected from the game. So was trainer Skip Thayer, who stood behind the bench waving his glasses while staring directly at Gregson.

Not that Thayer didn't have a, uh, perfectly plausible explanation for his actions. "I've always tried to be helpful, take care of the referees," he said. "If they have any needs ... and I thought Terry needed a little help tonight. I didn't say a word to him. He asked what I was doing and I said, 'Glasses are a little steamy. I'm just airing them out.' I guess he thought 10 minutes was too long to air them out."

Protesting the call nearly became a painful experience for Bowman. He almost lost his balance while perched with one foot on the bench, the other on top of the dasherboards. His wobbly act was caught by the TV cameras and, to the considerable amusement of his players, was replayed on a huge screen in Times Square the next morning when the Penguins' bus was pulling out to take them to the airport for the flight home.

But none of them were chuckling in the minutes that followed Rappleye's ruling. They contended the replays had been inconclusive, and Stevens cited the lack of physical evidence that the mesh had been breached. "If something goes through the net, there's usually a little hole," he said. "But there was nothing."

Bowman was also upset that Dave Newell, a supervisor of officials who attended the game, was not seated near Rappleye, and thus had no input on his ruling. "The supervisor is supposed to have access to the video," he said. "They're all ex-referees or linesmen, so they have a good feel for the game. But here, he couldn't do his work in the location where they have the video referee. I would say that if Dave Newell had been there, it would not have been ruled a goal."

But Newell wasn't in the replay booth, the goal was on the scoreboard, and a 3-1 loss was about to go on the Penguins' record. They had turned in one of their strongest efforts to that point of the season, however faint such praise might be, but had nothing except frustration and perspiration-soaked uniforms to show for it. "I thought we played fabulous," Paul Coffey said. "It's a tough loss, but what are you going to do?"

The ruling on Kocur's shot was unfortunate for the Penguins, but it was more than offset by a break they got at home two nights later against the Edmonton Oilers. They squandered a 4-2 lead in the final two minutes of regulation, but salvaged a victory when Stevens scored at 3:25 of overtime by tipping a Paul Coffey shot past Oilers goalie Bill Ranford. It was not, however, a typical deflection. Stevens scored while prone on the ice, where he had been pinned by Edmonton defenseman Kevin Lowe. And, oh yeah, his stick was pointed randomly at the Civic Arena ceiling when Coffey's shot struck it. Other than that, it was pretty much a set play.

A lucky goal? Nah. It was far more fortunate than that. Some cosmic force must have decided the Penguins were owed a break, and had paid it back with interest. "We're not known for doing things easy," Stevens said. Definitely not, but at least they were starting to get things done again. They had won three of four games, during which time they allowed just 10 goals.

The Penguins hadn't gotten back to the top of their game by any means, but they had come a long way in a short period of time. "Overall, I think guys are starting to get their confidence again," Gord Roberts said. "Things are a heck of a lot better around here than they were two weeks ago."

They were for most players, anyway, but you could forgive Ron Francis — and Penguins management — for wondering what had happened to his game during his contract dispute. He had been back in the lineup for eight games, and was chugging along on a pace for a zero-point season, a bit less production than the Penguins had been counting on.

Francis had finished 20th in the NHL scoring race in 1990-91, but now was tied for 21st place. On his own team. And one of the players he was chasing was Tom Barrasso, a goalie. Francis had to like his chances of overtaking Barrasso eventually, but catching some of those defensemen who had already stockpiled two or three points during the first six-plus weeks of the regular season was starting to look like too much to hope for.

"This is really frustrating," Francis said. "I've never had this happen before. The last three games, I thought we (his line) started to get some chances but, whether it's me not putting it in or the guys I set up not putting it in . . . maybe we ought to have a little seance here to get rid of the curse."

It wasn't surprising that Francis was feeling spooked by his inability to score, but his teammates didn't think he needed any unnatural intervention to break out of his slump. Just a little time to get his game back in shape after he had missed training camp and the first three weeks of the season. "He'll work himself out of it," Joe Mullen said. "I think as soon as he gets that first one, the doors will open."

Bowman also attributed Francis's scoring drought to the action he had missed, and worried that putting too much emphasis on getting points might detract from his overall game. "He's a real conscientious player, but he did miss the entire training camp," Bowman said. "You don't want to have him pressing, because he's a good player both ways."

Francis tried to look beyond the stat sheet, to see that his contributions included playing well defensively and winning key faceoffs. But he had gotten accustomed to being a consistent point-producer, and it was tough to accept a string of goose eggs as his personal linescore. "I have to keep telling myself that I missed two months, that I'm two months behind everybody else," he said. "In essence, this is my training camp. I can't get frustrated. I can't get down. It's only a matter of time before things start to happen."

His teammates hoped Francis was correct, and none felt more strongly about it than Mark Recchi. He too had gone through a protracted contract dispute and was caught in the quagmire of a scoring slump. If salvation was inevitable for Francis, then Recchi had to figure it would be coming his way as well.

Recchi had developed into one of hockey's top right wingers during the 1990-91 season, but by his own admission had sputtered badly through October and the early part of November. Recchi might have been hockey's biggest bargain when he earned $105,000 during the Penguins' run to their first championship; now that he was working on a four-year, $3.6 million deal, however, Recchi looked like he deserved something close to the minimum wage.

Recchi had five goals and eight assists in his first 19 games, a 55-point pace, going into the Penguins' game in Quebec November 18. Those were not the kind of numbers anyone expected, and his frustration only intensified Recchi's struggle to break out of his slump. He was trapped in a vicious cycle of underachievement. "He lost his confidence early in the season," Lemieux said. "It seems like every time he shoots on net, it doesn't go in. Last year, it went in."

Recchi's confidence plummeted, but his teammates didn't lose faith in him. They had seen him do too much to believe that his scoring touch was gone for good. "He'll turn it around," said Kevin Stevens, who had stumbled early in the season after receiving a large contract of his own. "He works hard, and if you keep working hard, it's bound to turn. And Recchs isn't a kid who stops working."

No one ever questioned Recchi's work ethic, and by mid-November, even Recchi began to believe the end of his slump was imminent, that he would be pumping up his point total before much longer. "It's going to come," he said. "I can feel it. It's just a matter of time before I start doing the things I did last year."

He couldn't have known just how little time it would take, however. Recchi didn't just break his slump that night in Quebec; he obliterated it. He got his first career hat trick and added three assists in Pittsburgh's 7-3 victory. It was the most productive night of his professional life, and probably one of the most satisfying. "I knew it was just a matter of time . . . I was hoping it was just a matter of time," he said.

That win closed out the first quarter of the season, during which time the Penguins hadn't put up many impressive numbers. They were 9-8-3 — none of those victories had come against an opponent with a winning record — and in fourth place in the Patrick Division. They had allowed more goals than they had scored (80-79), and their home record (3-4-3) was the third-worst in the NHL. Those statistics didn't require thorough analysis to be interpreted; the message they carried was that the Penguins had been no more than a mediocre team. "It can only get better," Bryan Trottier said. "That's the good news. We certainly know the areas where we need to improve."

Still, Pittsburgh realized it had ample time to salvage the season, that the remaining 60 games represented an opportunity to get rid of any sour taste that had developed during the first 20. "With everything that's gone on, it could have been a lot worse," Recch said. "I think talent carried us this far. Now we've got to start putting it together and playing our game."

Maybe it was a coincidence that the Penguins seemed to right themselves the day Baldwin's group purchased the franchise. Their victory in Quebec that night sparked a 5-0-1 run by a team that had struggled just to hang near .500 for the first six-plus weeks of the season.

More likely, it was a reflection of the stability, on and off the ice, that had finally arrived. Players were getting accustomed to Bowman's style of coaching, even if it was not quite as player-friendly as they had started to believe a few games into the season. Ownership wasn't an issue anymore. And Bob Johnson's ordeal had reached its tragic, but inevitable, conclusion.

And Pittsburgh surely got an emotional boost by a show of desire from defenseman Ulf Samuelsson. He had returned to Sweden after his father died November 3, and stayed there until the morning of November 24. His plane didn't touch down in Pittsburgh until late afternoon, yet Samuelsson hustled directly to the Civic Arena and told Bowman he was ready to get back into the lineup against the New York Islanders that night. "I came with that (playing) in mind," Samuelsson said. "When you set your mind to it, you can do it."

Who cared about jet leg? So what if he had spent the entire day wedged into airplane seats? What difference did it make how many time zones he had crossed?; it's not that difficult to reset your watch. But Samuelsson hadn't flown all those miles just to watch a hockey game. He could have stayed in Sweden and seen one on TV if that had been his objective.

"It was a pretty good illustration of wanting to play," Bowman said. "I didn't think he should play, but he said he slept all the way over." Of course, Samuelsson didn't have a tough time convincing Bowman to use him, considering that defensemen Gord Roberts and Grant Jennings were unable to play because of the flu. "I guess we looked at what we had, and the options weren't too good," Bowman said.

Samuelsson had not played since October 29 — a minor hip injury forced him to miss two games before his father died — but he didn't need much time to re-establish his presence. At 2:34 of the first period, he intervened in a scrap between Kevin Stevens and several Islanders and, before the Penguins' 2-2 tie went into the record book, delivered several thunderous bodychecks.

Samuelsson had made it clear he was back, even though there was no way of knowing just how long he would be staying in Pittsburgh. He was in the option year of his contract, and he was being wooed by his old team, Leksand, of the Swedish Elite

League. Samuelsson made no secret of being a hockey merce-
nary, with money as his main motivation for playing in North
America.

He said a good contract would be the pivotal factor in
determining where he played during the 1992-93 season, but
expressed a desire to remain with the Penguins because, "everybody wants to win, and I'm on one of those teams that would be
favored to win the Cup for the next few years." He understood
that while money can buy a lot of things, a Stanley Cup ring isn't
one of them.

The Penguins closed out November with a couple of resounding victories against Philadelphia, 9-3 in the Spectrum,
and 5-1 at the Civic Arena, and looked as if they were ready for
a run that would make another Patrick Division championship
possible. The first-place Capitals were just six points in front of
them when December began, and the Penguins remembered
how quickly they had closed a 12-point gap against the New York
Rangers during the final month of the previous season.

Pittsburgh was on a 7-2-2 roll and, with Stevens having
scored 17 goals in 13 games, seemed about to reclaim its place
among the league's elite teams. "It certainly looks like we've
started to put it back together," Francis said. "Right now, I don't
think it matters who we're playing," Joe Mullen said. "We just
want to try to keep our game going."

Maybe the identity of the Penguins' victims didn't matter to
Mullen, a relative newcomer, but it did to some of his teammates
who had played in Pittsburgh for a while. No team had tor-
mented them like the Flyers, and every victory against Philadelphia was precious payback for all the abuse the Penguins had
been subjected to during those interminable and agonizing seasons. And it was especially sweet when they defeated the Flyers
in the Spectrum, where the Penguins once had a winless streak
that spanned 42 games — a total equal to more than half a season
— and 15 winters.

Some of those losses were among the most humiliating in
franchise history, like the Penguins' 13-4 defeat on March 22,
1984, but those were not the ones that hurt the most. When the
Flyers had a vastly superior team, as was usually the case, an
occasional blowout was to be expected. The losses that stung
most, however, were the ones in which the Penguins were poised
to snap the jinx, only to see an apparent victory vanish like a puff

of smoke. Sometimes the critical play was a fluke goal. Sometimes it was a questionable penalty. Sometimes it was an untimely breakdown by the Pittsburgh defense. But it was always something.

The Penguins' utter futility in the Spectrum was so outrageous that it became the topic of a running joke between the Pittsburgh and Philadelphia media. Whenever the Penguins were in town, Jay Greenberg, the longtime hockey writer at the *Philadelphia Daily News*, would sidle up to this author and Tom McMillan of the *Pittsburgh Post-Gazette* in the press room as the opening faceoff approached. His expression solemn as an autopsy, Greenberg would look them in the eye and say, 'This is the night.' Then everyone would smile, because they all knew what Greenberg meant. And then he would be proven wrong a few hours later, as always. At least until February 2, 1989, when Pittsburgh left the Spectrum with something besides a heartache for the first time since 1974. But all those gruesome nights between victories in Philadelphia made a deep and lasting impression on the men who lived through them.

"There are a lot of teams in this league, but I can't think of one team I like beating better than Philadelphia," Phil Bourque said. "And it's twice as good when we beat them in their building, because I can remember coming in here and having like a 5-2 lead with five minutes to go in the third period, and they'd pull it out somehow."

The Penguins were streaking when word arrived that Johnson had died and, a few days later, Bowman publicly acknowledged for the first time that he likely would stay behind the bench for the balance of the season. The "interim" tag still was part of his title, but the reality was that there was no one lined up to step in as a permanent replacement for Bob Johnson. "I don't think they want to change a lot right now," Bowman said.

His players agreed, and had long since accepted that he would be the coach for the rest of the season. "I think Scotty took it as something that's going to last the year," Bryan Trottier said. "Scotty jumped on board knowing this was not going to be a month-to-month thing. That, I think, was made absolutely clear from the beginning, and I don't think anybody is going to second-guess that decision."

Bowman said he was trying to be as much a caretaker as a coach, that his objective was to preserve the team and style

Johnson had put together, not reshape it. "You try to keep what was here before and not get in the way," he said. "That's the main idea. The toughest part has been trying to preserve the team. There are cogs in the team that are different, and every spoke in the wheel is important."

Bowman wanted to keep that wheel rolling down the path that Johnson had charted for it but in many ways, that was an unrealistic objective. His approach to the job, as expected, was dramatically different from that Johnson had used. "Bob was unique," Trottier said. "There aren't going to be a lot of guys like Bob Johnson. Bob was very positive, very upbeat, very energetic. Scotty's a little more old-school. He's a perfectionist. He expects really good execution. He wants consistency."

When the Penguins arrived in Edmonton after attending Johnson's memorial service in Colorado Springs, they were greeted by deep snow, blustery winds that sliced through overcoats like a sabre saw and temperatures that felt like they had dipped a few degrees below absolute zero. A pretty typical winter day on the prairies. Which is to say, perfect weather for hockey. Or survival training in the sub-Arctic.

But the Penguins paid little attention to the conditions that met them in Edmonton. They were still preoccupied by thoughts of Johnson and his family, and the 13 1/2-hour journey from Pittsburgh to Colorado to Edmonton hadn't done much to help their focus. That was apparent during their 5-3 loss at Northlands Coliseum the next night. "You travel for 16 (sic) hours, it's obviously going to take something out of you," left winger Bob Errey said.

The subsequent legs of their road trip were less grueling even though, upon leaving Edmonton, Joe Mullen said, "it already feels like we've been on the road for a week, and it's only been three days." On that third day, the Penguins flew from Edmonton to San Francisco, with a change of planes and layover in Vancouver, to prepare for their first-ever game against the San Jose Sharks.

On paper, a game between an expansion team and the Stanley Cup champions sounds like a gross mismatch, and the Penguins made a concerted effort to avoid taking two points for granted. They talked about how the Sharks had beaten quality opponents like Calgary and Los Angeles, about the impressive work habits they had developed, about the 3-0-1 streak San Jose had pieced together. "There's a danger anytime you perceive an opponent as being inferior," Tom Barrasso said. "You open yourself up to be upset. We're the type of team that, if we get sloppy, can give up goals very quickly, and we don't want to do that."

"Anytime you play a team like this, you have to prepare yourself to play hard for 60 minutes, because most of their players are going to do that," Lemieux said. "I don't think we're going to take them lightly. They're playing very well as a team right now. It doesn't matter if they're an expansion team. You still have to go out there and work hard against every team."

The Penguins said such things often enough that they actually started to believe them, but they probably didn't have to bother. For if their game against the Sharks had looked one-sided on paper, it got infinitely worse when it was transferred to ice.

The Penguins put the Sharks through some of the most intense growing pains imaginable in an 8-0 victory at the Cow Palace. San Jose coach George Kingston used three goalies — Jeff Hackett, Arturs Irbe, and Brian Hayward — over the course of the evening. Unfortunately, he didn't try playing all three at once. When Kingston talked about how his team's "focus fell away in the second period," it was suggested the Sharks had been distracted by the red light that flashed behind their goaltender every few minutes.

Mario Lemieux had two goals and four assists to show for his night's work. Kevin Stevens picked up a hat trick — his third in eight games — and the power play converted five of 11 chances after scoring on just three of the previous 31. "These type of games are going to happen with expansion teams," Lemieux said.

If there was anything the Penguins didn't enjoy about this victory, it was that they had to go all the way to the West Coast to claim it. It's not that anyone in their traveling party objected to spending a few days in San Francisco, which quickly became one of the most popular stops on the circuit when the Sharks entered the league.

But people who make their living in hockey get tired of airports and hotels, of eating in restaurants and relying on long-distance phone calls to stay in touch with family members. Everyone understands that travel is an occupational hazard, but that doesn't mean they have to like it. Especially when your roommate on the road is a guy like Ulf Samuelsson, who has picked up a reputation as a world-class snorer. "If he gets to sleep first, you're in trouble," said Ron Francis, who pulled that duty on this trip.

But there can be more serious problems, too. While the Penguins were in San Francisco, thousands of miles and three time zones from home, Peter Taglianetti learned that his wife had been diagnosed with walking pneumonia. The Taglianettis had a nanny to help with the care of their three young children, but any crisis on the homefront is intensified when a player is out of town.

"It's tough because, especially with little kids, everything seems big," Taglianetti said. "The wives learn to cope with it. The first couple of years, the travel really gets to them, but when you've been doing it for five or six years, it's almost old hat."

So is trying to kill time when you're on the type of business trip the Penguins take so many times every winter. Some players read, sleep, or kibitz with fellow passengers on airplanes, but card games are the diversion of choice for many. "It makes the time go by," Frank Pietrangelo said. "If you had to sit there for three or four hours and do nothing, you'd go crazy." It's almost a Pavlovian response for some players; as soon as they hear a seat belt buckle, they crack open a deck of cards. The games are such a staple of travel that the assistant coach in charge of distributing boarding passes sets aside blocks of seats for players who wouldn't think of taking any flight without getting in a few quick hands.

Grant Jennings isn't especially fond of cards, but emerged as a pioneer in the field of mid-air recreation by taking a laptop computer on the road. It enables him to keep track of financial records and the like, but perhaps more importantly, can be programmed to play a variety of games.

His occasional sidekick at 30,000 feet is Jaromir Jagr, a product of the video-game generation. Jennings decribes Jagr as "pretty good" at playing chess on the computer, and Jagr's competitiveness comes through as he matches moves with the machine and vows he will not be beaten by it. "This," Jagr announces to anyone within earshot, "is just a stupid computer."

So the road show moved on to St. Louis, although the Penguins might have been better off to skip their 36-hour visit there. Several players' bags did not turn up on the luggage carousel after their flight touched down, and the morning skate was canceled because of a scheduling conflict at the St. Louis Arena. And those were the most enjoyable parts of their trip to Missouri. Things got really bleak once game time rolled around.

The Blues beat them, 6-1, and the Penguins played like a team that had been forced to hitchhike in from San Francisco. That was particularly true during the first 17 minutes, when St. Louis scored five goals. "We just came out flat," defenseman Jim Paek said. Which is a lot like saying the Titanic had a minor run-in with an ice cube.

That loss was a miserable end to a trip that spanned six-plus days, four time zones, two provinces, four states, and 5,897 air miles. But included no time for practices, outside of two game-day skates. "We haven't had a chance to really do anything except be in airports, be on planes and report to the games," Pietrangelo said.

The next western swing was a month away, and the Penguins responded well to being back in a more familiar setting. They beat the Rangers 5-3 December 10 in their first game after the trip, a victory that was especially satisfying because of the fierce rivalry that had developed between the teams. A victory against New York might not have been the greatest thing the Penguins could imagine, but it probably qualified for the top five. "Whenever we play the Rangers, we're drooling to beat them," Stevens said.

It was a good thing for the Penguins, then, that Bob Errey got some bad news on the morning of the New York game. Upon returning from the morning skate, Errey checked his answering machine and found a message that an arbitrator had awarded him a salary of $340,000. Which, by Errey's calculations, was about $60,000 less than it should have been. "I wasn't happy with the (arbitration) process, and I'm still not happy," he said.

And the Rangers were downright miserable, because Errey took out his frustrations on them, scoring a shorthanded goal and dishing out numerous hard hits. But it was Paul Stanton, playing for the first time since injuring his knee on October 31, who handed out the most memorable check of the evening. He flattened Rangers enforcer Tie Domi at 7:35 of the first period by driving his shoulder into him at center ice. It probably was an accident — Stanton does not play an overly physical game and had not been looking to lay out Domi — but that didn't make it any less impressive. Not much, anyway.

New York finished the game with far more completed checks than Pittsburgh, but the Penguins had the edge in the most important statistic: Goals scored.That is the ultimate objective in any game, and while most of the Penguins prefer to play a style that emphasizes finesse, they have learned to cope with opponents bent on beating them into submission. "If they want to do that, we'll win our games," Stevens said. "We had the same team last year, and we put a ring on our hands."

The Penguins didn't look much like champions in their next game, but the New Jersey Devils were even less impressive in a 4-3 Pittsburgh win made possible when Joe Mullen scored with 36 seconds left in the third period. The game was so dismal that Mario Lemieux was named the No. 1 star, even though his most memorable play of the evening had been failing to score into an empty net midway through the third period. "This team is capable of winning like that," Mullen said, "but any team is." Which, no matter how correct, is a chilling thought for anyone who appreciates a well-played hockey game.

But the Penguins found out one night later that winning ugly was a whole lot better than losing the same way as Washington beat them 7-2 at the Civic Arena. That gave the Capitals a 3-0 lead in the season series and a 21-4 advantage in goals. While Washington's upgraded offense deserved some of the credit for those numbers, they also reflected the level of Pittsburgh's performance against the Capitals, which pretty much fluctuated between awful and abysmal. "If we go out and play like we did tonight, they're going to smoke us every time," Larry Murphy said.

The loss snapped the Penguins' 5-0-2 streak and dropped them eight points behind the Patrick Division-leading Capitals. And Murphy was quick to clear up any doubts about whether Washington's impressive showings against the Penguins were a fluke, or questions about whether the Capitals could really be that much better than Pittsburgh. "They are at this point," he said. "They're obviously playing at the top of their game... we're not going to beat them unless we're playing at the top of our game."

There were reasons to believe the Penguins were about to develop a mental block about facing Washington, that they would enter future games against the Capitals convinced defeat was inevitable. "If you're going to be a successful team, you're going to run up against a lot of hurdles during the season," Murphy said. "And right now, this is a huge hurdle for our team, something we're going to have to overcome."

Tom Barrasso, however, said it was unlikely that Washington's success in the first three meetings would have any lingering effect on the Penguins, that any dents those defeats put in Pittsburgh's confidence were superficial and would have no future repercussions. "I think we're beyond that," he said. "Hopefully, we are anxious to play them again. This is getting very repetitious, and I think we'd like to put it to a stop."

There were not many stops in the Penguins' immediate future, however, because Barrasso, Frank Pietrangelo, and Wendell Young passed on an optional workout at Neville Ice Arena the next day. With no goalies available, Phil Bourque and Grant Jennings volunteered to go into the nets during the workout. Which meant there was still nothing remotely resembling a goalie in the building.

Jennings said he used to be a baseball catcher and that he likes to go in goal once or so a year. Bourque insisted that he was a former street hockey goalie, then showed his vast knowledge of the position by trying to strap his right pad onto his left leg. Nonetheless, using Jennings and Bourque in goal served two key purposes for the Penguins: 1) It kept Barry Smith, the only coach at the practice, from having to play the position and, 2) It did wonders for the confidence of any teammates who had been struggling to find their scoring touch.

"They (Jennings and Bourque) are suffering from sunburn, from the red light going on so often behind them," Bryan Trottier said. "Jenner was outstanding with his right foot. If you shot at his right foot, he could make a save. Anywhere else, you'd score."

Actually, using those guys in goal was a pretty good simulation of game conditions for the Penguins, considering San Jose was due in town a few days later for its only visit of the season. As had been the case earlier in the month, the Penguins all but conceded a victory to the Sharks in their pre-game observations. Maybe the Sharks weren't quite ready to be enshrined in the Hall of Fame en masse, but to hear the Penguins tell it, such an honor would be coming any day.

Murphy said, "San Jose can win, and they showed they can win in the past" and that the Sharks "are a much better team than they were at the start of the season." And, in one of the most impressive shows of self-discipline by a Penguin all season, he kept a straight face the whole time.

Or maybe Murphy was just saving his grins because, deep down, he knew the Penguins were in for another laugher and that he'd need an ample supply to get him through the evening. Dismembering the Sharks was turning out to be a habit Pittsburgh found hard to break, and San Jose hobbled out of the Civic Arena with another eight-goal loss, 10-2. It was a charitable gesture by Scott Bowman to settle for a field goal when he could have pressed for a second touchdown.

Eight of the Penguins' goals came during the second period, a franchise record, and San Jose coach George Kingston again had to grope for some positive facet to a crushing defeat. "It's all part of learning for us," he said. Presumably, the primary lesson for San Jose was to avoid being moved into the Penguins' division in any future realignment. And the Sharks might have caught on to the idea that giving the Penguins vast tracts of open ice to work with wasn't such a good idea, either.

"We had a lot of room out there," Lemieux said. "Anytime a team gives that much room to myself and Recchi and Stevens, we can do a lot of damage." Lemieux, Recchi, and Stevens made up the most menacing line in the league, so it wasn't surprising they could do unspeakable things to an expansion team. But the fact is, Bowman probably could have double-shifted the Marx Brothers in that game and had them put up big numbers, too.

The Penguins needed little time to detect the main weaknesses in the game of Sharks goalie Jarmo Myllys which, at least in this game, proved to be shots on goal. Anything headed in the general direction of those 24 square feet of net had a pretty decent chance of ending up in it.

Jamie Leach opened the scoring with a knuckleball that floated into the net, and Bob Errey closed it with a shot that hit Myllys in the glove — another vulnerable area, apparently — before dropping over the goal line. "For all the times you get really good wood on a puck, and the goalie never sees it, and it winds up in his glove, it's nice to get a break once in a while," Errey said.

Errey's teammates enjoyed seeing him score a couple of goals, too, because he doesn't turn up in the highlights very often.

Guys who make their livings the way Errey does, grinding along the boards and playing hard-nosed defense, rarely get the attention or adulation that goal-scorers do. "He's not one of those guys who's going to be in the limelight," Stevens said. "He knows that, but he knows what he means to the team."

Errey's second goal was the final entry on a thoroughly depressing scoresheet for the Sharks. This was another of those games that didn't figure to turn up in the San Jose highlight film, but was sure to be replayed in the players' memories for a long time. "We had a lot of young players on the ice tonight, and this was a lesson I'm sure they won't like, but they'll remember," Kingston said.

Ulf Samuelsson was one of the few Penguins who didn't have a big offensive night against the Sharks — he was recovering from elbow surgery a few days earlier and didn't play in the game — but management didn't seem to hold that against him. One day later, about the time the statisticians figured to be finished totaling the damage Pittsburgh had done to San Jose, Samuelsson was given a four-year contract reportedly worth $3.75 million.

The talk that he would return to Sweden for good after the 1991-92 season ended abruptly. Samuelsson planned to make the Civic Arena his home for at least four more years. "We put everything on a piece of paper and made the decision," he said. "There were so many factors for me to stay." By most informed estimates, approximately 3.75 million of them.

Samuelsson, however, said money was not the only thing that influenced his decision. He is idolized by the Civic Arena crowd — "The people and fans here are great," he said — and he sensed that there might be a sequel or two to the Penguins' 1991 championship. "It's a lot of fun to play if you're winning," Samuelsson said. "And this is, by far, the best team I've ever played on . . . or ever will play on."

Samuelsson had that thought reinforced while watching the Penguins' next game on television as he continued his recovery from the elbow surgery. What he and everybody in Boston Garden saw, was Jaromir Jagr take another step toward becoming a dominant offensive force. He scored two goals, one of them on a new addition to his ever-expanding repertoire.

Jagr, like many Europeans, disdains the slapshot, preferring to carry the puck close to the net and snap off a wrist shot. But five minutes into the third period, he unleashed a slapshot that went between the legs of Bruins goalie Andy Moog for the decisive goal in Pittsburgh's 5-4 victory. Jagr's teammates couldn't have been more stunned if he had stood up on the bench and recited the Gettysburg Address. In perfect English. Backwards.

Joe Mullen said seeing Jagr take a slapshot "surprised everybody" on the Pittsburgh bench, and nobody disagreed. "That's the first time I've seen that," Ron Francis said. "But if he's going to get the same results, he'd better take a few more."

Jagr, however, said he couldn't even think of doing such a thing again. "This is first and last," he said, "because I don't want to beat every goalie," Jagr laughed. It's easy to joke when you're so young, so talented, and growing oh-so-comfortable with your second language.

The Penguins followed their victory in Boston with a 7-5 loss to the Rangers at the Civic Arena, at which point Mullen made an indelible impression on this season. He is a quiet sort who rarely attracts attention, even though he is an outstanding two-way player and a consistent 40-goal scorer. But it's difficult to avoid the spotlight when you put together two games like Mullen did to bookend the Christmas break.

On December 23, he scored four goals during a 6-4 victory against the New York Islanders at Nassau Coliseum, not terribly far from his childhood home in the Hell's Kitchen section of Manhattan. After the game, his teammates marveled at his productivity, at how a player 34 years old could continue to compete—and excel—in the world's finest league. "He looks like he's timeless," Larry Murphy said. "He's playing like he's always played. I'm sure Father Time is going to catch up with him in six or seven years, but I don't think it's going to be anytime soon."

Mullen's torrent of goals deflected attention from a shocking personnel move by Scott Bowman. He removed Paul Coffey, the highest-scoring defenseman in NHL history, from his customary position at the left point on the No. 1 power-play unit and slid Ron Francis into that spot. And in the third period, Bowman replaced Coffey on the second unit with Ulf Samuelsson. Samuelsson's offensive abilities can charitably be described as modest, even though he got a goal in this game, so all the shuffling was not exactly a ringing endorsement of Coffey. Or an indication that this would be a good time to consider putting an addition on his home in Pittsburgh.

"We just wanted to go with Francis and Murphy, and then we felt Ulfie didn't get in a lot, so we went with Ulfie and Paul Stanton," Bowman said. "We're trying to get Stanton into the power play, and I think he's helping." Maybe that really was Bowman's rationale for removing Coffey from the power play, but few people bought into his explanation.

Instead, Coffey's demotion was widely interpreted as an experiment to determine if the Penguins could replace him on their power play; if so, it might be easier to part with him and his seven-figure salary. The early returns did nothing to increase his chances of staying in Pittsburgh: The Penguins scored on five of nine power plays against the Islanders. "Obviously, our power play was the difference," Larry Murphy said.

Three of Mullen's goals that night had come with the man-advantage, as he registered just the third four-goal game of his career. It was, however, only his first of the week. Perhaps for the benefit of anyone who missed his performance on Long Island because of holiday social commitments, Mullen duplicated it in a 12-1 victory against the Toronto Maple Leafs at the Civic Arena on December 26.

"One thing about Joey," said Toronto general manager Cliff Fletcher, who had been GM in Calgary when the Flames traded Mullen to Pittsburgh. "If he gets an opportunity, you know where the puck's going." And if you didn't know, it was easy enough to figure out. Just look for the flashing red light. Scott Bowman had a slightly different perspective on what Mullen had done — he wasn't the one whose team had come up on the wrong end of an 11-goal game — but didn't see any need to dispute Fletcher's assessment. "He doesn't seem to need many chances to score," Bowman said.

But Mullen was a little disappointed by his production. Four goals are nothing to mope about most of the time, but Mullen felt he had wasted an opportunity to score more. Turns out he hadn't put in every shot he had taken against the Islanders and Toronto, just the overwhelming majority of them. He was on an amazing run, but what Mullen had in mind was perfection. Perhaps it wasn't a realistic objective, but anything less meant he had something to work on.

So it wasn't much consolation that, if he continued on this pace, he had a chance to overtake Michael Jordan in the NBA scoring race by, oh, mid-January. Not when he had converted on just eight of 12 shots in the past two games. "I'm getting a lot of opportunities," Mullen said. "I even missed a couple of chances in both this game and the last one. And they were real good chances, too."

Having back-to-back four-goal games wasn't enough to get Mullen into the headlines again after the Toronto game, because his linemates had moderately productive evenings of their own. Kevin Stevens, the No. 2 scorer in the NHL, had two goals and four assists — and actually lost ground in the points race. Lemieux, who had gotten engaged to his longtime girlfriend, Nathalie Asselin, the previous day, celebrated the occasion with two goals and five assists to raise his lead over Stevens to three points. "I don't plan on catching him," Stevens said. The Toronto game made it apparent that, unless Lemieux's chronic back problems flared badly and often, no one else in the league could expect to, either.

The Penguins' attack was so fearsome against Toronto that, when the game was over, several Pittsburgh players went out of their way to express compassion for Maple Leafs goalie Grant Fuhr. He is one of the greatest goalies in recent NHL history and was a key component in the Edmonton Oilers' dynasty in the 1980s, but the Penguins subjected him to 60 minutes of non-stop abuse. "Seven or eight or nine goals we scored, he didn't have a chance," Lemieux said.

The Penguins scored on 12 of 32 shots, an astounding success rate of 37.5 percent. To put that feat into perspective, consider that their most accurate shooter going into the game was Lemieux, who had converted on 24 of 107 shots (22.4 percent). "It was crazy out there," Stevens said. "One of those nights where everything went into the net."

There was, however, a dark side to the Penguins' Boxing Day bashing of the Maple Leafs. Goalie Tom Barrasso got a bruised right ankle when he was kicked by Toronto forward Kevin Maguire during the first period. Barrasso stayed in the game and was outstanding — he stopped 30 of 31 shots for one of his finest showings in the first half of the season — but said his ankle was "sore beyond belief" after he removed his skate.

The injury was severe enough to keep Barrasso out of the lineup for two critical games in the final weekend of 1991. The

Penguins had to go to the Capital Centre and Madison Square Garden for games against the two teams they were chasing in the Patrick, and do it without their No. 1 goalie.

The Penguins were painfully aware of the 21-4 advantage in goals Washington had run up while defeating them in their first three meetings, even though most of them had trouble accepting the idea the Capitals were dominating them that way. Washington had not won a season series against Pittsburgh since 1985-86 and had been chased out of the playoffs by the Penguins in five games in 1991. "We owned them all the time," Troy Loney said. "We seemed to be doing something right against them, and we got it in their minds that they would lose to us . . . it's like we used to be against Philadelphia."

The Penguins had another reason to be concerned going into the game at the Capital Centre. Two nights earlier, Washington had a 6-1 lead at home against the Rangers, then fell apart and was beaten 8-6. Larry Murphy predicted the Capitals "had such a humiliating defeat that they're going to bounce back and be ready and determined," and Loney agreed the Penguins would have to be ready to bear the full weight of Washington's fury. "When you lose like that, you want to come out with a vengeance the next game," he said. "They're going to come out smoking, so we'd better be ready."

All the circumstantial evidence suggested the game would, at the very least, be lopsided, and that's the way it worked out. This time, however, things tilted in the Penguins' favor. Wendell Young, filling in for Barrasso, stopped 27 of 29 shots, and Murphy and Phil Bourque scored shorthanded goals, only the 11th time in franchise history the Penguins had gotten two in one game. "The two shorthanded goals killed them," Mark Recchi said.

This game was a total reversal of the previous three between the Penguins and Capitals. Washington had held the Penguins without a power-play goal on 20 tries in the first three games, but Pittsburgh capitalized on two of six chances and dominated all phases of the game. More importantly, the victory kept the Penguins within striking distance of Washington, who was tied with the Rangers for first place.

"We knew we had to win this game, because we've got to start closing the gap on them," Murphy said. "If we're going to stay tight with these guys and have a chance to catch them, we've got to win games like these. We let the other three slip away."

So the Penguins headed for New York, and another showdown with the Rangers. And their first regular-season game against Randy Gilhen, their former teammate who had been lost to Minnesota in the expansion draft a few days after Pittsburgh won the Stanley Cup. He subsequently was traded to Los Angeles, and then on December 23 shipped to New York for center Corey Millen.

Gilhen's ties to the Penguins were not severed when he left the team, or even when getting his Stanley Cup ring turned out to be almost as difficult as earning it had been. It was shipped to him a month or so into the next season, but the side bearing his name and number identified him as "19." That's the number he had worn when he joined the Penguins in 1988, but he changed to No. 15 after the Penguins signed Bryan Trottier. Gilhen returned the ring to the Penguins, who had the mistake corrected, but not before his former teammates had exploited the situation for weeks' worth of one-liners.

Gilhen was known to the Penguins as "The Great One," although the series of moves he had been forced to make in the previous few months had earned him the nickname "Suitcase," too. Some of Gilhen's closest friends, most notably Wendell Young and Peter Taglianetti, still played for Pittsburgh, which promised to make for an uncomfortable evening at the Garden. Gilhen would be playing his first game for a team that had cultivated an intense, sometimes ugly rivalry with the Penguins.

"It's definitely going to be different," he said. "Everybody knows about the rivalry between New York and Pittsburgh. It's going to be tough against Pittsburgh, but those guys (the Rangers) are my teammates now."

Gilhen, an accomplished defensive forward, laughed as he threatened to do whatever was required to keep players like Mario Lemieux and Kevin Stevens from scoring. "I'm going to be hooking and holding Kevin, and tugging on Mario's jersey," he said.

But there was nothing Gilhen or any of his new teammates could do to stop the Penguins in this game, particularly in the third period. Pittsburgh scored four unanswered goals in the final 20 minutes to beat the Rangers, 6-3. "In the third period, we played as (well) as we have all year," Bowman said. "We played a perfect two-way game."

Much of the post-game praise was directed at Young, who had stopped 52 of 57 shots during the weekend. "Wendell played outstanding again," Recchi said. Perhaps Young's most spectacular moment came when he thwarted New York forward Darren Turcotte on a penalty shot late in the second period. "That really gave our team a big lift," Bowman said.

Actually, Young never had to make a save on Turcotte, who made a deft move to his forehand after skating down the slot, but seemed to shoot the puck over the crossbar. "I took away the five-hole (area between the legs) and he went wide on me and threw it up," Young said. "I'm scrambling, basically. If it hit me, it was lucky. If he put it over (the net), thank you."

Turcotte had scored New York's first and third goals, but his failure to convert on the penalty shot was a pivotal moment in the game. Having dodged the very real danger of falling behind by two goals, the Penguins rallied to post their fifth consecutive road victory, most in team history. "It's confidence," Stevens said. "We feel we can go into any rink and beat anybody."

"We're a lot more patient on the road, and we seem to play hard for 60 minutes," Lemieux said. "We showed a lot the last two nights, back-to-back games against two very good teams at the top of our division."

He was right, but now there was another team hovering near the top of the Patrick; the Penguins were just three points behind the first-place Capitals, one in back of New York. "Everybody's talking about the Rangers and Washington, but we're right there," Stevens said.

The Penguins looked like they were ready to make their move, and they were. It just wouldn't be in the direction everyone was expecting.

CHAPTER SEVEN

A Free Fall to Nowhere

1991 had been the most exhilarating year in franchise history, but it ended in a thoroughly forgettable way. Which was pretty much the same way 1992 began. The New Jersey Devils, who were hanging eight points behind the third-place Penguins, came into the Civic Arena and humbled them 7-4 on New Year's Eve. It helped that Pittsburgh played like a team whose holiday hangovers had shown up a day early.

The Penguins didn't know much about Devils left winger Valeri Zelepukin, who had just been promoted from New Jersey's farm team, but they got a crash course during this game. Zelepukin scored two goals — the first of his NHL career — and was named the No. 3 star. Pittsburgh needed no introduction to Devils defenseman Scott Stevens, a long-time nemesis, but they were reminded of just how much of a force he could be when Stevens buried two pucks behind Wendell Young.

Pittsburgh fared no better in the rematch at Brendan Byrne Arena two nights later as New Jersey posted a resounding 4-0 victory that ended the Penguins' five-game winning streak on the road. The loss in New Jersey was noteworthy, and not only because it marked the midpoint of the regular season.

The Penguins would have set a franchise record for the best first half in their history if they had even split the games against the Devils, but instead hit the middle of the season with a 22-14-4 record and 48 points, one shy of the record. "It's too bad about the last two games, because we could have had a terrific first half," Scott Bowman said.

The Penguins had recovered nicely from their lurching start in the early weeks of the season, but nobody even thought of suggesting they had played well enough in those games to earn one point, let alone two, in New Jersey. "Fifty points would have been a lot nicer," Ulf Samuelsson said. "I'm not that good at math, but I know 50 and 50 make 100, and whenever you can get over 100 points in a season, you're on a good pace."

But Pittsburgh never gave itself a legitimate shot at hitting the 50-point plateau in New Jersey. The Penguins, who had averaged 4.77 goals in their first 39 games, were held to one shot in the first period and 16 for the game. And Mario Lemieux and Kevin Stevens, the driving forces behind the Pittsburgh offense, failed to get a point for the first time in 12 games.

Bowman gave a strange twist to an unusual evening by playing Paul Coffey, the most prolific defenseman in hockey history, on left wing, another unmistakable indication that his time in Pittsburgh was nearing an end. Coffey was used primarily on a line with Jaromir Jagr and Bryan Trottier, and from Bowman's perspective, fit in fairly well.

"He was the only guy we could really move up there and get some speed on that side," said Bowman, who had dressed seven defensemen for the game, one more than the normal complement. "He didn't look out of place at all." That, it should be noted, was an opinion not shared by many people. To most observers, Coffey looked like a player who had been thrown into a totally alien environment, a job whose responsibilities and nuances he understood in only the most peripheral way. Except for not knowing what he was supposed to do, when he was supposed to do it, and how it was supposed to be done, Coffey looked right at home on left wing. But hey, those minor kinks can be worked out.

Disturbing as the game — and most of its subplots — had been, things could have been much worse for the Penguins, because they nearly lost Lemieux. New Jersey defenseman Viacheslav Fetisov struck him near the left eye with his stick with just under three minutes left in the second period. Lemieux's legs were thrashing as he dropped to the ice, his face buried in his hands.

"I actually saw his stick hit my eye," Lemieux said. "It hit the bone first, then hit my eye, right underneath the lid. I was lucky. I opened my eye and I couldn't see, but my contact (lens) was off a little bit, so that's why I was blurry." The blow did more than just dislodge his lens, however. Lemieux had a gash near his left eye, and the area around it was discolored and swollen. Even his eyelid was bruised.

This was not the first time the Penguins lost a high-profile player because of Fetisov's stickwork. Coffey sat out several games during the first round of the 1991 playoffs after Fetisov jabbed him in the left eye. So predictably, the Penguins were outraged when they learned Fetisov, who received a five-minute penalty and automatic game misconduct, was joking with New Jersey reporters after Lemieux was injured. Fetisov was quoted as quipping that he commits stick fouls against "only the big names: 77 (Coffey) and 66 (Lemieux)."

The Penguins missed the humor in Fetisov's one-liner, however, and asked the league office to investigate the incident. Craig Patrick described the spear as "a very careless act with a stick." He declined to say whether the Penguins believed the incident had been intentional, but said, "we have our opinions."

The Penguins had their problems, too. Their cushion over the fourth-place Devils had been halved in little more than 48 hours, and the way they were playing, it was reasonable to expect it to shrink even more. "We played way below our standards the last two games," Samuelsson said.

But the Penguins raised the quality of play in the next game, a 3-2 victory against Winnipeg at the Civic Arena, and did it despite considerable adversity. Coffey missed the game because of the flu, and Lemieux was a late scratch after developing back spasms, which were rapidly becoming a personal trademark. "His back started to tighten up 10 or 20 minutes before we went on the ice," Scott Bowman said. "He started getting better halfway through the game, but then it was too late to take a chance."

The Penguins had long been aware that Lemieux's back could give out at any time. The most harmless-looking act, like bending over to tie his skates, could put him in excruciating pain. Lemieux spent so much time and effort nursing his back that his agent should have lined up a deal to have him endorse orthopedic mattresses.

Nonetheless, losing Coffey and Lemieux at the same time forced the Penguins to make some strategic adjustments. They abandoned the free-skating game they prefer for a tighter, defense-oriented approach, a style similar to what Winnipeg used every time the Jets reported for work. "They don't score many goals, but they don't give up many, either," Ron Francis said.

"That was great for us to win that type of game," Larry Murphy said. "Low-scoring games, we don't get too many of those." No more than a handful per season, actually. None of the Penguins looked bewildered when they ventured behind their own blue line, however, and most actually went there with commendable frequency in the Winnipeg game. Well, it never hurts to try something different, break up the routine a little.

The Penguins don't like playing a close-checking game — would an artist who specializes in creative works be expected to enjoy the drudgery of painting a house? — but the victory against Winnipeg proved again that they can do it well. "It's not typical of what we've had in the last little while, but when this team wants to play, we're better than any team in the league," Tom Barrasso said. "We just have to make sure we're motivated every night to play. If we do that, we're going to be pretty successful."

Lemieux, who had been told by doctors to expect occasional flare-ups from his back during the season, skipped the optional workout the next day, but Coffey was there. The previous night, a Canadian television report suggested he would be traded to Philadelphia within a week, and Coffey said he was convinced his departure was "inevitable," even if he didn't know when or where he would be traded. He couldn't have felt any other way; far too much smoke had been blowing around for far too long for it to turn out that there never had been a fire.

"I love it here," Coffey said. "There's not anybody who can question that. But if I'm not in their plans and I'm traded, that's fine, too. It's part of the business, part of the game. Any athlete has to accept that. I don't understand what's happened. Three weeks ago, things were perfect. Then, boom, I was pulled off the top power-play unit and the whole bit."

Coffey did not argue with the notion that Pittsburgh's vast array of talent at forward might make him expendable, that the team might be able to get by without the dimension he adds to an offense. "We do have a lot of talent up front," he said. "If they feel they can get by without me, that's the way it goes. I just want to play hockey. If a team is not happy with players, they should just get rid of them. Be manly about it."

Craig Patrick, for his part, continued to insist that a trade involving Coffey was not imminent, and that he was not actively trying to deal him. "There's nothing happening," he said. That was nothing Coffey hadn't heard before, and he didn't put any more faith in it this time than he had on previous occasions. He understood that Patrick doesn't like to deal in an open-air market, that any trade talks going on were not likely to receive a thorough and accurate airing in the public prints.

Patrick's passion for secrecy makes reporters wonder if they might someday have to invoke the Freedom of Information Act to get him to release even the most innocuous data, like who has signed a contract or which players are moving between Pittsburgh and the minor leagues. Factoids and transactions that most pro teams announce as a matter of course are sometimes handled like state secrets by the Penguins, although Howard Baldwin's keen sense of public relations has done wonders for the flow of information.

Coffey was back in his customary spot on defense for the next game, but Lemieux was a last-minute scratch again. Not that his presence would have mattered. Los Angeles goalie Kelly Hrudey stopped 40 of 42 Pittsburgh shots in the Kings' 5-2 victory and was in a groove the Penguins had no chance to knock him from. "You had the feeling Kelly wasn't going to let anything in," Los Angeles center Wayne Gretzky said.

Hrudey said his dazzling performance was motivated by fear as much as anything, that he knew Pittsburgh could do serious damage to a goaltender's statistics when its offense is in sync. "I was petrified," he said. "I've been watching their box scores. I've seen some of the games they've had. I didn't want to be on the receiving end of a 12-1 loss, like Toronto."

His concerns were understandable, but the way Hrudey played, the Penguins wouldn't have put a dozen pucks behind him if the game had gone on all night. Or for a week. "The ones he didn't see or make a great save on either hit him or went wide, or hit the shaft of his stick," Bryan Trottier said. "Luck was on his side, and he played a great game, too."

Maybe Hrudey should have had an inkling that this would be his game when Lemieux, who had skated in the warmup, had to be removed from the Pittsburgh lineup a few minutes before the opening faceoff. "I had a quick sigh of relief when I heard he was out," Hrudey said. "But just a quick one."

Lemieux accompanied the Penguins on a Western road trip that began the next day and skated with the team at the Calgary Corral on January 9, but obviously was discouraged that his back continued to bother him. He had looked fluid and limber while skating, but said the pain had not abated and was reluctant to predict when he might play again. "It doesn't feel real great," he said. "It doesn't feel strong. I've got to do what's best for the team, and for myself. If I don't feel I can help the team . . . or do the things I want to do, I shouldn't be out there."

So Lemieux spent the next evening in the Saddledome press box, and watched as goaltending was the decisive factor in the game, much as it had been in the Kings' victory a few nights earlier. This time, however, it was for an entirely different reason.

Wendell Young was given the start against Calgary and allowed the Flames to score on a play that surely made any goalie who saw the replay break out in a cold sweat, or at least caused him to feel sharp sympathy pains. It began in the Calgary zone, when Kevin Stevens took a shot that missed the Flames' net. The puck caromed out of the right corner and slid into the Pittsburgh end, where Young hustled to retrieve it in the left faceoff circle. He wanted to shoot the puck to Stevens at center ice, but it deflected off his stick and skidded into the net he had just vacated.

"It was an embarrassing moment," Young said after the Flames' 7-5 victory. "It changed the whole game around . . . We're trying to cut down the goals-against, and there's a bonehead play like that. I looked up and saw Kevin open at center ice and when I looked up at him, the puck just went off my stick. I picked a nice corner, too, right inside the post."

Young's teammates and coaches weren't nearly as hard on him. They dismissed the goal as a quirky twist of fate that came far too early in the game to have had a major impact on the outcome. "It was just an unfortunate play," Scott Bowman said. "Those (fluky) goals don't bother me as much as the other ones." And there were plenty of other goals to be upset about. Especially the two that Al MacInnis and Theoren Fleury scored in a seven-second span of the third period to turn a 4-4 tie into a comfortable 6-4 Calgary lead. "That's the game," Bowman said.

It is testimony to Young's mental makeup that he was willing to discuss at length, even joke about, the costly gaffe he had made, but the Penguins didn't need a show of class and character; they needed a victory. The Devils had closed to within two points, and the Penguins were faced with the grim prospect of a game at the Pacific Coliseum, where the Vancouver Canucks were 15-5-4 and interest in hockey among the paying public had been rekindled by the Canucks' unexpected surge to the top of the Smythe Division.

The Penguins' troubles were compounded when Lemieux flew home to have his back examined because it wasn't getting any better. Their prospects for getting out of the afternoon with a point or two looked even more bleak, when the Penguins were forced to get by without Phil Bourque (bruised left foot), Jim Paek (dislocated finger), and Larry Murphy, who returned to Pittsburgh after his infant daughter became ill.

The Penguins also hadn't won in eight days, but they snatched two points from the Canucks with one of their most solid performances to that point of the season. Tom Barrasso was outstanding in goal, particularly when Vancouver had a 12-4 edge in shots during the first period, and the Penguins had come up with the tourniquet they needed to keep the lifeblood from gushing out of their season."It seems like we had been at 50 (points) forever," Joe Mullen said.

Pittsburgh was able to sneak past the Canucks even though its injury list swelled even more during the second period, when Coffey went out with a pulled groin muscle. "I've never seen a team that can bounce back when it loses big parts like this team," Samuelsson said.

"It's a long season, and I don't like to put too much emphasis on any one game," Barrasso said. "But you've got to bring things to a stop at some point, and it was good that we did it today."

Winning at Pacific Coliseum made the day-long trip home far more pleasant for the Penguins, and their outlook improved even more when they got back to Pittsburgh. Lemieux's examination had shown that he was suffering from a new affliction, but not one that would jeopardize his career. Or even interrupt it for any length of time.

The diagnosis, reached after much poking and prodding and testing, was that Lemieux had come down with a severe misunderstanding, a second-degree sprain of the vocabulary. Oh, the pain in his back was real; there was no question he had been having terrible spasms. But that was the extent of his problem, and Lemieux's fears that he had developed a new condition were unfounded.

Dr. Charles Burke, an orthopedic surgeon and the Penguins' team physician, said the complication that had been preying on Lemieux's psyche was "more of a semantics problem" than a medical one. That Lemieux, upon hearing some unfamiliar terminology in a discussion of his problem a week or so earlier, had become concerned that his problem was more severe than he was being led to believe.

"It was a more descriptive word that turned into (the perception of) a new diagnosis," Burke said. He added that Lemieux had been pain-free during the examination, and that tests had confirmed his back was in reasonably good shape. "They looked better than his last (test) results ... before training camp," Burke said.

Burke said he fully expected Lemieux to get clearance to play in the All-Star Game later that week, that there was no reason to think he would do harm to his back in a game with so little body contact. Pittsburgh officials had convinced Lemieux to skip the Canada Cup tournament in 1991 because of fears he would hurt his back, but Burke said such concerns didn't apply now. "The All-Star Game is a little different than the Canada Cup," he said. "I don't think there will be much resistance if he's back to normal."

And Lemieux certainly seemed to be back to normal at practice the next day, when he skated for the first time in about a week. "He looked really good," Bowman said. "You could tell by the way he was handling the puck." Lemieux said he felt "pretty good" after the workout, and that he realized he was all but guaranteed of being bothered by back problems for the rest of his career.

"This kind of thing happens once in a while, especially when we play back-to-back games," he said. "But I've played a lot of games this year, and it feels pretty good. I've been fighting back pain for three or four years. I've got to take some time off from time to time. My back is not as strong as it used to be." Never mind that it was still strong enough to carry the franchise most of the time.

Bowman made a habit of limiting the strain on Lemieux's back on off-days, so much so that it was a fairly significant event when he participated in a practice. "We're careful not to use him too much in practice," Bowman said. "But it's hard to ask him to sit out a game. Mario likes to play a lot. He's playing 25, 30 minutes a game, killing penalties, working the power play. We try to have a lot of days during the season when he doesn't have to skate. Mario kind of goes along with that. If he were a football player, and he only had to play one day a week, it would be much easier."

Lemieux, his body rested and his mind at ease, returned to active duty when the Penguins visited Detroit on January 16, and set up Pittsburgh's first goal. But his comeback was almost obscured by the Penguins' failure to protect a 3-0 lead in the third period.

They played championship-caliber hockey for the first 40 minutes, and looked to be ready to run the Red Wings out of Joe Louis Arena. "Going into the third, we expected two points and wanted two points," Ron Francis said. The Penguins self-destructed during the first half of the period, however, and probably were fortunate to escape with the point they got for a 3-3 tie after Gerard Gallant, Ray Sheppard, and Steve Chiasson scored for Detroit in a span of just over nine minutes.

The tie at Joe Louis took the Penguins to the All-Star break, and most of the players got a rare weekend off. Not all of them, however; indeed, the All-Star Game at the Spectrum in Philadelphia January 18 could have been mistaken for a Pittsburgh intrasquad game. Mario Lemieux, Kevin Stevens, Jaromir Jagr, and Paul Coffey had been chosen as Wales Conference starters in fan balloting. Bryan Trottier was added to the Wales roster in the veterans category. And the Pittsburgh coaching staff was overseeing the Wales team, an honor earned by winning the conference during the playoffs the previous spring.

But one name was conspicuously absent from the Wales Conference roster. Joe Mullen, the No. 4 scorer in the league when the lineup was announced, did not get a place on the team. Perhaps it was because the Penguins had so many other players on the team. Surely it wasn't because Mullen's statistics weren't good enough — he had 26 goals and 30 assists in 42 games.

He was the only player among the NHL's top 14 scorers who wasn't invited to participate in the game, but Mullen reacted in character when the team was announced. There were no bitter outbursts, no spewing bile at the panel of general managers who had filled out conference rosters. Mullen likes to make an impact, not noise, and quietly shrugged off whatever disappointment he felt over being slighted. "If you make it, you make it," he said. "If you don't, you don't. I'm not going to dwell on it."

Some players view the All-Star Game as an annoyance, a meaningless exhibition that denies them a chance to get away from the rink for a few days. But Trottier was genuinely enthused about participating in the game for the eighth time in his career. "Playing in it is an honor," he said. "The excitement is there and the honor is there. The fun of playing in it outweighs the rest that even I know I need at this particular point. "

Lemieux, who was better-rested than he would have cared to be because of the time off his back forced him to take, laughed about his chances of winning a fourth car as the All-Star Game MVP. "I need another one," he said. Lemieux, like Stevens, said he was "pretty excited" about being in the game.

Jagr, meanwhile, seemed almost in awe of participating. "It's unbelievable that I made this team, that I will play with players like (Brett) Hull, (Wayne) Gretzky, Mario and Kevin," he said. "The best players. I can get a car . . . when I go buy one."

Stevens, however, projected Jagr as no worse than a darkhorse contender for MVP honors, because of his style of play. He figured a player with such outstanding one-on-one skills would thrive in a game with so little body contact. "It's his type of hockey," Stevens said. "There's not much hitting and there's a lot of stickhandling and a lot of offensive moves. That's why he's there. He's an exciting hockey player. He's going to be fun to watch."

But there would be no car for anyone from the Pittsburgh contingent—that went to Hull—and precious little glory, either. Trottier and Stevens got goals during the Campbell Conference's 10-6 victory, but the highlight for the Penguins had come one night earlier, when Lemieux beat Chicago goalie Ed Belfour on a breakaway to win a tiebreaker and give the Wales a victory in the annual skills competition.

The Penguins' nine-man entourage should have known it was in for something of a lost weekend when getting from Detroit to Philadelphia proved to be a complicated and drawn-out ordeal. The group was booked on a late-morning flight, but it was delayed because of mechanical problems. When it seemed that that flight was about to be canceled, the group hustled to reserve spots on another airline departing about 2 1/2 hours later. All that effort and anxiety proved to be pointless, however, when the original aircraft was repaired and able to take off about an hour behind schedule.

Before the skills competiton that evening, the Penguins' all-stars got to renew acquaintances with John Cullen, their former teammate who was Hartford's representative in the game. Cullen was — and is — one of Stevens' closest friends, and the two revel in the opportunity to exchange insults. The more bitter, the better. And Stevens got off an all-star-caliber shot at Cullen after Cullen broke in on a conversation about Jagr's improving grasp of English.

Cullen delivers words at a machine-gun pace, and occasionally leaves more than a participle dangling. Like a half-sentence. Or a thought. All of which gave Stevens the opening he was looking for when Cullen saw fit to comment on Jagr's handling of his second language. "You've got your own language," Stevens said, unsuccessfully trying to suppress a wide smile. "At least he's a Czech."

The All-Star break was timely for the Penguins, if only because it gave them a week with no losses. And because it had long since become apparent that the Patrick was the NHL's dominant division, any contender that got trapped in a protracted slump was in mortal peril of dropping out of the race for first place. "You've almost got to win every night to keep up," Mark Recchi said.

But when the games resumed, it quickly became clear that the Penguins hadn't forgotten some nasty habits during their few days away from the rink. On January 23, they ran up a 4-1 lead against Buffalo at the Civic Arena, but collapsed in the third period and lost 5-4 in overtime. "We had two points in our pockets, and they just came by and took them out," Wendell Young said. Well, not exactly. It was more a case of the Sabres taking what the Penguins were all too willing to give them, considering Donald Audette's game-winner against Young came on Buffalo's 50th shot, the most the Penguins had allowed at home since February 12, 1989. "You're not going to win too many games with 50 shots on goal against you," Young said.

Or when you can't protect a three-goal lead in the final period, which had happened to Pittsburgh in consecutive games; they had blown a 3-0 advantage in Detroit in the final game before the all-star break. "Twice in a row is definitely unacceptable," Larry Murphy said. Scott Bowman disagreed when it was suggested that the Penguins had gotten overconfident when they went up by three goals against the Sabres, but added that, "the way we played in the third, it looked like that."

The Penguins solved their nagging problem holding leads in an unconventional way two days later on Long Island; they didn't get one until less than a minute was left in the game, which meant they didn't have enough time to lose it. Mario Lemieux's goal with 56 seconds to play in the third period put them ahead of the New York Islanders, 4-3, and Ron Francis sealed the victory with an empty-net goal at 19:58. Even when its team defense was in its most shabby state, Pittsburgh could feel pretty confident about its chance of guarding a two-goal lead for two seconds. Six or seven seconds, now, that might not be so easy, but two seconds they could deal with.

Pittsburgh had been trailing the Islanders 3-2 after two periods, when Bowman decided to juggle his line combinations in an effort to jump-start the offense, to inject some life into what had been a fairly lame performance. He put Lemieux between Stevens and Jagr because "We needed something to get us really going, charged up."

It was a move Bowman had tried on several previous occasions — the unit was dubbed "The Pittsburgh Skyline" not long after it was   assembled for the first time — and it paid off big for the Penguins in this game when Jagr and Stevens made the passes that set up Lemieux's decisive goal. Stevens started the play by throwing an outlet pass that led to a two-on-one break for Jagr and Lemieux. "I saw those two break up the middle and just gave it to them," Stevens said. "It was a great two-on-one by them. When they get a two-on-one on a defenseman, good luck."

Or, in this case, good night. Jagr and Lemieux exchanged passes in the New York zone until Jagr eventually got the puck to Lemieux for a tap-in from the right side of the crease. "I thought he was going to shoot," Lemieux said. "At the last second, he slid it across. It was a great play. I didn't think he could make it."

A line blessed with so much skill and creativity is capable of doing almost anything, almost any time it wants to do it. It's pointless for opponents to concoct strategies for stopping the Stevens-Lemieux-Jagr line when it is intact; holding back the ocean tide with a tennis racquet would be easier. Other teams would be better served by having their tactics focus on damage-control, because shutting the line down for more than a few shifts just isn't a realistic objective most of the time. "Every guy on the line has got a lot of speed, is big and strong, can handle the puck very well and can shoot," Lemieux said. "We could be as good as we want."

The Penguins were upbeat when they headed for Washington after the game, almost didn't care that that part of the country had been paralyzed by a snowstorm. But the good feelings that the victory on Long Island generated vanished at the Capital Centre the next afternoon, when the Penguins lost more than a hockey game. They lost their composure during a 6-4 loss to the Washington Capitals, and as a direct result, they lost Jaromir Jagr for 10 games.

The Penguins felt the Capitals strayed far outside the rules all afternoon to impede the Stevens-Lemieux-Jagr line, and their frustration with referee Ron Hoggarth spilled out in the final minute of the third period. Seconds earlier, Lemieux had the puck in the Washington zone and was trying to set up a tying goal when the Capitals got the puck away from him using what the Penguins considered unacceptably creative defense. "Three guys tackled him from behind, lifted him up, spun his leg around," Stevens said. "I guess Hoagy (Hoggarth) didn't see that."

Hoggarth apparently didn't see Jagr on a collision course with him seconds later, either, after Kelly Miller had scored on a two-on-one break at 19:01 to give Washington a 6-4 lead. They made contact near the Pittsburgh net and, after consulting with linesmen Gord Broseker and Ryan Bozak when the game was over, Hoggarth decided Jagr had deliberately skated into him.

That was a violation of Rule 67, which covers physical abuse of officials, and guaranteed Jagr a suspension of at least three games. Lemieux said later he had been assured by Hoggarth at the time of the incident that it would not fall under Rule 67. Hoggarth did, however, issue 50 minutes worth of misconduct penalties to Lemieux, Jagr, and Stevens, which meant they beat most of their teammates into the shower by several minutes. "I haven't seen three guys get thrown out of a game like that since the Hansen Brothers in 'Slapshot,'" Ron Francis said.

No videotape of the incident ever surfaced, and Jagr insisted the collision had been accidental. "I didn't want to hit him," he said. "I'm not (an) idiot." The Penguins, however, made no effort to hide their displeasure with Hoggarth's work in this game. Lemieux said "it was a great game until the referees got involved," and labeled the NHL "a garage league" that condones the clutch-and-grab tactics some teams use to negate the advantage more talented opponents have.

"It's a skating game, a passing game, and I think that's what the fans want to see," Lemieux said. "I think the advantage is to the marginal player now . . . The good players can't do what they're supposed to do." That was a general criticism of officiating — and the league policies that guided it — Lemieux had made earlier, but he also added a customized blast at Hoggarth, who he said, "just can't keep up with us . . . he's so bad."

In addition to protesting his innocence, Jagr trashed Hoggarth's work in a blistering critique. "Look at the last shift," he said. "Kevin gave me a pass, two players hit me in my head . . . He (Hoggarth) is laughing all the time. When I talk to him about something, he tells me since I'm a European player, he can't call it."

Miller's goal clinched the victory for Washington and gave the Capitals the season series for the first time in six years, but the Penguins insisted the outcome was more a reflection of the referee's work than of the Capitals' superiority. "They didn't win this one on merit, I'll tell you that," Bowman said.

But no one denied that the Penguins felt like losers the next day, when they were notified that Jagr had been slapped with a 10-game suspension after league officials ruled the incident with Hoggarth was a Category II offense, which meant he had "deliberately applied physical force" to an official.

Jagr was so dismayed by the decision that he talked about returning to Czechoslovakia, and the Penguins said they were stunned by the severity of the penalty. Lemieux said it "doesn't really make sense" that Jagr got a 10-game suspension, while Viacheslav Fetisov had gotten five after hitting Lemieux in the eye with his stick.

"I don't think it's fair," Stevens said. "I think it was just kind of incidental contact. I was coming down one side and I think Hoggarth turned and pointed to me with his back turned and Jaromir came in from the outside and they hit. I think it's tough to call. I don't think Hoggarth saw him coming, and they just hit. It (the 10-game suspension) is definitely a setback. He's an offensive threat, and it's something the other team isn't going to have to worry about, so they can key on other players."

Players and management weren't the only ones upset about the league's ruling on Jagr, or by the way the season was deteriorating. Before the Penguins' next game against Winnipeg at the Civic Arena, security personnel removed a banner reading, "Get Rid of Bowman, Keep Coffey," from a balcony. And the atmosphere wasn't any more encouraging a few hours later, after the Jets skated away with a 4-0 victory that dropped the Penguins' home record to a wretched 10-10-4. "We've given a lot of games away this year," Ulf Samuelsson said. "We're a little better team, especially at home, than we've shown."

That was reassuring to hear, considering the loss dropped the Penguins to 1-4 in their past five games at the Civic Arena. For the season, they were 10-10-4 on home ice, a record that fell somewhere between dismal and deplorable. The idea of a home-ice advantage was sounding more and more like a cruel hoax, especially in view of the Penguins' routinely productive play on the road.

"It seems like every team that comes in here, all they want to do is clutch and grab us," Joe Mullen said. "For some reason, they've been very successful playing that style here. I don't think it's anything else. The crowd can't be blamed. We're the ones doing the playing. And I don't know why we'd feel like we were under more pressure at home. It's nothing like that."

Bad as the news had been, it was about to get worse. Lemieux had missed the final two periods of the Winnipeg game because of pain in his lower back and, the next day, acknowledged he had pondered the possibility of premature retirement because of his recurring back troubles. "If it's going to hurt me for the rest of my life, it's not worth it," he said. "I think everybody is frustrated because we can't figure out what's causing the pain. They can't figure out why the pain was there last night, and I get up today and it was fine."

Dr. Charles Burke, the Penguins' team physician, said Lemieux's exasperation was understandable. "As expected, he gets terribly frustrated by us, the doctors, because we can't make him better," Burke said. "It's frustrating to him and it's frustrating to us." Burke said Lemieux's condition would not threaten his well-being or cause him to retire, but that Lemieux was "still very down" mentally because of his problems, which would come and go with no warning, often for no apparent reason.

"There are periods like the beginning of this year when he did very well for 30 games," Burke said. "He's had a couple of setbacks where, just when he's feeling better, all of a sudden, it comes back. They (the spasms) always seem to come right after he's been feeling so good. It becomes so mentally difficult because just when he thinks things are going to get better, the pain comes back."

A week earlier, Lemieux had said that he was having no problems with his back, that it was "the best I've felt in months." That all changed when he bent over to tie his skates before the Winnipeg game and felt a sharp pain in his lower back.

"Once it starts, it gets worse and worse," Lemieux said the next day. "It's great today. That's why I can't understand what's the problem. It was the same thing in the playoffs last year. I don't know what to tell you. When I feel good, I should play, but the last two or three weeks, it's happened too often. I want to find out why before I go out on the ice."

Lemieux's teammates said they understood his anxiety and the frustration that prompted him to speak of retiring. "You're going to play the game for 10 or 12 years, but then you've got to live the next 30 or 40 years of your life," Ron Francis said. "You don't want to live 30 years of your life in pain. We'd rather see Mario enjoy life than go through the aggravation he is now."

Lemieux wasn't back for the next game, but the aggravation was. The Penguins were 4-0-1 in their first five games against the Islanders, but New York trampled them, 8-5, at the Civic Arena January 30. It was Pittsburgh's fourth loss in a row on home ice. Coach Scott Bowman said, "our last 10 games have been our worst 10 games," and his players were even more emphatic. None of them enjoyed losing, but it was about the only thing they were doing on a consistent basis.

"It's ridiculous now," Stevens said. "We've been giving games away. It's not the way we're supposed to be playing.

We're not playing with enough enthusiasm. We're not hitting anybody. We're not initiating anything. We're too worried about defense. Our game is offense. We're an offensive team.

"If we give up three goals, we give up three goals. What are you going to do? We can score five goals and win. Instead of us worrying about stopping them, we should just do what we're going to do. We should just worry about our game. It's gotten to the point where we're not doing anything out there. We should be worrying about playing like the Pittsburgh Penguins, not worrying about stopping the New York Islanders."

A few hours before the New York game, Craig Patrick was given a five-year contract and an additional title, executive vice president, that team president Howard Baldwin said would get Patrick involved in all "phases of the operation."

Baldwin said getting Patrick under contract was "one of our first priorities" after he and his partners assumed ownership of the team, but Patrick didn't sound like a man who had any intention of skipping town when his previous deal expired at the end of the season.

"I really like this organization, the city, and the fans," he said. "And I like our chances to be successful. I didn't have any desire to go anywhere else, and I really like the direction the new ownership is intending to take us. They're going to allow us to be as successful as we possibly can. I think we can have a very successful near future and long (-term) future."

Patrick would do much to enhance Pittsburgh's short-range prospects — and indisputably earn his upgraded paycheck — with a bold personnel move a few weeks later, but it would be longer than that before the Penguins could find a consistent cure for their struggles.

They beat St. Louis 4-1 at the Civic Arena February 1, thanks largely to the defensive work of left winger Bob Errey. He shadowed Blues right winger Brett Hull, who entered the game with a league-high 52 goals, and reduced him to a virtual non-factor with relentless checking. "To hold him to what we did was a great effort," Bowman said.

The Penguins' emphasis on containing Hull wasn't surprising. He entered the game with more shots on goal than any two of his teammates combined, and was becoming established as the top triggerman in hockey. "Anytime he's got the puck on his stick with an opportunity to shoot, it's a threat to be a goal," Ron Francis said.

But Hull didn't get the puck on his stick — or anyplace else — very often against Pittsburgh, particularly during the first 40 minutes of play. He had one shot in the first two periods, mostly because Errey was acting as if he had been Velcroed to Hull's chest. Playing such tenacious defense, Errey said, "is how I'm going to earn my credibility," and there was little doubt he had acquired a surplus of it against St. Louis.

The victory snapped Pittsburgh's four-game losing streak on home ice, where they had won just one game since their 12-1 mauling of Toronto on December 26. That had been little more than a month earlier, but it seemed like at least a dozen lifetimes to the players who had gone through the incessant drudgery and defeats of January. "Hopefully, it gets some of the pressure of having lost a bunch of games here away from us for a little bit," Tom Barrasso said. "We played a pretty successful team and I think we beat them soundly."

Quickly, too. St. Louis goalies Curtis Joseph and Guy Hebert faced 26 shots during the first period, a Blues record and one shy of the Penguins' record set during a 12-1 victory against Washington March 15, 1975. Pittsburgh had managed just two first-period goals in its previous three games, but scorched the Blues for four in the opening 20 minutes. "We really took it to them," Larry Murphy said. "We got some goals early, and we were able to control the game from then."

The Penguins also got some good news to go along with their two points. Tests had detected a weakness in the wall of one of Lemieux's back muscles, and doctors said it appeared to be the cause of the pain that had forced him from the lineup.

Dr. Charles Burke said the diagnosis of a herniated muscle was "as good a possibility as anything else," although there was "no way to prove" that it absolutely was the cause of his latest problem. Burke said the key to recovery for Lemieux was rest, and that it was possible the problem would heal itself. If not, he said, it could be surgically repaired. "When his pain gets better, he's going to try it and see what happens," Burke said.

Lemieux skated lightly during practice the next day and said he was not ready to play, but that "if I'm pain-free for a few days and don't get twinges like I had last week, I'm going to give it a shot. There's no sense staying off if I feel good." When

Lemieux resumed skating, the Penguins took a thoughtful precaution to make sure he didn't aggravate his condition: Locker room attendant Tracy Luppe was assigned to lace and tie his skates.

The diagnosis of a herniated muscle had been made in Washington, D.C. after Lemieux went there to be examined. Finding out that he didn't have a serious problem with his back freed Lemieux from gnawing fears that his playing future was in real jeopardy. "That was very important for me," he said. "I'd been searching since last year in the playoffs for what the pain was all about and where it was coming from. Now that I know the structural part of my back is good . . . that's what I was afraid of."

But even though Lemieux's mind had been put at ease, his back would not allow him to resume playing just yet. That meant Bryan Trottier, for years the No. 1 center of the New York Islanders, was charged with filling in for Lemieux on the No. 1 line with Kevin Stevens and Mark Recchi, with trying to fill the enormous void created by Lemieux's absence. "It's stimulating to be asked to step up and contribute to the offense," Trottier said. "I love it. It's not something I feel uncomfortable with."

It's something his linemates didn't have any trouble accepting, either, even though most of them were in youth hockey around the time Trottier was playing between Mike Bossy and Clark Gillies on the top line in the NHL. "He was unbelievable then, and I still can't believe I'm playing with him," Stevens said.

Trottier showed why teammates of all ages had confidence in his ability during the Penguins' next game, a 4-4 tie with Detroit at the Civic Arena. He scored Pittsburgh's second and third goals and assisted on the one Recchi got to tie the game. "He's filling a big void that needs to be filled," Recchi said.

So, for that matter, was Recchi, and the void was one that developed when he was struggling to score during the first six weeks or so of the season. But Recchi had long since rediscovered his scoring touch, and the goal against Detroit made him just the second player in franchise history to get 30 or more in each of his first three seasons. The only other one to do it was Lemieux, which meant Recchi was keeping some rarified company.

"I'm just playing like I think I can," Recchi said. And, he might have added, the way the Penguins expected him to when he signed that four-year, $3.6 million contract in the fall.

Trottier chalked up another three-point game in Madison Square Garden on February 5 — giving him 10 points in four games — but it wasn't enough to save the Penguins from a 4-3 loss to the New York Rangers. Adam Graves got the game-winner while New York was shorthanded at 8:31 of the third period, the third time in four games that Pittsburgh had given up a goal while on the power play. "Those goals hurt you a little more because you think you're on your way up," Ulf Samuelsson said. "Then you get your legs taken right out from under you."

Much as the loss hurt the Penguins — it dropped them 14 points behind the division-leading Rangers — it was even tougher on their bodies. Pittsburgh management accused New York forward Kris King of clawing Kevin Stevens' face during a fight with 15 seconds left in the game, and Samuelsson was on the receiving end of some wicked stickwork by the Rangers.

He was whacked by New York defenseman James Patrick and took a baseball-type swing just below the ribs from New York right winger Mike Gartner midway through the third period. Gartner, whom Samuelsson had cross-checked several times in the preceding seconds, received a five-minute major penalty and game misconduct, but Patrick got off with a minor for roughing.

Scott Bowman said he did not see the slash by Patrick, but that he was told by players it had been a flagrant violation. "I don't want to make a comment without looking at it, but the other people who saw it thought it was really bad," Bowman said. "Our guys said it was a vicious slash that easily could have been a major penalty. He (Patrick) just took a two-hander right at him."

Gartner, meanwhile, offered reporters an unusual explanation for the slash he gave Samuelsson. "I'm not the first guy who had taken a five-minute penalty on Samuelsson, and I'm sure I won't be the last," he said. Gartner undoubtedly was right, but that logic must have been lost on league officials, who ultimately gave Gartner a three-game suspension.

Samuelsson, typically, shrugged off the stick fouls as part of the game, but they illustrated the growing animosity between Pittsburgh and the Rangers. No one could have foreseen that the rivalry would get absolutely white-hot in a matter of months, but New York coach Roger Neilson already recognized that the

Penguins were a team he would prefer to avoid during the postseason. "They're a hard team to beat," he said. "One more team we don't want to meet in the playoffs."

The playoffs, however, were a long way off, and they were almost becoming more distant by the day for the Penguins. The surge that had carried them so close to the top of the Patrick Division in late December was ancient history, and their outlook, at least for the short term, was not particularly promising.

They still were playing without Lemieux, who continued to be bothered by an aching back and had targeted February 15 for his return. And Lemieux suffered a medical setback of sorts on February 7, when league officials gave him a slap on the wrist. It came in the form of a $1,000 fine for the harsh remarks he had made about referee Ron Hoggarth after the Penguins' 6-4 loss in Washington January 26.

"He indicated these remarks grew out of a series of frustrations," said NHL president John Ziegler, who presided over Lemieux's hearing in New York. "Despite provocation, public remarks critical of NHL officials must be penalized." Lemieux didn't argue that, but made sure to get his money's worth out of the meeting with Ziegler.

He rattled off his complaints about officiating in the NHL, most of them dealing with the way excessively rough play is handled, and expressed his interest in being one of the two NHL Players Association members who would sit in on a Rules Committee meeting when NHL coaches and general managers made their recommendations to that panel.

"There were no apologies," said Tom Reich, Lemieux's agent. "The most important thing to Lemieux is that he is going to get a chance to express himself on this whole range of issues. There were two separate areas. There was no action taken for what he said about the league." Which, of course, had been that it was a "garage league," a characterization that was rather opaque, but clearly not complimentary.

Lemieux might have been tempted to utter a few unflattering remarks about his team the next day, too, as the Penguins left Los Angeles left winger Luc Robitaille unchecked in front of their net with less than a minute to play in a tie game. Which, in a fraction of a second, wasn't a tie game anymore, as Robitaille threw a backhander behind Tom Barrasso for the game-winning goal in the Kings' 4-3 victory at the Civic Arena. "This would have been terrific, to pull out a point or maybe even two," Bowman said. "And you end up with nothing."

Less than nothing, actually, if you consider that the game cost the Penguins more than just another fresh notch in the loss column. Ulf Samuelsson got a bruised left foot when he blocked a Rob Blake shot during the first period and had to leave the game. He did not accompany the Penguins to Boston that evening, a major disappointment for his teammates and Bruins fans.

Samuelsson ranks high on the list of the most detested opponents among the sports devotees of Boston, somewhere between Bill Laimbeer and, well, anyone who ever played for the New York Yankees. And he might have become the ultimate arch-villain during the 1991 Wales Conference final, when his hits caused the thigh and knee injuries that sidelined Boston right winger Cam Neely for much of the 1991-92 season.

The *Boston Globe* marked his scheduled return with a major story and there was little reason to doubt Samuelsson would spend the afternoon having garbage, threats, and slurs heaved at him by the Boston Garden crowd. Not that Samuelsson really cared about the reception he would get.

"It doesn't bother me," he said a few days before being injured. "As far as my personal feelings, I don't have any. This isn't the first time I'm in that position. I put myself there a lot, so I'm used to it. If something happens, it happens. It's not going to affect me."

The Garden crowd, denied a chance to express its contempt for Samuelsson, had to settle for watching the Bruins dismantle his teammates, 6-3. The only positive development for the Penguins was that the game was followed by a five-day break in the schedule, which meant they were guaranteed to go the better part of a week without losing again.

But there were some distressing data for the Penguins to reflect on during their time off. Like how they had lost three games in a row and were 4-11-2 in their past 17. How they had held just one of the previous eight opponents to fewer than four goals. And how the fifth-place New York Islanders were creeping back into the Patrick playoff race, having sliced the Penguins' lead over them to nine points. "We all know where they are," Troy Loney said.

But that didn't mean the Penguins would be able to keep the Islanders there, a safe distance from serious playoff contention. "We've got to look behind now, but I think it's more of a case where we have to look at ourselves," Larry Murphy said. "We're going through a tough time now, and we've just got to pull it together."

Nice idea, albeit not in a literal sense, because the Penguins effectively split after the game in Boston. Some returned to Pittsburgh, others traveled to their hometowns, and many headed for Florida to escape winter. And maybe to get away from questions about how a defending champion could be struggling so badly less than a year after its victory celebration.

"If we had been on a roll, we probably would have said we'd be better off playing," said Scott Bowman, raising a thoroughly hypothetical concept. "As it turned out, it (the break) couldn't have come at a better time."

Too bad it couldn't have lasted a little longer. Getting away from the rink for a few days seemed to rejuvenate the Penguins, and some players even joked about their ongoing struggle. "The only place we're not slumping is in practice," Gord Roberts said. "We look good there." A little levity never hurts, but most of the Penguins saw nothing to laugh about in their predicament. "It's getting serious here," Stevens said. "It's not like we're sitting in first place and teams are chasing us. The teams on top are running away from us, and the teams on the bottom are coming up behind us."

The Penguins got some good news when they visited the Met Center in Bloomington, Minnesota on February 15 — Lemieux returned to the lineup and got extensive ice time with no apparent problem — but the word from the scoreboard was depressing as ever. The Minnesota North Stars beat them 5-2 to drop Pittsburgh to within five points of the Islanders. "We're not in the playoffs by any means," said Larry Murphy, who scored both Pittsburgh goals.

About the only thing the Penguins did well was to bicker about the work of referee Bill McCreary. Paul Coffey received two misconducts, a 10-minute and a game, at 13:25 of the second period after complaining to McCreary. Seconds earlier, Minnesota forward Mike Craig had charged into Coffey, but McCreary did not call a penalty, and that seemed to trigger Coffey's outburst.

Lemieux picked up an unsportsmanlike conduct penalty with 2:22 left in the game after giving McCreary some unsolicited advice about how he was handling his job. "I just told him what I thought was happening at the end of the game," Lemieux said. "We had a good shift, were buzzing around their net and every time we got into their zone, there was one of our guys on the ice with one of the Stars on top of him. It happened about six different times, and he didn't make the call."

The bottom line to it all: McCreary didn't reverse any of his non-calls, and Lemieux said he expected to be summoned back to John Ziegler's office again "pretty soon" to be punished for criticizing officials.

Just when it seemed as if the Penguins' relationship with the officials couldn't deteriorate any more, it did. Dramatically. The Penguins' dealings with referee Paul Stewart had been strained for a long time before he worked their game in the Spectrum on February 16, but the events of that evening turned a bad relationship bitter.

After the Penguins' 3-3 tie with the Flyers, Lemieux told Bowman and several teammates that Stewart had made veiled threats about his future dealings with Lemieux and/or the Penguins during a brawl with 16 seconds left in overtime. Several players said Lemieux spoke of a "surprise" Stewart said he had for the Penguins, and Stevens said, "Mario told me he (Stewart) said he's going to get Mario in some way, or our team in some way."

When Bowman heard of Lemieux's allegations, he asked Wally Harris, the NHL's assistant director of officiating, to discuss the situation with Stewart. "He said Stewart's interpretation was that he was going to surprise everybody by throwing them all off (after the brawl)," Bowman said. "He told Mario he had a surprise for him, and the surprise was 10 ejections. I just wanted to make sure his 'surprise' wasn't intended for later on (in the season). Wally Harris assured me that he went in the room and he (Stewart) said, 'No,' that things are said in the heat of the game and that he was going to surprise everybody and give them all two-and-10s (minor penalties and misconducts)."

Most of the Penguins didn't seem to put much credence in Stewart's explanation, but at least the evening hadn't been a total loss, for the first time in quite a while. "It's good for us to get a point," Joe Mullen said. Rare, too, considering Pittsburgh had lost four games in a row before visiting Philadelphia.

But the game against the Flyers served another purpose, too. It got the Penguins to recognize that their frequent, ugly run-ins with officials were accomplishing nothing. Nothing good, anyway. It made them realize that publicly chastising referees — and doing it so frequently — was not likely to bring about the changes they were seeking. "I don't think they're happy with us," Kevin Stevens said. "And I don't think we're happy with them."

Finally, it registered with the Penguins that fighting with officials was counterproductive, that there was nothing to be gained by alienating referees the way they had been. "The referees have a very, very low tolerance for our team," Tom Barrasso said. "That's not to say it's undeserved, but I think we get calls against us — particularly misconducts — quicker than any team I've been associated with . . . I think it's only human nature that if you attack someone, whether it's verbally or physically, there is always a backlash, whether intended or not."

Lemieux, whose scathing "garage league" remark instantly became a part of hockey's lexicon, agreed the running feud with officials was having some unpleasant side effects. "You can see that all the referees are after us now," he said. "They're trying to make a point on their side and it showed the last couple of games. Especially late in the game, they won't call anything (against Pittsburgh opponents)."

The Penguins didn't need much help from referee Kerry Fraser when Toronto visited the Civic Arena February 18. Joe Mullen had a hat trick and Pittsburgh scored the first six goals of the game en route to a 7-1 victory. It was the Penguins' first two-point effort in more than two weeks, but the result was little more than an afterthought in the locker room when the game was over. Word had begun to circulate that a trade was imminent, and that it wouldn't be the kind you'd have to read the fine print in the newspaper to learn about.

Paul Coffey, the prevailing wisdom had it, was gone, on his way to Philadelphia or Los Angeles. Mark Recchi's name made it into a few whispers, too, with the Flyers his apparent destination. The shake up that had been speculated on for months was about to hit. And the aftershocks would be felt for months.

CHAPTER EIGHT

Putting the Pieces Together

Paul Coffey had known it was coming. Had expected it since the early days of the season. He had long since resigned himself to changing area codes and employers. But in the early-morning hours of February 19, after he had gotten word that the deal was finally done, he couldn't leave the Civic Arena. Not just yet, anyway.

He stuffed his feet into his undersized skates for one last whirl around the rink that had been his home for most of the previous five seasons. One last chance to relive the memories that had been made there. It would be 2 a.m. before Coffey could bring himself to head home.

He was back in the locker room later that morning, after his teammates had learned the details of the deals. Coffey was being sent to Los Angeles for defensemen Jeff Chychrun and Brian Benning and a first-round draft choice. Recchi and the first-round draft choice would be dispatched to Philadelphia for right winger Rick Tocchet, defenseman Kjell Samuelsson, goalie Ken Wregget, and a conditional draft choice. The intent of the trade was obvious: The Penguins were giving up finesse players to get some physical ones.

"Our objective was to improve our team defensively and to improve our physical presence on the ice," GM Craig Patrick said. "We wanted to improve our chances to repeat as Stanley Cup champions."

If you buy into the axiom that defense wins championships, the Penguins clearly had enhanced their odds of repeating. Tocchet, whose grit had earned him the role of Philadelphia's captain, was renowned for his solid two-way play. Samuelsson, best known for his pterodactyl wingspan, had a reputation for being thorough and sound in his own end. And Chychrun had the capacity to give Pittsburgh some much-needed muscle on defense.

Still, there is a personal side to all personnel moves, and the trades obviously altered the Penguins' locker-room chemistry by changing the blend of personalities there. A few players openly questioned the wisdom of the deals, even while acknowledging the newcomers would give the team better balance. Kevin Stevens was particularly dismayed because Recchi is one of his closest friends, and less than a year had passed since another close friend, John Cullen, had been traded to Hartford.

"People say that athletes look out for themselves, that all they want is more money," Stevens said. "Here's an instance where Recchs turned down more money (from Philadelphia as a free agent) to stay here and help us win. It just goes to show that you've got to watch out for yourself . . . The players coming in here are great hockey players, don't get me wrong. I'm not saying anything negative about any one of those players. I'm just talking about our team and what we had here, how we won it last year. They were a huge part of that."

And Pittsburgh had become a major part of both players' lives. Coffey told a throng of media before flying to Edmonton, where he made his Kings debut that night, that he has "a lot of fond memories . . . I had five great years here." Coffey had months to brace for a trade, but Recchi was caught completely off-guard by word that he was being transplanted to the other side of Pennsylvania. He cried openly as he said goodbye to the men who had just become his ex-teammates and, in the words of Ulf Samuelsson, "was just destroyed." Recchi's reaction was not unexpected. He had dedicated every speck of energy, every fiber of his being to the Penguins from the time he joined the team, and now he was being told that he had become an expendable commodity. He could not see the trade as a professional transaction; to Recchi, it was a personal affront.

Despite the reservations expressed by some players, not all reaction to the deal was negative. Most of the media greeted it with cautious optimism, and Mario Lemieux endorsed the moves, saying it "was probably time for a change." Having Lemieux's approval was important, not only because of his stature on the team but because of his close relationship with Recchi and Coffey. If he had chastised management for sending away two close friends, there could have been a rift in the locker room that would have taken months to heal, and that was time the Penguins didn't have.

Patrick, meanwhile, defended the trades as a key step toward Pittsburgh's impending title defense in the playoffs. "We're moving two quality people, no question, but we wouldn't even consider it if we didn't think we were improving our hockey club," he said.

There was a similar reaction on the other side of the state, where Tocchet had been a longtime fan favorite, and Samuelsson was a fixture on the Flyers' defense. Getting Recchi, a proven goal-scorer, and Benning was an important part of the Flyers' rebuilding program that later would include prying super-prospect Eric Lindros from the Quebec Nordiques.

"Sure, trading within your division is not done much, but maybe I haven't caught on to that," Flyers GM Russ Farwell told reporters. "But our focus was narrowed on a young goal-scorer, and we have to be more concerned about our team and not so particular about how we got him. Recchi is a legitimate 100-point scorer. He has done it, and it's been a long time since the Flyers have had a 100-point scorer."

"I know we gave up a lot, but with all due respect to Tock and Sammy, our future looks a lot brighter," Flyers goalie Ron Hextall said. Of course, Hextall had no way of knowing then just what his role in Philadelphia's rebuilding program would be; he was part of the package Farwell shipped to Quebec during the offseason to secure the rights to Lindros. Hextall described Recchi as "an opportunist with a great set of hands, and this team really needs a good set of hands."

Samuelsson said he was disappointed about being traded, but understood the Flyers were rebuilding "and I'm not part of it at my age (33)." Tocchet had been under excruciating pressure to carry the Flyers in Philadelphia and joining the Penguins could have eased much of his burden, but Tocchet chose to keep his expectations high. "The players, management, and fans expect stuff out of me, and I'm going to give it to them," he said. "That's pressure I want. I used to have it in Philly and I want to have it here."

Tocchet, like his close friend Coffey, had been the subject of endless trade speculation since early in the season, and said he was relieved something had finally been settled. "It got to the point where I was getting nervous on the ice and I started taking the game home with me, which I never did before. Now I'll get the chance to play with a lot of great players, and I'm excited about that."

That was not a universal sentiment on this day, however. Frank Pietrangelo and Wendell Young, the incumbent backups to No. 1 goalie Tom Barrasso, were outraged at the idea Ken Wregget would be joining them on a depth chart that was already full. Having four goalies around can make for an awfully crowded crease.

Pietrangelo said the acquisition of Wregget was "a slap in the face to us," and Young predicted a trade that would break the logjam of bodies at their position was imminent. "Something else is going to happen here," he said. "I don't think any of the goaltenders are happy. They (management) must not be happy with the goaltending."

Patrick did not address overcrowded conditions in goal until March 10, when he shipped Pietrangelo to Hartford for future considerations. Wregget became entrenched as the No. 2 goalie, and Young was limited to less than 52 minutes of playing time in the 22 regular-season games that followed the trade.

Getting a new backup for Barrasso was not Patrick's main intent when he worked out the three-team deal with Philadelphia and Los Angeles; solidifying the Penguins' defensive infrastructure was the obvious objective. And no one should have been surprised that nearly a month passed before Patrick put together a trade to unload one of the excess goaltenders. His management style is painstakingly deliberate, often to the exasperation of players, agents, and even staff members who deal with him.

But Patrick's patience should not be confused with reluctance to make monumental changes to his team. Less than a year before Coffey and Recchi were traded, Patrick swung a deal with Hartford that galvanized the Penguins for the drive through the playoffs.

The cost had been steep — he gave up Zarley Zalapski, a young defenseman with wondrous potential, and John Cullen, one of hockey's most gifted playmakers, along with minor-league player Jeff Parker — but the returns were enormous. The Whalers sent Ron Francis, Ulf Samuelsson and defenseman Grant Jennings to Pittsburgh. Not coincidentally, the Penguins' first Stanley Cup followed a few months later.

Jennings was a nice addition to Pittsburgh's rather lackluster defense corps, but Francis and Samuelsson were the keys to the deal. Francis gave Pittsburgh a sound two-way center who was the perfect complement to Mario Lemieux, and Samuelsson brought muscle and grit that the defense needed so badly.

Francis had been the cornerstone of the franchise in Hartford, a perennial fan favorite who commanded respect because of the consistency and quality of his game. There were no fundamental flaws in his game, but Francis' attitude was every bit as important to the Penguins as his ability.

He had to make the transition from being the focus of attention with the Whalers to playing a supporting role with Pittsburgh. Ego is an important element in most athletes' success, but Francis was willing to accept a reduced role for the good of his new team. His slice of glory became smaller, but his sacrifices were rewarded with a Stanley Cup ring less than three months after he joined the Penguins.

"When I came here, Bob Johnson told me, 'We have this guy (Lemieux) here already and we'd like to keep him the No. 1 center,'" Francis said, smiling. "I think anybody who plays the game plays because they want to win . . . This team is so talented, you have to understand that. Mario is one of the best — probably the best — ever to play the game, so you're not going to take his ice time away. And with all the other talent we have, you have to accept the role they give you and work with it."

"We've asked him to play a role on our team that's important," Scott Bowman said. "He knows it, and he knows the most important thing is trying to get wins."

The Penguins were able to win — and win big — at least in part because of the dimension Francis brought to their lineup. He was qualified to fill a role no one else in the organization could. "We had Mario, but we didn't have a No. 2 center who could play both ends of the ice the way Ronnie can," Bob Errey said. "He wins the big draws and shuts the other team's top center down. And he's a great scorer when he has to be."

Cullen had been a crowd favorite at the Civic Arena, but fans there were quick to accept Francis, too. Samuelsson became a cult hero almost from his first shift. His rugged, unyielding style had a strong blue-collar appeal, and every hit he delivered on home ice was greeted with chants of "Ulf, Ulf, Ulf."

The reception was a little different on the road. If Samuelsson isn't the most-hated player in the National Hockey League, he's at least on the short list of finalists for that distinction. "He'll throw those quick rabbit punches in your face, maybe give you 'the wash,' which is sticking his glove in your face and washing your face," left winger Phil Bourque said.

"On the ice, he's a jerk to a lot of people," Pittsburgh defenseman Peter Taglianetti said. "I think if you polled 500 people in the league, they're going to say the exact same thing. Except for the 20 guys on his team." And nowhere is Samuelsson more despised than in Boston, where his long-running rivalry with Bruins right winger Cam Neely, an exquisite power forward, hit full boil during the 1991 Wales Conference final.

Samuelsson and Neely had numerous Richter Scale-rocking collisions during that series, including one the Bruins contend caused the thigh and knee problems that forced Neely to miss most of the 1991-92 season. Many months after the series, the Bruins' raw hatred for Samuelsson was evident when they reflected on his pitched battles with Neely.

"Boston's the one team that really dislikes him," said Garry Galley, whom the Bruins traded to Philadelphia during the 1991-92 season. "And the Neely thing last year just added fuel to the fire. He (Samuelsson) has that aura about him that makes you want to run him . . . I think it's just a matter of time before he gets caught in a vulnerable spot."

"There have always been guys in hockey who picked their spots, but he thinks it's OK for him to tear a guy's leg off or blow someone's knee off," Bruins winger Lyndon Byers said. "Such is the way of life. Payback is a bitch, and that's why it works out in the end."

For his part, Samuelsson insisted he has no malice toward Neely, that he was simply filling his role as the guy designated to neutralize the opponents' most dangerous winger. He said he had an assignment to contain Neely, not a mandate to maim him.

"Anybody who looked at the replay saw I didn't stick my leg out intentionally or anything," Samuelsson said. "I was trying to hit him hard . . . as hard as I could. And I will do that against any player, because I think that's part of my job. Most of the time, I initiate all the stuff that goes on. You try to initiate, not retaliate."

That attitude makes him something of a novelty, considering Swedish players had long been reputed to have little tolerance for a physical game. Someone once speculated that if defenseman Inge Hammarstrom went into the corner with a dozen eggs in his pocket, he could emerge without having broken any. A profile in *The Pittsburgh Press* suggested that if Samuelsson tried to do that, he would "come out with yolk on his stick, shell fragments on his elbows and a dead chicken in his hand."

And for all the abuse he dispenses, Samuelsson probably absorbs even more. Neely has pummeled him in several fights over the years—"He can hammer away pretty good," Samuelsson said—and opposing players routinely commit stick fouls against him, but Samuelsson shrugs it all off as nothing more than part of the game.

"Ulfie takes his knocks," Bryan Trottier said. "He gets slugged in the head, he gets whacked, he gets butt-ended, he gets speared, and I haven't heard Ulfie complain to anybody about cheap-shotting him. He takes his knocks, and I guess he accepts that as part of the game. Ulfie's created his own mold, and he's going to crack and break it by himself, too. Because I don't think we're going to see another Ulfie for a long time."

The Hartford trade made the Penguins' first championship possible, but was just one of several deals over the years that brought in key components of the Cup-winning team. During his tenure as general manager, Eddie Johnston relied heavily on draft choice to rebuild the franchise on the rubble he inherited in 1983. But while good drafting laid the foundation of future success, trades were vital to assembling Pittsburgh's Cup-winning talent.

Johnston made the first one on November 24, 1987, when he sent Craig Simpson, Chris Joseph, Dave Hannan, and Moe Mantha to Edmonton for Paul Coffey, Dave Hunter, and Wayne Van Dorp. The deal established a pattern that would hold through most of Pittsburgh's major trades over the next few years: Former first-round draft choices didn't have much hope of finishing their careers in Pittsburgh. In that case, the Penguins parted with two, Simpson (1985) and Joseph (1987).

Tony Esposito, who succeeded Johnston as GM in a controversial move by owner Edward J. DeBartolo in the spring of 1988, traded two more in November of that year. He shipped Doug Bodger, one of Pittsburgh's three first-rounders in 1984, and Darrin Shannon, the No. 1 pick in 1988, to Buffalo for Tom Barrasso and a third-round draft choice. And Patrick did the same on March 4, 1991, when he included Zalapski, the No. 1 choice in 1986, in the six-player deal with Hartford.

Barasso was a critical acquisition, because he gave Pittsburgh the top-quality goaltender every championship team needs. Buffalo drafted him out of Acton-Boxboro High School in Massachusetts with the fifth pick in the 1983 draft, and Barrasso dominated the position during his first year in the league. He was the Rookie of the Year, the first-team all-star and earned the Vezina Trophy as the NHL's top goalie.

No goalie ever had been taken so high in the draft, and it's doubtful any in the future — no matter when they're chosen — will be a high-impact player just a few months after graduating from high school, the way Barrasso was. Most young goalies, no matter how gifted, can count on being well into their 20s before they get to the NHL.

"I would be thoroughly amazed if it ever occurs again with an 18-year-old goalie," Barrasso said. "I was never intimidated by it. I never sat back and said, 'Hey, I'm playing in the National Hockey League.' I expected to do well. I expected to go in and be able to do the job. I never doubted that, and it was evident in my performance. I treated it like I was still in high school. I showed up to play every day. I wanted to excel. Really, hockey was all I did. It was the driving force in me at that time, and that was a big part of being able to have success."

But he never repeated his success of that first season, at least not in Buffalo, and eventually became the scapegoat for the Sabres' repeated inability to get past the first round of the playoffs. Goaltending is the most critical variable in post-season play, so when management and fans in Buffalo began to look for an explanation for their early exit from the playoffs each spring, Barrasso was a convenient target.

The Sabres deemed him expendable when Daren Puppa showed signs of developing into a quality replacement, and

Esposito, himself a former all-star goalie, did not hesitate to work out a deal to acquire Barrasso. A few years later, Buffalo still hadn't reached the second round of the playoffs, and Barrasso was starting a nice collection of Stanley Cup rings. And it had been shown that the playoff pressure so many people in Buffalo felt made Barrasso crack, actually brought out the best in him.

Maybe that's because Barrasso had matured as a player since leaving the Sabres. Maybe it's because he learned that there are issues infinitely more significant than hockey when his young daughter, Ashley, had an extended, life-threatening bout with cancer. In any case, he has shown little reluctance to accept the excruciating pressure that is inherent in his line of work. Doubters need only consult his record from the 1991 and 1992 playoffs. In Games 5-7 of Pittsburgh's eight playoff series in those years — the games in which the pressure to perform is most intense because the stakes are highest — Barrasso has a 10-0 record and 2.00 goals-against average. The goalie hasn't been born who wouldn't love to have those numbers on his resume.

"Goalie is the most pressure-filled position in hockey," he said. "Any mistake a forward or defenseman makes can be made up by the goalie. But when a goalie makes a mistake, it usually costs his team a goal. But I don't let the pressure bother me. It's how you handle it. Myself, with what I've been through with my daughter, it has changed my outlook a bit. What's pressure to somebody else might not necessarily be pressure felt by me. This is what I do. It's my choice and I try to enjoy it, because I won't be doing it forever."

Barrasso was labeled arrogant earlier in his career and still comes across as being aloof at times, but his steady, confident approach to his job is a key ingredient in his success. "Tommy really seems to keep himself on an even keel," Ron Francis said. "When he's playing really well, he doesn't seem to be overly cocky or mouthy; he's very relaxed and laid back. Conversely, when things aren't going well for him, he doesn't seem to be totally down in the dumps. That's very important for a goaltender. You can't be on the emotional roller-coaster, because your confidence level seems to go with it."

Barrasso long ago resigned himself to the reality that he is unlikely to rank among the statistical leaders at his position, regardless of how well he plays. Inflated numbers are a given for any goalie playing behind an offense-oriented team like the

Penguins. "Every goalie wants good numbers," Joe Mullen said. "But the bottom line is wins, and if you can get good numbers there, that's what everybody's going to be looking at."

Barrasso's victory total should be enough to quiet the critics most of the time. And if that doesn't work, he can always show them his collection of rings, the ones with the diamonds. The ones that prove he deserves a place among hockey's top goaltenders, no matter what his regular-season statistics might say.

"I'm just tired of taking criticism that, true or false, is irrelevant," Barrasso said after the Minnesota series in 1991. "I'm just tired of being criticized. When I came in (to the league), I had these labels put on me, and you can't shed them until you do something like win this Cup."

Despite all the precedents, the Penguins didn't have to give up a first-round draft choice in every significant deal that went into building their championship teams. On June 16, 1990 — about an hour after drafting Jaromir Jagr — Patrick shipped Pittsburgh's second-round choice to Calgary for right winger Joe Mullen. The price seemed high for a 33-year-old, but Patrick was acting at the behest of Bob Johnson, who had coached Mullen in Calgary.

"He has some years left in him, I'll tell you that," Johnson said. "He can play. He's dangerous when you don't think he's dangerous. In front of the net when he's leaning over or laying down — when most players are completely out of the play — that's when he'll score."

Patrick made an uncharacteristically bold prediction when the deal was done: "I think he'll score 40-plus goals for the next two years." His projection was a little off in 1990-91, when Mullen got 17 goals, but missed nearly half the season after undergoing surgery to repair a herniated disk in his neck. Patrick looked prophetic the next season, however, as Mullen scored 42 times, the seventh time he had gotten 40 or more goals. He joined Hall of Famers Gordie Howe, Phil Esposito, and John Bucyk as the only players in league history to score 40 or more after turning 35. Which might explain why his teammates sometimes wonder if there is a typographical error on Mullen's birth certificate. Sure, he has the hairline of a man in his mid-30s, but Mullen plays with the enthusiasm of a guy 10 years younger. And there's no signs of old age from his hands or legs, either.

"You're only as old as you feel and only as old as you play, and Joey looks like he's 19 again," Ron Francis said. "You don't really realize how good a player he is until you actually play with him. He does all the little things right, defensively as well as offensively."

"I'm sure if you look in the yearbook, it says 35 next to his name, but it's hard to believe," Larry Murphy said. "I've never thought of him as 35, and I'm sure he doesn't consider himself to be 35. He's got the attitude of a 15-year-old, and the body of a 25-year-old."

"I know this is late in life for a hockey player, but I try not to think about age," Mullen said. "Once we put on our uniforms, we're all the same age. Everyone's a kid. I think my enthusiasm is what keeps me going. If I ever lost that, I might slow down a little. But I still love to play the game. I love to go out and do the best I can every night. I have the same enthusiasm as when I started, and I can't see myself giving (the game) up, even though some day I know I'll have to." Just not anytime in the foreseeable future. Like, say, anytime before the 21st Century.

But Mullen contributes more to his team than just offense and enthusiasm, as if those wouldn't be enough. He is an intelligent and dedicated defensive forward and an accomplished penalty killer, versatile enough to contribute in any situation that arises during a hockey game.

"He's a complete player," Scott Bowman said. "If one part of his game runs into a problem, he still has a lot of value. Mentally, he's got things in hand so he probably could take a reduced workload at the right time. He's the ultimate team guy."

Mullen had a much greater impact than most people expected when the Penguins acquired him, and the same was true of what looked to be a medium-magnitude deal Patrick made on December 11, 1990. He sent two defensemen, Jim Johnson and Chris Dahlquist, to Minnesota for two others, Larry Murphy and Peter Taglianetti. Johnson and Dahlquist were solid, albeit unspectacular, players, especially in the defensive zone, and the book on Taglianetti was much the same. Murphy, however, was widely regarded as a player who could contribute regularly to the offense, but was a liability in his own end. In Pittsburgh, he was best known as the defenseman Mario Lemieux had scorched for a spectacular overtime goal during the final weekend of the 1987-88 regular season.

But Murphy would chisel out a major niche with the Penguins, prove to be equally effective and valuable in both ends of the rink. He generated the offense the Penguins were counting on — 77 points in 77 games in 1991-92 — and his defensive work was a revelation. Murphy does not play an overtly physical game, but his intelligence, reflexes, and instincts allow him to play an almost mistake-free style. And his ability to do little things that are often overlooked, like holding the puck in at the point during power plays, add an important facet to his game. The Penguins hoped Murphy would be a pretty good defenseman for them; he's turned out to be one of the best in the National Hockey League.

"He's really been above all expectations for myself," Scott Bowman said. Bowman credited Bob Johnson for coaxing maximum productivity from Murphy, for shattering the perception that he was a one-dimensional player. "I think that all changed last year," he said. "When Murphy came here, Bob decided to play him under any circumstances, and he just carried over. A new lease on life started for him last year, and he's just kept it up."

"The first day I got here, Bob told me he needed me," Murphy said. "In Washington, I was basically just a role player. In Minnesota, all they wanted me for was the power play. When I got to Pittsburgh, they told me they needed me in every situation. This is an ideal situation for me. The personnel here is great, and they've given me a lot of responsibility. I've been given a big role on this team, and I really appreciate it."

Much the way the men who play with Murphy appreciate the way he handles any job he's given, consistently and effectively. Gord Roberts, Murphy's frequent defense partner for most of two seasons, said, "He does everything you ask him to, and he does it every night." Defenseman Jim Paek said Murphy "brings everything to the team. He brings offense and defense. He plays on the power-play and penalty-killing teams. And he's a good guy to sit next to and talk to. When he talks, everybody listens."

But when people talk about Murphy — and there was a lot to say during the 1991-92 season — few outside Pittsburgh seem to hear. He tied Al MacInnis of Calgary for fourth place in the scoring race among NHL defensemen and his plus-minus rating of plus-33 tied for fifth-best in the league, but Murphy wasn't even named one of the three finalists for the James Norris

Trophy, given to the league's top defenseman.

Never mind that Kevin Stevens said Murphy had a year "as good as any defenseman in the league" and deserved "a lot more credit" for the Penguins' success than he received, or that Bowman felt Murphy had "absolutely the best year of his career." But that wasn't enough to make an impression on many voters, and the problem was compounded by all of the high-profile players in Pittsburgh's lineup. Even really good players can get overlooked in the forest of great ones that fills the Pittsburgh locker room.

Murphy, who played on Canada's championship teams in the 1987 and 1991 Canada Cup tournaments, said he doesn't feel slighted by the lack of attention — and respect — around the league, that "if somebody really worried about something like that, they should hire a PR firm to promote them."

Perhaps he didn't care because there really wasn't space on his mantel for a piece of hardware, like the Norris, that he could win from the league. Or perhaps because he has spent parts of two seasons in Pittsburgh, and has two Stanley Cup rings to show for it.

JAROMIR JAGR
Some fans think it's no coincidence that by mixing the letters of his first name you get "Mario Jr."

Goalie **TOM BARRASSO** stopped 27 shots for his second career playoff shutout during the finals with Chicago.

The Penguins matched the Boston Bruins' high-priced offer to keep Massachusetts native **KEVIN STEVENS** in Pittsburgh.

JOE MULLEN became the first American-born player to score 400 career goals during a game against Edmonton in March.

MARIO LEMIEUX'S chronic back problems flared throughout the season, but he was still recognized by the hockey world as one of its all-time premier players.

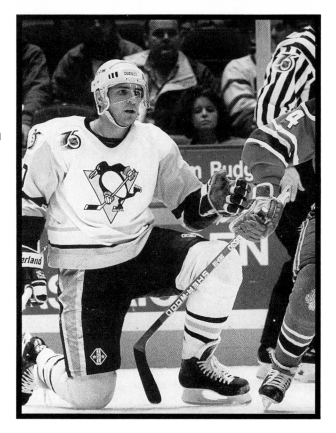

RON FRANCIS scored the Cup-clinching goal in Pittsburgh's 6-5 victory over Chicago.

ULF SAMUELSSON was assigned a bodyguard for protection while the Penguins were in Boston; a testament to Bruins fans' dislike of the aggressive player.

In March, RICK TOCCHET showed his toughness by scoring two third-period goals to pull out a 4-3 victory in Chicago, even though his jaw had been broken by a Lemieux pass earlier in the game.

The Penguins delayed raising their championship banners in 1991, hoping that Bob Johnson would soon be well enough to attend the ceremony.

In December of 1991
LARRY MURPHY
became one of only ten
defensemen who have
reached the 700-point
level in their careers.

(l to r) **KEVIN STEVENS, TOM BARRASSO, BRYAN TROTTIER,** and **RON FRANCIS** celebrate back-to-back Stanley Cup Championships.

The Pittsburgh Penguins proved that the first time around was no fluke by clinching the 1992 Championship in a four-game sweep of Chicago.

MARIO LEMIEUX received the Conn Smythe Trophy as the Playoff MVP for the second year in a row—only the second player in league history to accomplish this feat.

CHAPTER NINE

Down the Stretch

The Penguins' monumental trade with Hartford in March of 1991 had produced immediate and impressive results. The first night that Francis, Samuelsson, and Jennings were in the lineup, the Penguins, who had been 0-4-1 before the deal, beat Vancouver, 4-1, at the Civic Arena. That launched them on a 9-1-2 rampage that enabled them to overhaul the New York Rangers and claim their first Patrick Division championship before the end of the month.

But no such jump-start would coincide with the arrival of Tocchet, Kjell Samuelsson, Chychrun, and Wregget. There would be no instant gratification, no string of victories that underscored the need for such a shake up. Or justified the risks Patrick took by making moves that redefined the personality of his team.

The day after the trade, the Penguins were never able to get a lead and had to settle for a 4-4 tie with Quebec. Any point is cherished during the final weeks of the season, but considering that the Nordiques had gone into the game with a road record of 0-22-6, the outcome didn't have anyone proclaiming that Pittsburgh had found the formula that guaranteed a spot in the finals again.

Tocchet, still recovering from a heel injury he had suffered in Philadelphia, needed only a few shifts with his new team to grasp the magnitude of the adjustment he would have to make. After playing a plodding style for years with the Flyers, Tocchet experienced something akin to culture shock while playing alongside Mario Lemieux and Kevin Stevens.

The game was still hockey, but it bore little resemblance to what Tocchet had gotten used to on the far side of the state. After spending years on an off-ramp, Tocchet found himself in the fast lane, and keeping up with the traffic flow was difficult in that first game. "I noticed a few times I had the puck and Mario and Kevin were flying up the ice," Tocchet said. "In Philadelphia, guys would be behind you and you would be tic-tacking up the ice and dump it in."

The Penguins' level of play rose considerably in their second game after the trade, but the results didn't improve. In fact, they got worse, courtesy of Montreal goalie Patrick Roy. He was unceasingly brilliant, stopping 26 shots in a 2-1 Canadiens victory at the Forum. The Penguins had done everything but win the game, but at this juncture of the season, getting two points was all that mattered. Moral victories meant nothing, even though the Penguins were fairly certain they had gotten one at the Forum. "I really thought we outplayed them," Tocchet said. "Roy was the difference. We would have liked to have won this game. It would have been a real character-builder. But I still think we outplayed them."

Roy wasn't around when the Penguins visited the Capital Centre a few days later, but Pittsburgh could detect no significant difference between him and Washington goalie Don Beaupre. Beaupre made 24 saves in Washington's 5-3 victory, and the Penguins were on a 1-6-3 free fall that dropped them to within three points of the fifth-place New York Islanders. "There's no excuse for losing," Larry Murphy said. "We've put ourselves in a tailspin, and it's something we have to overcome. Time is of the essence now. The Islanders are right behind us. Critical time is here."

So was the stretch drive. The game in Washington marked the start of the final quarter of the regular season, and already the Penguins had been all but mathematically eliminated from the race for first place in the Patrick Division. Their only realistic objective during the closing weeks of the season would be to hold onto a playoff spot, maybe sneak past New Jersey into third place. In October, none of the Penguins had expected to be little more than a distant dot in the rear-view mirrors of the division leaders by late February. "I don't think anybody here would have thought that (when the season began)," Troy Loney said. "Up to this point, it's been a frustrating year for us."

If Murphy was right about the critical time of the season having arrived, the Penguins must have forgotten to set their watches, because they looked like a team caught in a time warp during their next game, an 8-4 loss to Hartford at the Civic Arena. The performance was vintage Penguins, circa 1983-84. The difference is, they were the worst team in hockey then; now, they were the defending Stanley Cup champions. But the distinction was becoming blurred at best.

"I have to go back in the memory banks to remember the last time it was this bad in this organization," said Phil Bourque, who had signed with the Penguins as a free agent in 1982. Ulf Samuelsson said it was "the worst game I've played as a Penguin, and the worst game I've seen the team play." The Penguins had plunged to the statistical definition of mediocrity — 27-27-8 — and their lead over New York was whittled to one point when the Islanders beat New Jersey the next night.

The Penguins' margin for error had all but vanished at that point, lost in a hailstorm of defeats and disappointment. And while it wasn't quite time to push the panic button, it didn't seem like a bad idea to get a finger or two on it, because the season was on the verge of deteriorating into a full-scale disaster.

"Something's got to change in the way we're playing, and it needs to change pretty quick," Tom Barrasso said. "Otherwise, we're going to be in a lot of trouble. We've gone this far playing this poorly, and we're still all right, which is pretty frightening when you think about it."

Well, the Penguins were still alive, but they weren't exactly all right. The truth is, they were spiraling toward a premature — and lengthy — offseason at a terrifying speed. They still owned fourth place in the Patrick, but that one-point lead over New York was nothing more than mathematical life support.

The situation might even have been more scary than the Penguins realized, but that humbling loss to Hartford proved to be a pivotal point in their season. The resurgence that would turn out to be their salvation began two days later with a 5-2 victory against Buffalo at the Civic Arena. Pittsburgh burned the Sabres for at least a half-dozen breakaways and turned in the type of solid defensive effort seldom seen during the previous two months. "Everything fell into place," Larry Murphy said. "Our forwards were taking it right to them and Tommy (Barrasso) made the big saves when we needed them."

The Penguins had tumbled to the very brink of fifth place before righting themselves. If they had lost to the Sabres and the Islanders had beaten New Jersey later in the day, Pittsburgh would have plummeted out of the playoff picture, at least temporarily. "The team reacted well to the pressure of the situation," Bowman said. "Good teams do that; mediocre teams fall apart."

Bowman's players took their strong showing as a sign that they could indeed still respond in a desperate situation, that they could react to a challenge with resolve, not unconditional surrender. And that it was a promising portent for the rest of the season.

"The games we need to play well — when our backs are absolutely against the wall — we always come up with the right kind of effort," Barrasso said. "It has been the other games, where there hasn't been the pressure, that we've been lax. As time goes by, every game is important, and I think we're starting to realize that, because we're running out of time to get ourselves prepared. Hopefully, with that realization in mind, we're all going to show up to play, night in and night out. I like to think our players have the character to do that."

The Penguins understandably were relieved to get a victory, but were in no position to relax. They were about to embark on a road trip to Calgary, San Jose, and Los Angeles, a grueling trip under the best of circumstances. And these were nowhere near the best of circumstances. Not when the trip from Pittsburgh to Calgary included a change of planes in Dallas, a move made to secure lower airfares for the trip. One observer couldn't resist pointing out that the Penguins were practically going to Mexico to get to Canada.

If nothing else, the trip gave the players plenty of time to reflect on the observations of Phil Bourque, who said the Penguins would do well to call upon the legacy of Bob Johnson for inspiration during their current crisis. He pointed out how Johnson would even have found something good in the thoroughly depressing loss to Hartford. "I just keep thinking about Bob," he said. "How would Bob handle this situation? He'd find the positive ... You've got to think like that, because that's what won us a Cup, positive thinking."

But there was little positive energy coming from Craig Patrick's hotel room at the Skyline Plaza hotel in Calgary the next day, when he summoned the players for a no-holds-barred meeting. He told them to leave diplomacy and their inhibitions in the hallway, that he wanted nothing but unvarnished candor from everyone. From all indications, he got it.

Any topic was open for discussion, but players said later Scott Bowman became virtually the sole focus of the meeting. There were complaints about his habit of going home to Buffalo on non-game days. About the way he ran the bench during games. About the way he interacted with players. About nearly everything, it seemed, except his choice of socks, and somebody probably muttered a few disparaging syllables about those, too.

Frustrations that had been building inside some players for months spilled out in angry torrents of criticism, all aimed at the man who had been thrust into his job by the cruelest of circumstances. Bowman wasn't present — he was flying in from Buffalo when the meeting was held — and Patrick told the players not to discuss the session with reporters. Several who requested anonymity did, however, and said Bowman was subjected to some scalding attacks.

Predictably, players had been reluctant to go public with their criticisms of Bowman; blasting your boss in the newspapers doesn't do much for job security. But players who had left the team made it clear the personal bond that existed between Bob Johnson and the players was missing, that the relationship with Bowman was strictly superior-subordinate. "Bob cared about you off the ice as well as on the ice," Mark Recchi told Philadelphia reporters after he was traded. "With Scotty, you're lucky to get a hello out of him."

In some ways, the meeting between Patrick and his players changed nothing, because Bowman still was the coach and was empowered to run the team as he saw fit. But in other ways, it changed everything. The session dissolved the tension that had been building for months, and the atmosphere in the locker room at practice that day was as loose and relaxed as it had been in autumn.

That was most apparent when center Jiri Hrdina taped "68" to the back of a practice sweater, put on a baseball cap with a pigtail attached (no assembly required) and went for a quick pre-practice skate at the Saddledome. Hrdina's impersonation of Jaromir Jagr left his teammates wobbly with laughter, and Jagr was sufficiently amused that he appropriated the cap when Hrdina returned to the locker room.

Of course, it didn't hurt the Penguins' attitude to know that they would be facing an opponent that had been struggling almost as much as they were. The Flames were coming off an 11-0 thrashing in Vancouver, the most lopsided loss in franchise history. Not surprisingly, that game had not gone over well with the good people of southern Alberta. Two headlines in the *Calgary Sun* the next morning — "THIS IS PATHETIC" and "HUMILIATED" — captured the spirit of the moment rather nicely.

Things didn't go quite that badly for the Flames in their next game, but they weren't all that much better, either. The Penguins played without Mario Lemieux and Ulf Samuelsson, both of whom were felled by the flu, but beat Calgary, 6-3, to record their first back-to-back victories since December 28-29. "It's a good thing we came in here and got a win, because we haven't exactly been the hottest team in the world," Kevin Stevens said. "We went out and did what we had to do. It's tough without Mario and Ulfie, but our team pulled together."

And did it at a time when the Flames looked to be falling apart. Doug Risebrough resigned as their coach after the game, purportedly to concentrate on his duties as general manager. Some thought he had stepped down as coach to avoid being stripped of both titles. And the chaos that started in the Calgary front office made it all the way to the ice, where the Flames looked ragged and distracted. "They're a team that's kind of confused right now and trying to get untracked," Bob Errey said. "Just like we have been."

Well, the Penguins were getting untracked and, a few nights later, they would be unleashed. The NHL schedule-maker gave the Penguins an inadvertant, but timely, break in the guise of another visit to the Cow Palace. Another evening with the San Jose Sharks, the team they had burned for the first 18 goals in the season series. The team they had held scoreless for more than 112 minutes.

The Penguins again said all the right things about fearing San Jose before the game, although no one who had seen Pittsburgh dissect the Sharks in their previous two meetings was swallowing any of that "on-any-given-night" routine. And no one was buying it after the game, either. Not after seeing Rick

Tocchet get a hat trick — the first goals of his Pittsburgh career — in the Penguins' 7-3 victory.

That offensive splurge was a major breakthrough for Tocchet, who was starting to wonder if he had forgotten to pack his scoring touch when he moved to Pittsburgh. He said finally getting a puck into the net was "a relief, like getting a piano off your back," and nobody in the Cow Palace could have missed his exuberance when it happened. "You could see he was pretty excited about it," Lemieux said.

When the game was over, and Sharks goalie Jarmo Myllys had been skinned by the Penguins for the final time during the 1991-92 season, the only question was who had turned in the most stirring performance of the evening. Was it Huey Lewis and the News, who did a brilliant rendition of the national anthem? Or was it Lemieux, who turned in a virtuoso effort of his own?

Lemieux voted for Huey — "That was unbelievable," he said. "It was great" — but that probably was a minority opinion, because Lemieux had a goal and three assists to run his three-game total against San Jose to five goals, eight assists. If the Penguins had been in the Smythe Division and played the Sharks more than three times a year, he might have wrapped up the scoring championship by Christmas.

The Penguins closed out the road trip with a 5-3 loss in Los Angeles one night after they beat San Jose, and again, Kings goalie Kelly Hrudey left his fingerprints all over the final score. This time, he stopped 35 of 38 shots to hand the Penguins their sixth loss in a row at the Great Western Forum. "It seems like every time he plays against us, he's making those types of saves," Lemieux said.

The Penguins weren't happy about the outcome — neither was president Howard Baldwin, who took the players and staff out for a post-game dinner — but neither did they feel the need to dwell on it, because no longer were they flirting with imminent disaster. Their confidence had been restored, and the diverse facets of their game were coming together. Not as quickly as they might have liked, perhaps, but the signs of progress could not be missed.

Craig Patrick made a few long-term investments as the March 10 trading deadline closed in. He sent Frank Pietrangelo, the disgruntled goalie, to Hartford for future considerations, and shipped the rights to right winger Scott Young, who had spent the season in Italy, to Quebec for defenseman Bryan Fogarty.

There wasn't much risk involved in the Quebec deal, because the consensus was that Young had no chance to be more than a name near the bottom of Pittsburgh's depth chart at right wing, and there was the possibility Fogarty would blossom into the high-impact player so many projected him to be when the Nordiques drafted him in 1987. "We felt the downside for us was nil," Patrick said, "and we feel the (potential) upside is tremendous."

Fogarty had entered the NHL with impeccable, almost unparalleled, credentials. He was hailed as "the next Paul Coffey" after setting Ontario Hockey League records for points and assists by a defenseman while playing at Niagara Falls. But Fogarty's career began to dissolve into the blurry haze of alcohol abuse, and he missed part of the 1990-91 season while undergoing rehabilitation.

Nonetheless, the Penguins figured that in the worst-case scenario, they had given up a player who wasn't going to play for them in exchange for another who would be unable to. But the best-case outlook, which was more than a little bit of a reach, was that they had acquired a player who just might mature into an offensive force on the blue line, maybe even fill the void left when Coffey was traded.

"Bryan's got exceptional talents, especially offensive talents," Patrick said. "That's what appealed to us. We had a fellow here for a number of years, Paul Coffey, who had similar qualities and was very successful. We feel Bryan, in time, can come in, and with a little tutelage from people here, develop into that kind of player."

When the trade was finalized, Patrick said he believed Fogarty had "made a lot of strides" toward beating his drinking problem, but Fogarty had a relapse a few weeks after reporting to the Penguins' farm team in Muskegon, Michigan. He was enrolled in another rehabilitation program, and team officials began to talk less about what part Fogarty might play in the Penguins' future, and more about how they were interested in seeing him salvage his off-ice life.

The trading-deadline deals, unlike the ones on February 19, had few repercussions inside the Pittsburgh locker room. Most of the Penguins were happy to see Pietrangelo join a team for which he could play regularly, and few expected to play alongside Fogarty, at least for the rest of the season. And there wasn't much time to dwell on transactions, anyway. The Penguins' grip on fourth place and a playoff berth was getting stronger, but was still somewhat tenuous.

They preserved their four-point edge over the Islanders with a 5-2 victory against Calgary at the Civic Arena March 10, thus giving the Penguins victories in consecutive home games for the first time since November 27-December 10, when they had won three in a row. As major feats go, that wasn't much, but it gave the Penguins reason to believe that home ice would be a little less hostile for the rest of the season.

"We had a tough time here for most of the season, but that's all behind us now," Lemieux said. "We've just got to look forward. We want to establish that for teams to come in here and take two points from us is going to be tough."

That must have sounded ominous to the rest of the league, which already had to be concerned about the way Tocchet was fitting in with the Penguins. He scored two goals against Calgary, running his total in three games to six, and continued to raise the level of his play toward the lofty one set by his linemates. "Playing with 66 (Lemieux) and 25 (Stevens) helps," he said. "I have confidence now. I go out there and I know I'm usually going to get a couple of chances a game." And, more importantly, turn those opportunities into numbers on the scoreboard.

So the Penguins were on a 4-1 roll as they entered their most critical game to date, a collision with the Islanders at the Civic Arena March 12. A victory would swell their lead over New York to six points and be a mortal blow to New York's playoff prospects. But if the Islanders won, the cushion would shrivel to two points, and the Penguins could be one losing streak away from spending the first round of the playoffs on a golf course. "We're not trying to make it suspenseful," Bob Errey said. "Winning would go a long way toward securing a playoff spot."

"People use the phrase 'biggest game of the year' kind of loosely, but this is it for us," Larry Murphy said. "When the situation started to develop where both teams . . . looked like they'd be fighting for the last spot, I think both looked forward to this game. It's kind of like, you're fighting a team for a playoff spot. Well, let's play each other and determine it."

While both teams recognized the enormity of the stakes in this game, neither played like they did. The game was an artistic disaster, but the Penguins were able to survive their self-inflicted wounds better than New York, and escaped with a 6-4 victory. "We won ugly," Tocchet said. "You've got to win these games. Good teams win when they don't play that well."

Don't misunderstand. The Penguins were grateful for the victory. They were just glad there hadn't been any style points at stake. "We'll take the two points, but we definitely can play a lot better," Lemieux said. So could the Islanders, but they realized they might not get another chance to chisel away at Pittsburgh's advantage in the standings. "I'd rather be in Pittsburgh's spot, that's for sure," New York defenseman Tom Kurvers said.

Ironically, the game-winning goal in that most critical game against the Islanders had been scored not by Lemieux, Stevens, Mullen, or Tocchet, but by defenseman Kjell Samuelsson, who is much better known for his long arms than for what he does with the hands at the ends of them.

Scoring goals wasn't part of his job description with Pittsburgh, but he didn't mind chipping in with some offense every now and then. "He (Patrick) brought me in to play defense, but if I can score goals, that's the fun part," Samuelsson said. "Playing defense is just dirty work."

Beating the Islanders had expanded the Penguins' comfort zone considerably, but their momentum was shattered two nights later. They visited Toronto and were beaten 6-3 in a game in which their goaltending was almost non-existent. Tom Barrasso did not play because of back spasms, rapidly becoming the official ailment of the Pittsburgh Penguins, and both of his backups struggled badly against the Maple Leafs.

Wendell Young allowed three goals on 17 shots before being replaced by Ken Wregget, who gave up two on four shots. The empty-net goal that Maple Leafs forward Glenn Anderson scored with 42 seconds left in the game might have been the toughest Toronto got all night, considering that it took Anderson two tries to get it into the net.

It was a demoralizing defeat, and the prognosis was not promising as the Penguins boarded their charter flight after the game. They were on their way to Chicago Stadium, one of the most intimidating rinks in the NHL, and would spend the next night battling the Blackhawks, whose physical style was tailored to exploit the undersized ice surface in their arena. Chicago was 9-0-4 in its previous 13 games at the Stadium, where Pittsburgh had won just seven times in the previous 24 years.

So no one was surprised when, six minutes into the third period, the Blackhawks were protecting a 3-1 lead. The chances of Pittsburgh overcoming that deficit seemed almost microscopic, especially when Tocchet had left the game after having the left side of his jaw ripped open by a Mario Lemieux pass late in the second period. The puck gashed Tocchet's face, and it was learned later, broke his jaw. It was the type of injury that should have put him out of the game and into an emergency room. Instead, Tocchet returned to the bench at 2:34 of the third period.

He then proceeded to orchestrate one of the Penguins' most impressive comebacks of the season. At 7:27, he beat Blackhawks goalie Dominik Hasek to make it 3-2. At 14:50, he tied the game with what Tocchet described as "a typical 'me' goal," when he charged toward the net and had a Ron Francis shot deflect off him and go into the net. Larry Murphy gave the Penguins their first lead of the night with a power-play goal at 16:17, which held up as the game-winner in their 4-3 victory. They had quieted the crowd, silenced the Stadium foghorn and proven to themselves that they could hold up under extreme adversity. "Anytime you can come back on the Hawks and win in this building, it's got to be a character win," Tocchet said.

The two points the Penguins had earned were critical, but Tocchet's show of determination might have been even more important. No one could have blamed him if he stayed in the locker room; it probably would have been the smart thing to do. But the competitive fires inside him burn with white-hot intensity, and Tocchet didn't just return to the game, he helped to shape its outcome.

Ron Francis, who had been Tocchet's teammate with the Sault Ste. Marie Greyhounds in the Ontario Hockey League, wouldn't have expected anything less. "He's a Greyhound, through and through," Francis said. "You knew he was going to come back. He's the type of guy who'll take a hit like that and worry about fixing it after the game."

Almost overlooked because of Tocchet's riveting effort was that the Penguins had moved to within four points of the New Jersey Devils, which meant they were closer to third place than to fifth for the first time in weeks. Pittsburgh was on a roll, and any team that wandered into its path was in serious danger of being flattened. "We want to keep climbing," Stevens said. "Now instead of people talking about the Islanders catching us, we can talk about catching Jersey."

X-rays showed that Tocchet had a hairline fracture in his jaw, and doctors projected that he would be out for about a week. Not surprisingly, Tocchet said he hoped to be back in "24 hours, 48 hours," which would have meant missing just one game. It turned out that he sat out three. Grudgingly.

The Penguins did not like the idea that overhauling New Jersey for third place was the most they could accomplish during the rest of the regular season, but were beginning to focus on a more long-range goal. The playoffs were still several weeks away, but Pittsburgh was on a 6-2 run and was beginning to look like a pretty formidable 20-man unit.

"The team is playing pretty well in all zones," Barrasso said. "When we're losing, it's because we're not playing well defensively, and I think that's pretty much our history. We need to be patient in regard to where we finish, and we need to stay focused on the ultimate goal, which is having a successful playoff."

"At this point, you've seen us start to gel," Joe Mullen said. "You've seen us become a better defensive club, and that's what they were looking for when they made the trades (with Los Angeles and Philadelphia). We can all still play a lot better, and we can still gel a lot better, but it's not going to come overnight. We've still got 10 more (regular-season) games to get it going. This team's still capable of scoring a lot of goals. And if we can play our defensive game like we did last year, there could be a very similar outcome."

The Penguins took another step in that direction when they sliced their deficit against the Devils to two points with a 6-5 victory against Edmonton March 17, even though Lemieux was stopped on a penalty shot for the first time in six career tries. The Penguins wiped out a 4-2 disadvantage in the final 15 minutes of the third period, as Mullen became the 39th player in NHL history to get 400 career goals, and Francis swiped in a Bob Errey rebound at 14:02 for the decisive goal. It was far from their finest performance of the season, but signs that they were getting their game in order continued to turn up.

"We're not kidding ourselves," Larry Murphy said. "We still have to get to a higher level. But the positive thing is, we're finding ways to win. When we were a championship team last year, we found ways to win. Maybe that piece is back. There's obviously some work to do, but we're moving in the right direction."

Edmonton Coach Ted Green had pretty much the same perspective on the Penguins. "They've been a sleeping giant for a while, and they seem to have woken up," he said. "They're going to be a tough team to beat. They look like they have a lot of determination . . . to prove a lot of people wrong."

They didn't necessarily have anything to prove when Quebec stopped by the Civic Arena two nights later, but it was apparent from the first shift that the only uncertainty about this game would be Pittsburgh's margin of victory. The Penguins had an almost unthinkable three-on-zero break 11 seconds into the first period, and even though Kevin Stevens failed to convert on that chance, it pretty well set the tone for the evening. "Every time our offensive players were on the ice, there was no defense," Nordiques coach Pierre Page said. "When we made a mistake, it was always a two-on-one, a breakaway or, a three-on-one."

The Penguins scored two shorthanded goals on one penalty for just the third time in franchise history, and the Nordiques did a passable impersonation of the 1983-84 Pittsburgh team that finished with 38 points. "That's reminiscent of the first couple of Penguins teams I was with," said Bob Errey, who came to Pittsburgh in 1983. "Teams that tried to work hard, but the bounces didn't go your way . . .giving up shorthanded goals . . . a young team just trying to get somewhere, looking for direction."

Finding their direction wasn't a problem for the Penguins anymore. They were 8-2 in the past 10 games and had claimed a share of third place for the first time since February 3. "We've been trying to build momentum for a long time," Scott Bowman said. "We have it now, and we want to keep it up."

But there would be a few more speed bumps along their path to a spot in the playoffs, like when the Penguins needed third-period goals by Lemieux and Stevens to salvage a 2-2 tie in Hartford on March 22. Of course, Pittsburgh probably shouldn't have complained too much about that score, considering the Whalers had beaten them twice at the Civic Arena earlier in the season. "That's hockey," Lemieux said. "You can't say that just because it's Hartford or San Jose or Quebec, you're going to win every game."

But there was more to Hartford's success against the Penguins than some quirk of hockey fate. The Whalers played a plodding, defense-oriented style, which strained the Penguins' patience and made them vulnerable to mistakes born of frustration. And the fact that Hartford's lineup was laced with names the Pittsburgh players did not even recognize added to the problem.

"We took them lightly the first two times in Pittsburgh," Tom Barrasso said. "I don't think we gave them any consideration, as far as being able to play with us. But they're a grinding team. They hook, they hold, they make it difficult for a team like ours to get skating. And if you're not persistent and don't fight through the hooking and holding, it will be a long night."

The Penguins were glad to be finished with the season series against the Whalers, and not only because burglars had hit assistant coach Rick Kehoe's hotel room in Hartford and made off with about $1,500 in per diem and expense money. Playing in a game whose pace is dictated by the Whalers can be pretty exasperating for a team with such a high-intensity attack.

But it would be a while before the Penguins would have to worry again about being dragged down to — or below — the level of an inferior opponent. They were about to enter a stretch in which four of five games would be against division leaders. The results, they figured, would be a pretty good litmus test of whether they were ready to make another serious run at the Stanley Cup. "It's going to be a good measuring stick," Paul Stanton said.

"It will be a good gauge for a lot of players, and for the club as a whole," Bryan Trottier said. "It's a heck of a challenge. If we go into it with the right attitude — and I think our mindset is pretty good right now — and stay with good habits and good concentration, we'll come out of these games pretty good."

The Penguins took a healthy attitude into the first of those games, against Detroit at Joe Louis Arena, but they forgot to take an effective power play with them. They failed to score on five chances with the man advantage in their 4-3 loss to the Red Wings, while Detroit capitalized on two of five opportunities. And Lemieux, among others, said the disparity in those power-play numbers was not some cosmic accident.

"We just don't practice it," he said. "You've got to spend some time on it. That's up to us to go on the ice and practice it, the five, six seven guys who are on the power play. We haven't spent much time on it this year, and you can win a lot of games late in the season with special teams."

It went without saying that bad special teams can cost you a lot of victories, too. At least the Penguins didn't have to look for some subtle flaw in their strategy on the power play, to search for some tiny facet that was malfuntioning a bit. It was breaking down big-time. All over the place. "I think everything's not working on it, to tell you the truth," Stevens said. "I don't think there's one good thing we're doing. We can't get the puck out of our zone, we can't get the puck into their zone."

The only thing that prevented the Detroit game from being a total waste for the Penguins was a unique, two-pronged milestone. Stevens got his 50th goal on an assist from Lemieux, whose point was the 1,000th of his career. That raised questions about who got custody of the puck to commemorate their milestone, but Stevens offered a simple solution: "I guess we're going to cut it in half."

It had been evident that Stevens was destined for a 50-goal season for months, just as it was obvious that only a major breakdown by his back could prevent Lemieux from becoming the 35th player in NHL history to pile up 1,000 points. And he did it in 513 regular-season games, faster than anyone except Wayne Gretzky, who needed just 424. "To get 1,000 points, you have to get out there and pretty much do your job every night," Lemieux said. A lot of nights, anyway. By the time he reached the 1,000-point plateau, Lemieux had missed 121 games, the equivalent of more than one-and-a-half seasons, because of injuries. "I certainly should have been there sooner," he said.

Tocchet, wearing an astronaut-style helmet like the one Buffalo center Pat LaFontaine put on earlier in the season after his jaw was shattered by a high stick, was back in the lineup for the game in Detroit. He got an ugly welcome during the first period, when Red Wings defenseman Vladimir Konstantinov took a swing at his jaw, a move Bowman said sarcastically "takes a lot of courage." Tocchet, however, dismissed that cheap shot as a part of the game, and issued a not-so-subtle warning to Konstantinov about hockey's system of justice. "He got away with it," Tocchet said. "Next time, he might not. Next time, I might get him."

The Penguins approached their next game, against Vancouver at the Civic Arena, with some degree of trepidation. Not only because their power play was sputtering, but because Canucks rookie Pavel Bure was establishing himself as a game-breaker extraordinaire. He joined the Canucks after the season began, but was able to emerge as a solid contender for the Calder Trophy, despite the late start. Going into the Pittsburgh game, Bure had scored 17 goals in the previous 17 games.

Bure is an all-around offensive threat, but it was his speed that earned him the nickname "The Russian Rocket," and that gave the Penguins their greatest cause for concern. "He's real quick," Bowman said. "He can accelerate as quick as (anybody) I've seen in a long time. A lot of guys can skate, but they can't skate with the puck. He can skate just about as fast with the puck as without it."

But Bure wasn't as much of a blur as the Penguins had feared, at least not in this game. Or perhaps it's just that nobody noticed, because of the stellar performance of the Stevens-Lemieux-Tocchet line in the Penguins' 7-3 victory. The line combined for 14 points and a plus-minus rating of plus-11 in the Penguins' 7-3 victory against a good defensive team some considered a legitimate challenger for the Stanley Cup. "Obviously, our job is to provide offense," Tocchet said. "If we don't, we let the team down."

It's safe to assume that none of them went to bed that night feeling guilty. Lemieux and Tocchet had six points each, and Lemieux ran his lead over Stevens in the NHL scoring race to six points. Which, by Stevens' calculations, meant the race for the Art Ross Trophy as the league's top scorer was all but formally over. "That pretty much ends everything," he said. "It's been fun."

The good times, however, were about to go on hold for all of hockey. A strike by the NHL Players Association, which had been without a collective bargaining agreement since September 15, looked imminent. The possibility of a work stoppage had been dominating locker-room conversations for several weeks, and the Penguins went into their home game against Montreal March 28 not knowing if it would be the final time they would play this season, because a walkout had been tentatively scheduled for March 30. "Just when we get something good going, something (bad) might happen," Tocchet said.

Something that could be even worse than it sounded, because one of the few things both sides could agree on was that if the season were disrupted, it might be months before hockey was played again. "If there's a strike, I don't think it's going to be a short one," said Stevens, the Penguins' player representative. "If there is a strike, I'm not sure there would be hockey until next fall," Penguins president Howard Baldwin said. "If it happens, I think both sides will dig their heels in."

But if this was to be their last game of the season, the Penguins made sure to stockpile a summer's worth of good memories. They clinched a spot in the playoffs and ran off their seventh home victory in a row, beating the Canadiens, 6-3. Pittsburgh had managed just two goals in its previous two games against Montreal, but matched that total in a span of less than four minutes during the first period.

The Penguins eventually drove Canadiens goalie Patrick Roy, their long-time nemesis, from the game with four goals on nine shots, and outclassed Montreal in every phase of the game. "It would be a heck of a finish (to the season)," Larry Murphy said.

Their season would not end on this night, however. The NHLPA pushed its strike deadline back two days, so the Penguins would have one more game before swapping their sticks for picket signs. And it would be against Philadelphia, which meant Mark Recchi would return to the Civic Arena and Rick Tocchet and Kjell Samuelsson would face their former teammates for the first time.

Recchi anticipated that returning to Pittsburgh, the city he didn't want to leave, would be difficult. "It should be a pretty emotional game," he said. "I'm looking forward to it, but it will be tough in a way, too." Recchi said he would "love to get a couple of goals" against the Penguins, and made it clear he still was bitter about being traded. "I was disappointed with the way it was handled," he said. "I was pretty loyal to the team during the summer (by passing on a superior offer from the Flyers) and I lost a lot of money over it. Why didn't they let me go in the summer? Obviously, their feelings changed."

But Recchi's fervor for his first game in Pittsburgh wasn't shared by many of the players on either team, including others who had been involved in the trade on February 19. Nearly everyone was preoccupied by the impending strike, and the hard reality was that the game wouldn't have a significant impact on the Patrick Division standings. "It's not really an important game to either team," Samuelsson said. "They are out of the playoffs, we have made the playoffs. It's just another regular-season game."

Well, it didn't quite work out that way, either. The game, as expected, lacked any semblance of intensity — "Guys were leaving men open all over the ice," Tocchet said — but Pittsburgh defenseman Grant Jennings collected two goals in a 6-5 victory. That doubled Jennings' output for the season and, coupled with the two assists and plus-5 rating he had had against Montreal, suggested he was ready to be a factor in the playoffs, if needed. "We've got to worry about him," Tocchet said. "He might cross the picket line, the way he's playing."

There would be no picket line for Jennings to cross, but there would be no hockey for a while, either. At 3 o'clock the next afternoon, arenas across North America went dark. The strike that almost nobody wanted had happened. And much of the burden for trying to end it would fall on the Penguins.

CHAPTER TEN

One Strike, And They're Out

Bryan Trottier's skills and innate feel for the game earned him a confirmed reservation in the Hockey Hall of Fame long before he joined the Penguins as a free agent in the summer of 1990. A trophy case full of Stanley Cups and a niche among the top scorers in NHL history are enough to make a pretty favorable impression on the nominating committee.

But it wasn't Trottier's playing ability or the success of his team, the New York Islanders, that made him a natural to succeed Tony Esposito as president of the NHL Players Association. That was more a credit to his business instincts and knack for working with people, the same qualities that made many project him as prime front-office material when his playing days ended. And Trottier made no secret of his desire to stay in the game long after hanging up his skates for the final time.

So it looked as if Trottier was facing a potential conflict of interest when the NHLPA membership walked out and shut down the league on April 1. As the association's president, he had an obligation to help executive director Bob Goodenow get the best possible deal for the players. But as one who aspired to a career in management, Trottier faced the prospect of negotiating a CBA that could make his life more difficult when he swapped his uniform for a business suit. True to his nature, however, Trottier did not see the possibility of a problem, just a chance to prove himself to the people on the other side of the issues. The same people he expected to be working with in the not-so-distant future. Maybe in a few years, maybe in a few months.

"I would love to be on the other side of the table (eventually)," he said. "But I think if I didn't give it my all while I'm in this position, I wouldn't be able to give it my all if I'm in the other position. I can't play the fence in this situation . . . Anybody in this position would feel the same way. When it's all said and done, and should the opportunity come when I could be on the other side, I think I'll have a little more respect from that side because we battled eyeball-to-eyeball."

And there was a lot of staring going on in the days immediately before and after the strike began. The issues under negotiation were diverse and complex, ranging from free agency to dental benefits, trading-card revenues to revisions in the waiver rules. And while both sides professed that they were eager for a settlement, neither was willing to grant the concessions that would have made one possible.

The Penguins, who had generated so much momentum in the preceding weeks, had a particular interest in avoiding a walkout, but insisted they were willing to put their sticks and skates aside for as long as it took to get an agreement they could be happy with. And if the dispute cost them a chance at another Stanley Cup, well, sometimes you have to sacrifice things. Even dreams.

"Everybody says, 'Hey, we all want to play this game and hockey's taking off right now,' " Troy Loney said. "It's a great way to make a living, but we've got to get something done that's going to benefit all of us, regardless of what the short-term losses or gains may be."

The league-wide strike authorization vote was 560-4, an overwhelming show of support for the NHLPA. That might have been a surprise to management, considering the players waited so many months after the CBA expired before taking serious action. And that this was the first time in its history that the NHLPA had even come close to walking off the job to show its displeasure.

"To have put it off as long as they (management) have shows they really didn't take us very seriously, and with good reason," Tom Barrasso said. "In the past, the Players Association really hasn't done anything dramatic to show that we were a solid unit. But I think the vote was a pretty good indication of how we feel about ourselves and how we feel about our union."

The show of solidarity aside, some players had major concerns about the strike. None of them had to worry about where their next meal would be coming from, to be sure, but the strike resurrected some grim memories for those who had gotten a first-hand look at other labor disputes. Like Ron Francis, the son of a steelworker from Sault Ste. Marie, Ontario. He could remember some tough times his family went through when his father's union was on strike. Once, their family of four "basically lived off $25 a week strike pay" during a three-month work stoppage; another time, Francis's father was threatened with the loss of his job after a wildcat walkout.

Nonetheless, Francis said those childhood experiences taught him the importance of presenting a united front during negotiations. "It's not a pleasant thing to go through, but one thing you learn is that the union has to stick together," he said. "That's your bread and butter, if everybody hangs together."

The Penguins practiced a little togetherness with a team meeting at a suburban restaurant on April 2, but some cracks in their unity showed a day later. Players organized an informal workout at a rink in suburban Monroeville, but only seven showed up to skate. And none of those looked terribly serious about having a quality practice.

Kevin Stevens appeared wearing a Team USA jersey and New York Jets hat; Phil Bourque wore a Penguins sweatsuit and a Bob Johnson baseball cap. Equipment was sparse, almost primitive, and local youths had to be recruited to play goal, since none of Pittsburgh's regular goalies were inclined to serve as a target for their teammates in this type of setting.

And it wasn't exactly one of those high-tempo practices coaches cherish; the best proof of that was the five goals Ulf Samuelsson scored during a brief scrimmage. "The first time I've ever scored five goals in a year," he said.

Samuelsson laughed, but the players' supply of smiles was getting perilously low. By this time, the threat that the season would be called off was depressingly real, and that would mean the Penguins wouldn't get a chance to defend their championship. They were willing to give up the chance for a second Cup if it came to that, but no one was eager to see it happen. "If there are no playoffs this year, it would be a major setback for this organization because we have to be one of the top dogs," Phil Bourque said.

"We're the defending champions, and we want the opportunity to defend," Francis said. "And secondly, we feel — especially the way we were playing lately — that we're capable of making another successful run for the Cup. This is what we all play for. You want to win the Stanley Cup, and we feel we have a great chance to win it again."

But as the strike dragged on, it appeared increasingly likely the Penguins wouldn't get the opportunity to try. The sides exchanged charges and allegations more often than proposals over the next few days and by April 7, no less an authority than Howard Baldwin said "there's no question in my mind at all" that the season was about to become history. "This is the most ridiculous thing I've ever been involved with," he said. "And you're talking with someone who was involved in the WHA (World Hockey Association)."

Shortly thereafter, NHL President John Ziegler announced that unless a settlement was reached by 3 p.m. April 9, Baldwin's bleak prediction would be accurate. The season would be terminated. Immediately and irrevocably. Craig Patrick began preparing a contingency plan for his staff, arranging new assignments for men who had expected to be coaching in the playoffs. Assistant coach Pierre McGuire would work with the Penguins' Muskegon farm team. Assistant Rick Kehoe would monitor the American Hockey League playoffs. Assistant Barry Smith would go to a tournament in Switzerland and the world championships in Prague, Czechoslovakia.

But Patrick, like Baldwin, was determined to seek a resolution to the strike. On the evening of April 8, Patrick and Paul Martha, the team's general counsel, were allowed to address the players during a team meeting and tried to clarify management's position in the talks and answer questions about it. "They didn't try to convince us (to accept the owner's latest offer)," Stevens said. "We just talked about different issues. They talked from their perspective, and we talked from ours."

There was a lot of talking going on in New York, too. Trottier, who was on the players' negotiating committee, was in the midst of it, and Stevens had taken part when NHLPA executive director Bob Goodenow summoned the player reps a few days earlier, too.

Even so, at 3:01 p.m. on April 9, a message from Ziegler came across the fax machine in the Penguins' offices.

The language was terse and stilted and read, in part, that "the NHL owners' final offer was not accepted upon the expiry of the date and time established for its acceptance . . . " All of which meant that the deadline was past. The 1991-92 season was over.

Well, that's kind of what it meant. It turns out the 3 p.m. deadline, like so many others set during the dispute, had been chiseled in slush, not granite. Forget the fax; negotiations continued after the deadline, and into the evening. Baldwin told a Civic Arena press conference that "we're right down to the last half of the ninth inning with no room left," but said "the good news is that we're still talking, and as long as the two sides are talking, I'd have to say there is a ray of hope."

Maybe, but it wasn't bright enough to blind the players to their objectives. They still were not happy with proposals on topics ranging from licensing to the ownership of more than $7 million in surplus pension funds. "Unless some of the stuff is changed, there won't be an agreement," Stevens said.

Martha, who had helped to negotiate an end to the National Football League strike in 1982, and whom Baldwin said had been "intimately involved" in the talks with the NHLPA, said the players' interest in the strike had increased as the threat the season would be called off became more real. "Players are players," he said. "When they have to pay attention to something, they will. And up until now, they really haven't had to set their minds to it. They're more aware. They're more informed right now."

A day later, the strike was over. The season had been saved. And the Penguins had averted a major financial setback, because Baldwin said the team projected lost revenues of between "$1 million and $2 million" if the playoffs were not held. And the Penguins had played a leading part in getting the strike resolved.

Trottier and Stevens had prominent roles on the players' side, while Baldwin was one of a group of "moderate" owners who had been pushing for a settlement, and Martha had served on the owners' negotiating committee. "It's safe to say, looking at it objectively if I could, that this franchise played a major role in the settlement of this strike," Martha said. He said the Los Angeles Kings and New York Rangers also had played important parts.

Stevens went out of his way to praise the efforts of Goodenow, Trottier, and the rest of the NHLPA executive committee, even though some observers felt players like Wayne Gretzky and Mark Messier had brought about the settlement by getting involved in the negotiations when the outlook was especially bleak.

"You've got to give those guys (Goodenow et al.) all the credit in the world," Stevens said. "For people to come in and say that when Gretzky and Messier got into it, that's why we got this deal done is ridiculous. Obviously, they're big parts of the league, but to have Bryan and that committee working 16 hours a day and all of a sudden two guys . . . I respect them for coming and doing it, but I'm going to stand up for Bryan and those guys, because they're the ones who stuck with this thing for nine months."

Not surprisingly, the agreement was rooted in compromise by both parties. Neither got everything it sought, but neither was a clear-cut loser, either. And the sides had something else in common: An experience neither would cherish. "This certainly has not been a pleasant experience for anybody," Baldwin said. "Players, ownership, front office, media, fans, but it's something the league probably had to go through. I think the end result is, we'll probably all be better off for it."

The aftershocks of the dispute rattled around the league for months — criticism of his handling of the strike appeared to be a major factor in Ziegler's decision to step down as NHL president — but the Penguins had more pressing concerns. Like getting their team back together and getting ready for the renewal of their season, set for Brendan Byrne Arena in New Jersey April 13.

Mario Lemieux, like several teammates, was so convinced the strike would not be settled that he went on a golfing excursion to Florida a day before the settlement was reached. That meant he had to grab an early-morning flight to be back in Pittsburgh in time for the team's first post-strike workout the next afternoon at the Civic Arena.

That practice was, in many ways, reminiscent of the first day of training camp. Not as many bodies, perhaps, but the quality of play was about what you'd expect after an extended layoff. "Eight days?" Paul Stanton said. "It felt like eight months I'd been off." Scott Bowman anticipated such problems, and employed a plan that combined training-camp and regular-season workouts. The first half was devoted to skating and drills designed to increase stamina, the second to fine-tuning skills.

The strike proved to be a great equalizer for players who do not rely on finely honed puckhandling or shooting abilities to keep the paychecks coming in. "The worse everybody feels, the better it is for guys like me because I just plod along anyway," Troy Loney said. "The guys who really skate (well) feel like they're laboring. To me, it just feels normal."

The Penguins had three-regular season games left, and even though they were battling New Jersey for third place in the Patrick, they felt it was imperative that they get their overall game in order for the playoffs, not focus on where they would finish in the standings. That seemed like a healthy approach after their first game back, as they turned in a sloppy, uninspired 60 minutes in a 5-1 loss to the Devils.

The Penguins had expected a lackluster performance, but several players were troubled by what they perceived as a lack of intensity from their teammates. That was the sort of shortcoming that could knock them out of the playoffs almost as soon as they got into them. "I don't mind that we're not in sync, but we still have to have the effort," Bob Errey said. "I don't think that collectively, myself included, we had a 100-percent effort."

He was correct, but the Penguins had even bigger problems. Kjell Samuelsson sat out the game because of what Bowman described as a "wrenched neck" that had been troubling him on and off since January. And Mario Lemieux missed most of the third period after being hit by Devils defenseman Ken Daneyko and dropping onto his right elbow. His injury was announced as a bruised right shoulder, but it proved to be a mild separation. And it also turned out that the regular season was over for Lemieux.

It effectively ended for his teammates two nights later, when they beat Washington 4-1 at the Civic Arena. That win clinched third place and a first-round playoff berth opposite the Capitals. It also ended whatever miniscule chance Stevens had of overtaking Lemieux in the scoring race, because he was ejected for intervening in a fight between Rick Tocchet and Washington right winger Dino Ciccarelli during the first period.

Stevens charged across the ice and splattered Ciccarelli with an obviously illegal hit, even though there was little reason to believe Ciccarelli posed a clear and present danger to Tocchet, broken jaw or not. "I can protect myself," Tocchet said. "Nobody was taking a cheap shot. Kevin didn't have to come in." Probably not, but perhaps helping Tocchet wasn't Stevens' main motivation.

He knew Washington was Pittsburgh's probable opponent in the first round, and likely saw an opportunity to intimidate Ciccarelli, maybe convince him to keep a low profile during the playoffs. That wasn't likely to happen, of course, because Ciccarelli competes with the tenacity of a sled dog, but Stevens obviously figured it was worth a try.

Stevens returned for the regular-season finale at Madison Square Garden the next night, too, but plenty of his teammates didn't make the trip to New York. Larry Murphy and Ulf Samuelsson stayed at home, along with Mario Lemieux and Tom Barrasso. And while the Penguins' 7-1 loss to the Rangers was forgettable in just about every way, Scott Bowman injected a bit of strategy that made for a fairly memorable night.

He switched goalies Wendell Young and Ken Wregget an average of three times per period, once even changing them "on the fly." That involved Wregget dashing to the bench while Young hustled to the crease to stop a three-on-one break. "We wanted to give them both some work, and sometimes you don't know what kind of games these (will be)," Bowman said. "The first period, you could have a lot of shots and then you don't have any (later). So we decided we'd change them every five minutes."

It's doubtful Bowman would have used such tactics if the game had been of any consequence, but Pittsburgh's first-round opponent had been settled, and there was nothing at stake in the New York game except statistics. The loss cost the Penguins a chance to add to their franchise-record total of 18 road victories and to match the team record of 89 points in a season, set three years earlier.

Pittsburgh finished with a record of 39-32-9, tying Chicago for the sixth-best record in the league. Nobody paid much attention, but the Penguins earned an edge against Chicago in the standings tiebreaker by virtue of having more victories. That stat would be significant only if the Penguins and Blackhawks met in the Stanley Cup final, and not many people were predicting such a matchup in mid-April.

Still, the Penguins were confident they had a reasonable shot at earning a second Stanley Cup. If they played to their potential and got the breaks any champion needs, they felt they could earn another banner for the Civic Arena ceiling. They just hoped it wasn't a portent that the bus that was supposed to take the team from Madison Square Garden to LaGuardia airport after the regular-season finale for a charter flight home broke down on 33rd Street in Manhattan, forcing the players to flag down a series of cabs.

Maybe that was just a fitting end to a mostly frustrating season. In any case, the playoffs had been a long time coming, and the Penguins were ready to plunge into them. Anxious to show that their Cup from the previous year should not carry an asterisk, that there was nothing accidental about what they had accomplished in 1991. "We can't wait," Bob Errey said. "We couldn't be more ready."

CHAPTER ELEVEN

The Best, By Any Name

The regular season was a six-plus-month gauntlet of trials and tragedy, of occasional high points and countless hurdles for the Penguins. But finally, the playoffs had arrived. It was the time of year all hockey players enjoy most, and the time when Mario Lemieux pushes his game to levels most players cannot fathom, let alone reach.

That was Eddie Johnston's most cherished fantasy when he drafted Lemieux in 1984, that Pittsburgh was getting a player who could be the cornerstone of a championship franchise, a player who would prove his true mettle in the crucible of the postseason. The regular season is for setting records and making money; the playoffs are a test of greatness under pressure.

There were times when it seemed doubtful Lemieux would ever get the chance to prove his pedigree during the postseason; the Penguins did not qualify for them during his first four seasons in the league. That wasn't surprising, considering the decrepit state of the franchise when Lemieux joined it. And it is testimony to Johnston's unwavering faith in Lemieux's potential that Lemieux ever wore a Pittsburgh uniform.

In the days leading up to the draft, Johnston turned down a series of lucrative trade proposals. All he had to do was give up the rights to Lemieux, and Johnston could give his franchise instant respectability, a commodity it lacked to an excruciating degree. Quebec made an offer that reportedly included the Stastny brothers; Peter, Anton, and Marian. Montreal, who had gambled it would have a shot at Lemieux by acquiring a 1984 first-rounder from Hartford late in 1981, also put together an attractive package. Johnston considered every proposal, then rejected them. In about half a heartbeat. He was convinced Lemieux was a player a championship team could be built around, and others in the NHL concurred.

"Mario Lemieux is the most talented player in the draft," said Barry Fraser, Edmonton's director of player personnel. "By a mile." Jimmy Devellano, then Detroit's general manager, said Lemieux is "certainly the No. 1 rated player." A few weeks before the draft, no less an authority than Wayne Gretzky said he expected Lemieux to "do very well in the NHL . . . There's no question he has the ability to be a great hockey player."

But Gretzky, then the cornerstone of a developing dynasty in Edmonton, pointed out that Lemieux would be carrying a burden that went far beyond producing points and victories for his team. "He's going to have a tremendous amount of pressure put on him," he said. "He's 18, and he's going to be expected to lead that team to a championship . . . I only hope people realize he's only 18, and they just let him play and not try to change his style."

But while Gretzky projected Lemieux to be a high-impact addition to the league, not everyone was sold on him as a potential franchise player. Some people in hockey questioned his work ethic, suggesting he would prove to be little more than a lazy underachiever in the NHL. Others wondered whether his junior hockey statistics — 133 goals and 149 assists in 70 games in his final season with the Laval Voisins — had been grossly inflated by the offense-oriented style of play in the Quebec Major Junior Hockey League. One school of thought held that other highly ranked players like Kirk Muller or Ed Olczyk would be a safer selection for the Penguins.

"I think Lemieux and Muller are very, very close," Los Angeles General Manager Rogie Vachon said a few days before the draft. "Then you're moving down a step in the next four or five (prospects)." Neil Smith, a Detroit scout who later would become general manager of the New York Rangers, was even more blunt after the Penguins chose Lemieux first overall and

New Jersey took Muller second. "To me, Kirk Muller is the best player in the draft," he said. "The Devils really did it right."

It can safely be assumed that Smith, an astute judge of talent, has since revised his opinion. Muller developed into an all-star caliber player with New Jersey and later, Montreal, but his name isn't often mentioned alongside Lemieux's, unless the speaker is reflecting on prospects from the Class of 1984. Muller became a very good player; Lemieux has begun to earn support as one of the greatest in hockey history.

But getting Lemieux's name on a contract proved to be much tougher than deciding to draft him. Lemieux sparked a firestorm of controversy on draft day when he refused to join Pittsburgh's management at its draft table and put on a team jersey, as tradition dictated. "I didn't go to the table because the negotiations are not going well," he said. "I'm not going to put on the sweater if they don't want me bad enough."

Oh, the Penguins wanted — and needed — Lemieux badly enough, and about a week after they drafted him, they made a contract offer that proved it. He signed a deal worth about $700,000 for two years and an option, by far the biggest contract ever given to an NHL rookie at that point. He also got a promise that the Penguins would give him the freedom needed to take full advantage of his offensive skills. "We're not going to take Mario, who is a thoroughbred, and make him into a plow horse," coach Bob Berry said.

It didn't take long for the wisdom of that approach to become obvious, for the first chapter in the Lemieux legend was written during his first shift in the NHL, early in the Penguins' season-opener in Boston Garden. Lemieux stole the puck from Raymond Bourque, the Bruins' perennial all-star defenseman, and broke in alone on goalie Pete Peeters, another all-star. He faked Peeters to his knees and flipped the puck past him at 2:59 of the first period. First shift. First shot. First goal. In the span of a few seconds, Lemieux had validated all the hype, all the outrageous dreams Pittsburgh fans began to have when he was drafted.

"You know, every college basketball team has one guy who can pass or shoot better than anyone else on the team, and they usually call him, 'Slick,' " Boston Coach Gerry Cheevers said. "That's what I'd call this kid, 'Slick,' because that's just what he is."

Lemieux made the point again a few nights later during his first game at the Civic Arena in the long-awaited "Lemieux Debut." The game attracted a crowd of 15,741 — the Penguins had averaged 6,839 the previous season — and no one was asking for a refund when the night was over. Lemieux made a deft pass to set up a Doug Shedden goal 18 seconds into the game and, about two minutes later, pummeled Vancouver's Gary Lupul after Lupul jabbed him in the stomach with his stick. Twice. "Two spears in the stomach is not the way to play hockey," he said. Lemieux had about eight inches and 30 pounds on Lupul, and used it to such an advantage that Canucks goalie John Garrett felt obliged to intervene on behalf of his teammate, even though that assured Garrett would be ejected from the game.

Pittsburgh won the game 4-3 and while Lemieux was not pleased with his performance the rest of the evening ("I'm not really satisfied. I could have played better.") he had transformed another group of cynics into believers. But converting critics is a long and arduous process, and even being named to the Wales Conference team for the NHL All-Star Game in Calgary wasn't enough to quiet many of them. The most outspoken was Don Cherry, the former Boston and Colorado coach working as a broadcaster in Canada. About a week before the All-Star Game, Cherry described Lemieux as "the biggest floater in the National Hockey League."

But it was Lemieux who got in the last — and most emphatic — word with Cherry. He scored two goals and set up another during the Wales' 6-4 victory at the Saddledome, then dedicated his performance to Cherry. "That game was for him," Lemieux said. Cherry got a verbal slap and one of Lemieux's brothers, Richard, got the car Lemieux received for being named MVP of the game. "I guess I'm going to have to give it to him, because he asked me for it," Lemieux said.

But during his rookie season, Lemieux got a lot more than he gave, mostly in the form of physical abuse. Trying to intimidate him became an integral part of many opponents' strategies. He was tackled. High-sticked. Punched. Cross-checked. Almost every night. Almost every shift.

The ugliest assault came in late February, during a game against the Winnipeg Jets at the Civic Arena. With 6:41 left in the second period, Lemieux engaged Jets defenseman Tim Watters in a shouting match during a stoppage in play. As that unfolded,

Winnipeg defenseman Jim Kyte approached Lemieux from behind, then dropped him with a sucker punch Lemieux never saw coming.

Kyte, who would be traded to Pittsburgh a few years later, said the blow was in retaliation for a cross-check he claimed Lemieux had given Watters earlier in the game; Jets coach Barry Long characterized the punch as "a powder puff" and said, "anybody and their dog could take it." Nonetheless, it was enough to give Lemieux a mild concussion and knock him out of the game.

Lemieux accumulated numerous bumps, bruises, and welts during his first season, but he also piled up a lot of goals and assists. He picked up his 100th point during the Penguins' season-finale, a 7-3 loss in Washington, to join Dale Hawerchuk and Peter Stastny as the only rookies in NHL history to reach that plateau. He received the Calder Trophy as the NHL's Rookie of the Year and earned a berth on the all-rookie team, the first in a string of honors that would continue through his career.

The next season, he had 141 points and was named to the second all-star team. In 1986-87, he missed 17 games because of injuries but still managed 107 points and a spot on the second-all-star team. And his fourth year in the league proved to be a breakthrough season. Lemieux led the NHL in goals (70) and broke Wayne Gretzky's chokehold on the Art Ross Trophy, given to the league's top scorer, by racking up 168 points. He also supplanted Gretzky as the winner of the Hart Trophy, which goes to the NHL's MVP, and as the center on the first all-star team.

But Lemieux would not reach the peak of his production until 1988-89, when injuries that caused him to sit out four games were the only thing that prevented Lemieux from joining Gretzky as the only players in league history to record 200 points in a season. Lemieux led the NHL in goals (85), assists (114) and points (199) even though, remarkably, Gretzky reclaimed the Hart. During that season, Lemieux became the only player in history to score five different types of goals (shorthanded, power play, even-strength, penalty shot, empty-net) in one game, during a victory against New Jersey at the Civic Arena on New Year's Eve.

The highlight of his year, however, was participating in the Stanley Cup playoffs for the first time. Chasing a championship had been his goal since 1984, but he didn't get an opportunity to do it until his fifth season. "Mario missed a lot of playoff series because the team was being rebuilt," Scott Bowman said. "He didn't get the chances to show what he could do in big games that other great players have had."

There would be no titles for the Penguins in 1989, but Lemieux's work in those playoffs was an indication of the postseason greatness in his future. He concentrated on playing well defensively during the Penguins' first-round sweep of the New York Rangers, but shifted the focus more toward offense during Pittsburgh's second-round meeting with the Philadelphia Flyers. The Flyers ultimately won the series in seven games, but Lemieux's performance in Game 5 of that series was one of the most extraordinary in playoff history, as he had five goals and three assists.

When the despair of losing to Philadelphia faded, the Penguins realized they might be on the cusp of greatness. They had a quality goaltender, Tom Barrasso. A prolific offensive defenseman, Paul Coffey. And most of all, they had Mario Lemieux. Eventual triumph, it seemed, was almost a given.

But history had shown there were no gimmes for the Penguins, and the 1989-90 season would be one of the most painful — in almost every way — in franchise history. Not only because the season ended in a way that was sickeningly sour, as the Buffalo Sabres beat the Penguins in overtime of the final regular-season game to knock them out of the playoffs, but because Lemieux's recurring back problems flared to a degree that put his playing future in serious doubt.

He played with severe pain for much of the season and, in perhaps the most staggering feat of his career, had put together a 46-game scoring streak — just five games shy of Gretzky's NHL record — when he finally was immobilized by the pain during a game against the New York Rangers in mid-February. He went to Los Angeles for therapy on a herniated disk and a secondary bone problem and sat out 21 games, returning to Pittsburgh about 24 hours before that decisive game against Buffalo. Lemieux's goal and assist that night were not enough to save the Penguins from a 3-2 defeat, however, and Lemieux entered the offseason unsure about his prospects for the next season.

In early July, Lemieux returned to Los Angeles to be examined by Dr. Robert Watkins, who had overseen his treatment there. He, like Dr. Charles Burke, an orthopedic surgeon and the Penguins' team physician, recommended surgery to relieve pressure on the nerves in his back, which had been responsible for the pain in his back, legs, and buttocks.

"I don't think it's career-threatening," Lemieux said upon arriving back in Pittsburgh. "The surgery is 95 percent sure, and there's not a lot of risk involved. I think it was important for me to give it (a rehabilitation program) a chance, to try the therapy for a while. Obviously, it didn't work out too well, and we have to think about something else. I can't go on a day-to-day basis anymore, (where) one day it's good, and one day it's bad."

"We knew that, ultimately, there was a very high chance he'd end up with surgery," Burke said. "But we felt it was important to cover all the potential treatments and start with the most conservative one." Burke said the chances of the proposed operation resulting in a "major problem" probably were "under one or two percent," and that "complications from this type of surgery — despite the delicacy of it — are very small and very rare. I know that's sort of hard to understand, but this is a routine operation done very, very commonly."

And so, early on the morning of July 11, Lemieux checked in at Montefiore Hospital in Pittsburgh, where Dr. Peter Sheptak removed the herniated portion of his disk between the fourth and fifth lumbar vertebrae and some bone from Lemieux's spinal canal. The surgery was described as a "micro lumbar discectomy with bone decompression."

Shaptak termed the operation "technically, a success," and said that, "judging by what I saw at the time of surgery, I feel very optimistic about nothing going wrong. I anticipate a fast recovery." Sheptak said that, during the course of the surgery, he detected a secondary bone condition that might have contributed to Lemieux's back problems, at least to some degree.

"He did have a mild crack in a supporting structure of the bone that was related to some old trauma, probably from hockey," Sheptak said. "That could make him more susceptible to some backaches and discomfort in the future, but the operation should have been successful in relieving his buttock and leg pain, which was really causing him the most trouble."

Lemieux told a press conference a few days later that "I think I can be a better player now that I will be 100 percent. Hopefully, I can come back and have my best season." He predicted he would be on skates in "six or seven weeks" and predicted he would be ready for the start of training camp September 7.

Lemieux knew there would be at least one complication, but he was willing to deal with it. He has a well-known passion for golf — and a single-digit handicap — and realized he would have to give up the game while recovering from surgery. "Next year, I'll be able to play at least 36 (holes) a day," he said, laughing. "So that's no problem."

Lemieux's optimism about being ready to return by the start of training camp was understandable, especially in view of Sheptak's upbeat analysis after the operation, but it proved to be misguided. Lemieux was plagued by pain during camp, and eventually left the team during an exhibition-game swing through Texas. He returned to Pittsburgh for tests, where doctors determined there was an infection in his back, near the site of his surgery.

The infection was reported to be a form of vertebral osteomyelitis, which attacks the bony portion of the spine. Burke said it is a "very serious condition," although he predicted Lemieux would make a complete recovery.

Burke said tests showed some damage to the fourth vertebra and, while he couldn't specify the extent, it appeared to be "a very small amount." He added that the keys to Lemieux's recovery prospects were "how he heals, the damage that's been done by the infection, and how long it takes him to heal. If he doesn't heal completely, then Mario can have some real problems. There are indications that he is healing well, but we won't know until we run some tests."

Burke said there was a "definite possibility" Lemieux's career was in jeopardy, but that several factors gave cause for optimism. "The things Mario has going in his favor are that the bone damage was not extensive, it was diagnosed quickly, treatment started quickly, and he has responded to that treatment as fast — or faster — than we expected," Burke said. "The fact that he's a high-performance athlete in very good condition, I would expect him to be able to go on and heal his problem and make a complete recovery."

But there was a dark, uncertain side to Lemieux's outlook, too. "The fact that you've had two major insults to the back in a very short time can give people all sorts of back problems," Burke said. "A person can have one episode of back pain and never be the same again. Well, Mario has had a (herniated) disk and a disk-based infection in six months."

The treatment prescribed for Lemieux's condition was total rest for an indefinite period, with rehabilitation after that. It would be December before Lemieux, carrying several extra pounds, would be able to ride an exercise bike, and late December before he could strap on skates for the first time. And he would not play his first game of the 1990-91 season until January 26 in Quebec, but he made it a return worth waiting for. Lemieux had three assists in Pittsburgh's 6-5 victory at Le Colisee and, more importantly, reported no major problems with his back. "I felt pretty good," Lemieux said. "I'm just a little sore, but that's muscle soreness."

Lemieux came by his aches honestly that night; he played well enough to be named the game's No. 1 star. "It's going to take him a little while to get in game shape," Mark Recchi said. "And when he does, it's going to be scary."

But much of the season was history by the time Lemieux was healthy enough to play and, statistically, 1990-91 was the worst of his career. He failed to get at least 100 points for the first time — Lemieux had 19 goals and 26 assists in 26 games — but he was a major force during the stretch drive, when the Penguins wrapped up the first division championship in their history. Ironically, however, he was not on the ice when Pittsburgh clinched the title with a 7-4 victory in Detroit March 27. Lemieux sat out that game because one night earlier, he had been clipped in the eye with a stick during a 3-1 victory in Philadelphia, and the eye had swollen shut. Lemieux's teammates didn't feel he had cheated them, however; after all, he had scored all three of Pittsburgh's goals in Philadelphia.

Besides, there would be plenty of time for redemption in the playoffs, and getting to them for just the second time in seven seasons inspired Lemieux to raise his game to the most rarified level imaginable. This time, there would be no disappointment, as Lemieux thrived under intense pressure. He won the Conn Smythe Trophy as the playoff MVP while leading the Penguins to a Stanley Cup, which seemed unthinkable just a few months earlier. He led the playoffs in points (44) and assists (28), despite missing Game 3 of the Stanley Cup final against Minnesota when his back spasmed while he was tying his skates just minutes before the opening faceoff, and got at least one point in 22 of the 23 games in which he participated.

He had earned the respect that comes only with a Stanley Cup ring, the respect some critics had been so reluctant to give him. The "selfish" label some had tried to pin on him was gone forever, shredded by the championship he had done so much to forge.

Oh, Lemieux's problems didn't end on that heady night at the Met Center in Minnesota when the Penguins secured their first Cup. Winning can help a lot of things, but it can't do much for a bad back. The pain, the tightness, the spasms that caused Lemieux to sit out most of the 16 games he missed during the 1991-92 regular season weren't affected at all by his successes of the previous spring. Bones and muscles didn't have much of a memory.

Still, the recurring back problems weren't enough to keep Lemieux from winning his third scoring title — he had 44 goals and 87 assists in 64 games — or to prevent those who watch him play from realizing they were seeing an athlete of the most impeccable pedigree. It's not just Lemieux's skill level that is so overwhelming; he has instincts, a feel for the game, that simply cannot be taught. "Mario amazes me every time I see him play," Craig Patrick said. And Kevin Stevens paid Lemieux perhaps the ultimate tribute: "Bobby Orr was my hero when I was growing up, but now Mario's my hero."

So the Penguins were justifiably upbeat as they prepared for the 1992 playoffs. They had the confidence from being defending champions. They had the knowledge that when they were on their game, they could match, or surpass, any team in the league. And they knew they had Lemieux, perhaps the most volatile one-man strike force in history. "You have to be lucky to be good," Rick Tocchet said. "And with 66, we're already lucky."

Lemieux's value goes far beyond his individual skills. He has the ability to raise his teammates' level of play, to coax maximum production from those around him. "He just drags his game up to a new level and drags as many (teammates) as he can with him," Ulf Samuelsson said. That knack, more than any other, explains how Lemieux was able to help transform the tragicomedy that was Pittsburgh's legacy into triumph. To explain why June 9, 1984, the day the Penguins drafted Lemieux, will be remembered as the pivotal date in the franchise's first 25 years.

"They used to be the worst team in the league," Boston General Manager Harry Sinden said. "And then they got Lemieux."

Lemieux's niche in history is secure, if not quite defined yet. Statistics are not the only way to measure a player's impact on his team or the game, and the back problems that have impeded Lemieux for so many years are sure to shorten his career and hold down his offensive totals.

But Lemieux, more than any other player, has been evaluated on a scale of one-to-Gretzky since he entered the league, and it is a comparison in which Lemieux has fared quite nicely in recent seasons. Some Gretzky devotees — and Lemieux-haters — will never be swayed, but those who see Lemieux on a regular basis realize they are witnessing something very special every time he goes over the boards.

They are convinced the English translation of his surname, "The Best," is entirely accurate. Scott Bowman called Lemieux "the best player I know of the past 25 years," and no one would dispute that there have been a lot of supremely gifted people to pass through the league during the time. Or that Lemieux is qualified to stand alongside, and probably above, them all.

"He's the best player in the world," Ron Francis said. "And people who refuse to recognize him as such are missing the boat." Rest assured, you won't find any of those people in the Pittsburgh locker room.

"He's the best player, probably, to ever play the game," Stevens said. "He's the best player in the world, by far."

CHAPTER TWELVE

A Capital Achievement

By the end of the regular season, Lemieux had his third scoring championship and growing support as the dominant figure in the National Hockey League. But he also had some severe limitations. While it's popular in Pittsburgh to believe Lemieux can do anything, that simply isn't the case. He hasn't, for example, ever gotten so much as a single point when he's spent an evening in the press box.

And the Penguins had some serious concerns that that's where Lemieux would spend at least the early part of their first-round playoff series. The shoulder injury he had received in Game 78 of the regular season when he was checked by New Jersey's Ken Daneyko had not healed as Game 1 of the Washington series approached.

Lemieux got back on skates for the first time two days before the opener, but was not optimistic about his chances of being ready when the series started. "When I tried to skate, I couldn't move my shoulder very well," he said. "It's still a little sore."

His teammates, however, did not rule out the possibility Lemieux would be in the lineup for Game 1. Their hopes were based on equal parts of wishful thinking — they knew Lemieux would be the single-most important player in their drive for a second Stanley Cup — and precedent. The Penguins had gotten accustomed to seeing Lemieux play with intense pain, and be more effective than most players could be in perfect health. "He couldn't move last year and missed Game 3 (of the Stanley Cup final because of back spasms)," Errey said. "And the next thing you know, he scores three in the next game."

But there was an additional concern this time. The Capitals have some bruising hitters, and there was little doubt that Lemieux's bad shoulder would be targeted for extra attention. Early and often. "Once we get into the playoffs, we expect a very physical game," Lemieux said. "I'm sure I'll have to go in there and take a check to make a play, or give one. It doesn't matter if the shoulder hurts. You've got to go in there and do it."

Even if Lemieux had been healthy, the Penguins recognized Washington posed a formidable threat to their chances of repeating as champions. The Capitals had the second-best record in the NHL during the regular season, 45-27-8, and had beaten Pittsburgh five times in seven meetings. For years, Washington had emphasized team defense at the expense of everything else, and the lack of scoring was a major factor in the Penguins' five-game victory against the Capitals in the 1991 Patrick Division final.

But Washington general manager David Poile retooled his team for 1991-92, and the Capitals scored 330 goals, more than any team except Pittsburgh (343). The Capitals got consistent scoring from forwards Dino Ciccarelli, Dimitri Khristich, Michal Pivonka, Dale Hunter, and Mike Ridley, but it was the offensive dimension provided by their defense corps that most concerned the Penguins. Defensemen Kevin Hatcher, Al Iafrate, and Calle Johansson routinely got involved in the offensive rush and frequently gave Washington an odd-man advantage in the attacking zone.

Paul Coffey had used a similar style to become the highest-scoring defenseman in league history, so the Penguins were painfully aware of the problems offensive defensemen could create. They also understood that unless they backchecked with the fervor of a TV evangelist, the Capitals would be able to barrage Tom Barrasso with quality scoring chances.

Barrasso had stopped 97 of 100 shots in three appearances against Washington during the 1991 playoffs and realized that, while it was unlikely he would duplicate that phenomenal performance, the quality of his work would be a decisive factor in the playoffs. Goaltending always is, and the likes of Ken

Dryden, Bernie Parent, Grant Fuhr, and Bill Smith had made a lasting impression with their efforts under postseason pressure. Much as Barrasso had during the spring of 1991.

"It's certain that good goaltending can demoralize the other team and, at the same time, pick your own team up," Barrasso said. "That's not a perception. That's a real advantage . . . I recognize that adequate goaltending during the regular season is suddenly substandard goaltending during the playoffs."

There was nothing wrong with Barrasso's play in Game 1 against the Capitals; he stopped 28 of 31 shots. But Washington's Don Beaupre was even better, allowing just one goal on 33 shots in the Capitals' 3-1 victory at the Capital Centre. "That's the type of play we have to have from him," Washington coach Terry Murray said.

The Capitals got a few other things they needed to be successful against Pittsburgh, too. Like two goals from Peter Bondra, who had scored just twice during the final nine regular-season games. And a physical, clutch-and-grab performance by nearly everyone Murray sent over the boards. That style can be tedious to watch, but it is the best antidote to the Penguins' high-powered offense. It's hard to be creative with the puck when your arms are being held, or to pull away from an opponent when his stick is buried in your mid-section. "You've got to change your ways a little bit to overcome Washington's approach," Scott Bowman said. "Fight through them . . . and scream (at the referee) a little more."

Murray, meanwhile, said the Capitals' strategy of impeding Pittsburgh was vital to their chances of surviving the series. "If we execute well and take the body . . . I think we emphasize that a little more against Pittsburgh than any other team because of the talented players they have," he said. "They're very capable of doing a lot of good things one-on-one, and if you start getting mesmerized by the puck, they can beat you in a one-on-one situation pretty quickly."

No one can do that faster than Lemieux, but he had to sit out Game 1 because of his shoulder injury. Bryan Trottier took his place between Kevin Stevens and Rick Tocchet on the No. 1 line, and that unit threw 10 shots at Beaupre, but was unable to score. Trottier understood that, while he was filling in for Lemieux, he wasn't replacing him. "No one can fill those shoes," he said. "I certainly wouldn't try, nor would anyone else. I have to play like Bryan Trottier or I won't be effective at all."

Knowing that Lemieux would likely be back for Game 2 took some of the sting out of this defeat. So did remembering that they had lost the opener in all four series' in 1991, but still won the Stanley Cup. "We know how to come back," Stevens said. "It's not like we haven't been in this position before."

The Penguins spent the day between Games 1 and 2 searching for their offense, which had disappeared during the NHLPA strike. Since the strike was settled, they had been held to one goal in three of four games. Not coincidentally, all three were losses. "We know we're going to have to score more than one goal to win," Barrasso said. "We're the type of team that can explode for four or five a night, and that's what we need to do."

Lemieux returned for Game 2, but the Penguins' vaunted attack remained AWOL in a 6-2 loss. Lemieux set up power-play goals by Stevens and Larry Murphy in the first 7:08 of the game, but seemed to tire as the evening progressed. Not that the Capitals minded that he spent more time than usual resting. "There's no doubt he picks up the intensity of the game," Beaupre said. "He came out and took charge and got them the early lead."

But their 2-0 lead dissolved, and Washington ran off six unanswered goals to take a 2-0 edge in the series. And no one in the Pittsburgh locker room disputed that it was an advantage the Capitals had earned and deserved. "They've played that much better than we have," Larry Murphy said. "You can't hide that fact."

There was another reality that could not be dismissed, however. Pittsburgh had faced an identical deficit in the 1991 Wales Conference final after losing Game 1 and 2 in Boston Garden, then ran off four victories in a row. The Penguins had been far more competitive in the early part of that series against the Bruins than they were against Washington, but having a precedent for such a comeback helped to bolster their morale. Barrasso said, "We know what we are capable of," and Stevens added that, "If you don't think you can come back, there's no sense going to the rink tomorrow. We think we can come back, and we think we will."

But Stevens' words seemed to lack some of the conviction of his remarks after Game 2 against Boston, perhaps because the

Penguins were finding it nearly impossible to get pucks past Don Beaupre. He stopped 65 of 68 shots in the first two games — a phenomenal save percentage of .956 — and repeatedly thwarted the Pittsburgh offense. "He's been on top of his game," Stevens said. "We've got to find a way to crack him."

And if the Penguins didn't have enough problems, Tocchet had left Game 2 with a separated right shoulder after absorbing a hard check from Washington's Kelly Miller. Early indications were that he might sit out the rest of the series.

So the series shifted to the Civic Arena, where the Penguins had won their final nine regular-season games. The home-ice advantage figured to be a plus, and Pittsburgh remained adamant about believing its lineup was superior to Washington's, regardless of what Games 1 and 2 might have indicated. "I think we've got more talent," Phil Bourque said. "And we learned a good lesson last year on how to win. We just need to reach down a little deeper and remember what it took to win those games."

What winning many of them required was an all-out effort by Lemieux, and he came up with yet another in Game 3. He set up the Penguins' first three goals and scored their last three in a 6-4 victory to spare Pittsburgh the burden of trying to become just the third team in playoff history to win a series after falling behind, 3-0. Statistically, it was not the most productive game of his playoff career — he had eight points in a second-round game against Philadelphia on April 25, 1989 — but, considering the circumstances, it was one of the most impressive.

The Penguins had turned to the player they rely on more than any other, and he had responded in a manner too outrageous to imagine. "It's ridiculous, some of the things he can do," Stevens said. Never mind that Washington was matching two lines and its top four defensemen against Lemieux every time he stepped onto the ice. No strategy, regardless of how well-conceived, can slow, let alone stop, Lemieux when he is on his game, as he was this night. "He did pretty much what he wanted to out there," Murray said.

If anyone had as much of an impact on this game as Lemieux, it was referee Don Koharski. He gave Pittsburgh 12 power plays and Washington 11, which meant the game had little flow and only a handful of shifts of five-on-five hockey. "That wasn't really a hockey game," Washington's Kelly Miller said. "If I was a fan, I'd want my money back."

The Game 3 victory was Bowman's 115th in the playoffs, making him the winningest coach in NHL playoff history. But he got a verbal broadside, not congratulations, from Murray, who was upset when Bowman sent little-used right winger Jay Caufield into the game in the waning seconds of the third period. Caufield is an enforcer — he had no points and 183 penalty minutes in 52 regular-season games — and Murray was visibly dismayed when he appeared for the final shift of the game. "I said to him, 'What's going on, Scotty?'" Murray said. "The game was over. I was very surprised."

But perhaps he shouldn't have been. Tempers rise and nerves fray as a playoff series progresses, and emotions in this one were getting close to the flashpoint. That was evident when Joe Mullen, a perennial candidate for the Lady Byng Trophy, awarded for gentlemanly and effective play, traded vicious slashes with Washington center Michal Pivonka late in the third period of Game 3. "After a couple of games in a playoff series, guys aren't real friendly anymore," Barrasso said.

The Penguins, however, were downright hospitable in Game 4. They gave Washington a 7-2 victory, a 3-1 advantage in the series, and anything else the Capitals asked for. They spotted Washington a 3-0 lead in the first period, and allowed Dino Ciccarelli to score four times before the game was over. Elimination from the playoffs was just 60 minutes away, and it was inevitable if the Penguins didn't immediately lift their game from the depths to which it had sunk. Even Washington could not get over the ease of its victory, the way it was able to thoroughly dominate the Penguins in a building where they had won 10 games in a row.

"You never think a game like this would happen," Murray said. The Pittsburgh fans never imagined it, either. The few who remained until the final buzzer hooted the Penguins off the ice, convinced there would be no more hockey at the Civic Arena until autumn. That the dream of a second Stanley Cup was all but officially dead.

Ciccarelli issued the customary warning that "this series is not over," but there seemed little doubt that it would be in less than 48 hours. Only eight teams in playoff history had come back from a 3-1 deficit, and the Penguins could not survive unless they won two games at the Capital Centre, where Washington had dominated them all season.

It was a predicament that would have unsettled anybody, with the possible exception of Bob Johnson. And so, with a premature offseason staring hard at them, the Penguins invoked the memory of the Badger, the man who had taught them to cope with even the most staggering adversity. The odds of beating Washington three times in a row seemed almost nil, but the Penguins knew that Johnson, if he were coaching, would be totally convinced Pittsburgh would be going to the second round. And that he would expect the players to feel the same.

"We're all missing Bob, and he did have a big influence on us, but if we were taught — and we were taught right — we should remember what we learned and put that back into our game," Joe Mullen said. "I know we can play better. We've got to do it now. The way we played last year, and the way I know we can play makes me think we can do it. For us to win, and win consistently, we're going to have to get back to the same things we did last year."

Mostly, that meant playing team defense like they actually cared about it, instead of allowing the Capitals to roam the attacking zone at will. That was the major topic of discussion in a team meeting with the coaching staff before Game 5 and Lemieux, hockey's premier offensive talent, did much of the talking. He knew that getting points was nice, even important, but that the Penguins' only hope of winning the series was to limit Washington's offense.

It had taken a while for the Penguins to get that message, but it sank in quickly once it arrived. The Capitals had averaged nearly 33 shots during the first four games, but were held to 23 in Game 5, and the Penguins won 5-2. "We tried mainly to play a solid defensive game," Bowman said. "When you're in the position we're in, there's no margin for error."

Especially not when the Penguins' lineup had been pock-marked by injuries. Tocchet, who had made a premature return in Game 4, was deemed out of action indefinitely and not particularly hopeful about being back soon. "It doesn't feel very good at all," he said. "I can't reach to wash my left armpit right now. It was separated going in (to Game 4) and you could see when I played I couldn't accomplish much. And I hurt it a little bit more." What's more, a wrist injury prevented Kjell Samuelsson from dressing for Game 5.

But while the Penguins were short a few bodies, they had no lack of motivation. They wanted to win not just to stay alive in the series, but to prove that the fans and media members who had written them off after Game 4 were wrong. "We didn't want to give up on ourselves and never will," Stevens said. "It seems that a lot of people have." That included almost anybody who had looked objectively at the first four games of the series. Throw out Lemieux's extraordinary performance in Game 3, and Washington might have swept the round.

What might have been didn't matter, however. All that counted was that the series would go back to the Civic Arena for Game 6. The Penguins' chances of reaching the second round weren't alive only because of sheer mathematics, as had been the case after Game 4, but neither were they in command of the series. "I'd rather be in their position than our position," Barrasso said. "We have to win two, they have to win one. That makes it a lot easier for them."

There was an ominous footnote for Washington — the Capitals had played Game 5 in 11 previous playoff series, and the winner of that game had gone on to capture the series every time — but it did little to shake their confidence. "We're still up 3-2," Michal Pivonka said, "and have a couple of chances to put them away."

The Capitals had two chances to win one game, pretty decent odds for a team with so much talent and such a fundamentally sound approach to the game. Washington's locker-room closet was jammed with the skeletons of past playoff disappointments, but this was a new team with a new style and a new attitude. Unfortunately for the Capitals, however, they hadn't come up with a solution to an old problem — how to contain Mario Lemieux.

He singlehandedly extended the series to a seventh game, scoring two goals and assisting on three others in the Penguins' 6-4 victory. Lemieux had watched his team stumble to the brink of disaster and look over the edge, then swooped in to pull it back from the precipice of elimination. It was, by any measure, a magnificent individual effort. Unless it was Lemieux doing the measuring, in which case it was just an honest night's labor. "I just go out there and try to do my job every night," he said. "Some nights I'm able to do it maybe a little bit better than other nights."

And then there are nights like this one, when he does his job better than anyone else in the world ever has. Or could. "That's why they pay him $2.5 million a year," Barrasso said. And why no one who watches him play on a regular basis ever accused Lemieux of stealing a paycheck. He has the ability to raise the level of his play in tandem with the stakes of a game. Maybe he'll drift through a meaningless game or two during the regular season, but put Lemieux in a critical game during the postseason, and you're asking to be awed. "He loves the big games," Stevens said. "We're just lucky to have him here, so we don't have to try to stop him."

Lemieux had run up 15 points in his first five games against Washington, and the Capitals had no doubt he was the reason there would be a seventh game at the Capital Centre. "You've got to have key people playing well in the playoffs," Terry Murray said. "Those are the guys who make the difference in the outcome of the game. As you saw by Pittsburgh's performance, it was Lemieux who really got excited and made some real quality plays."

Stevens contributed a few of those, too. He wasn't much of a factor early in the series, but was reunited with Lemieux for Game 6 and got two goals, two assists, and a team-record 12 shots on goal. He had talked to a couple of former teammates, Barry Pederson and Mark Recchi, after Game 5, and had picked up a few pointers. Pederson told him to stop chasing people; Recchi suggested he shoot high on Beaupre. Stevens didn't just listen to their advice; he acted on it. And it worked.

There had been some anxious moments in this game — the Penguins had a 2-0 lead before Washington reeled off four unanswered goals to take a 4-2 lead in the second period — but the momentum shifted in Pittsburgh's favor when Joe Mullen beat Don Beaupre on a breakaway to cut the deficit to one. The goal was set up by Ron Francis, who pressured Washington's Kelly Miller and forced him to make a blind pass through the neutral zone. Mullen intercepted the puck and, seconds later, the Penguins were back in the game. And the series. "I didn't see Mullen," Miller said. "I was trying to make too big a play. I made a bad mistake."

So had his teammates. They had taken this species of killer Penguins to the cusp of extinction, then had given them a stay of execution. They had given Pittsburgh a chance to play a one-game season, and the Penguins had proven they were comfortable in a winner-take-all setting. "Game 7, you never know what can happen," Lemieux said. "A fluky goal here or there, some bad breaks. But we'll take our chances."

The Penguins downplayed the importance of the momentum they had seized by winning two games in a row — "We'll have them where we want them if we beat them (in Game 7)," Barrasso said — and both teams dragged some historical baggage into Game 7. The Penguins were trying to become just the second franchise in NHL history to win a seventh game on the road after falling behind 3-1 in a series; the New York Islanders did it in 1975 against Pittsburgh and in 1987 against Washington. The Capitals, conversely, were playing in a seventh game for the first time since that Islanders series, when they lost a quadruple-overtime heartbreaker at home.

Not that precedent would dictate the outcome of this game. History, by its very definition, is about the past, not applicable to the present; the Penguins proved that in 1991 by shedding their shabby tradition and winning the Stanley Cup. "Most things that are talked about as far as experience and about the (seventh) game are meaningless," Bryan Trottier said. "Because nothing happens the same way twice in a game. There are reactions in a game that have absolutely nothing to do with experience."

Both teams agreed that neither Washington's home-ice advantage nor the Penguins' knack for winning key games would be a factor in Game 7. They also shared the idea that the losing team would be in for a difficult offseason after having its season end so abruptly. "It's going to be tough for whoever loses," Stevens said. "But it will be a lot better if they lose."

A sign outside the Washington locker room before Game 7 read, "Anyone can make promises . . . Winners make commitments." The Capitals made one that night, but it was not enough. Not when the Penguins played a brilliant defensive game that limited Washington to 19 shots. They made the type of patient, intelligent effort so vital to success in the playoffs. "We couldn't have played better defensively," Bob Errey said. "For this team to win — and we showed it last year in the playoffs — we have to play some form of defensive hockey."

Getting timely goals helps, too, and the Penguins got a couple of those from Lemieux and Jaromir Jagr. Lemieux scored shorthanded, and Jagr converted on their only power-play opportunity of the evening. And after Mullen threw the puck into an empty net at 19:27 of the third period to clinch the Penguins' 3-1 victory, they were sent to the locker room to a thunderous ovation from the approximately 5,000 Pittsburgh fans who had made the five-hour drive to Landover, Maryland.

Down the hallway, there was stark, stunned silence. Another chapter had been added to Washington's legacy of playoff frustration, a tale so chilling it reads like something from Edgar Allan Poe. Less than a week earlier, Washington had had a 3-1 lead in the series and a veritable chokehold on a berth in the second round. Now the Capitals had nothing but a lot of unwanted time off to deal with.

"I really thought this was the year," Don Beaupre said. "I thought it was the year for the team and for myself. We blew a chance. The biggest chance I had, we blew." Murray described the Capitals' collapse as "very disappointing" and said, "this type of scenario should not happen. A great season was tainted. You're measured by how you finish, not how you begin."

That Washington's season had ended so suddenly was testimony to many things, but none more than the magnificence of Mario Lemieux. He finished the series with 17 points, two shy of the single-series playoff record set by Boston's Rick Middleton against Buffalo in 1983. And he did it despite sitting out Game 1 with a bum shoulder. "I have coached a lot of great players," Bowman said. "But I have never seen a guy play so inspired."

"I give all the credit to Mario Lemieux," Washington defenseman Al Iafrate said. "Period. Exclamation point." "We were beaten by just one guy," Murray said. "Lemieux was just too good."

CHAPTER THIRTEEN

"More Guts Than Brains"

The Penguins were understandably relieved to have survived their harrowing series against the Capitals. They even had a chance to revel in their triumph after Game 7 for perhaps 30 seconds or so. Because two nights after the Washington series ended, the second round would begin. And that best-of-seven series would be against a team many regarded as the finest in the National Hockey League.

The New York Rangers finished the regular season with the league's best record, 50-25-5, and their lineup featured some of the premier players in hockey. Like center Mark Messier who, after being acquired from Edmonton in October, had put together a 107-point season that established him as a heavy favorite to be named the league's MVP. And Brian Leetch, an almost-consensus choice as the NHL's best defenseman in 1991-92. And Tony Amonte, a serious Rookie of the Year candidate. And then there were goalies Mike Richter and John Vanbiesbrouck, gifted forwards such as Mike Gartner and Darren Turcotte, and quality defensemen such as James Patrick and Jeff Beukeboom.

Somehow, a series against the Rangers didn't seem like a fair reward for what the Penguins had achieved against Washington. New York had gotten a seven-game scare from the New Jersey Devils during the first round, but no one denied the Rangers had enough talent to merit a prominent place on the short list of Stanley Cup contenders. "They didn't finish first overall for nothing," Lemieux said.

The Rangers, however, had a few potential flaws. Coach Roger Neilson's history suggested an affinity for giving his enforcers, such as Tie Domi and Joey Kocur, significant ice time, and the Penguins felt that, if they played with composure and discipline, they could get a bounty of power-play chances. They also hoped to exploit the habit Leetch and Patrick had of getting involved in the offense. Their ability to operate in the attacking zone was a big part of what made Leetch and Patrick so dangerous, but the Penguins thought they might be able to trap them out of position and capitalize on quick counter-attacks.

New York, like the Capitals, had a 5-2 advantage in the season series and home-ice advantage against Pittsburgh. The Penguins, however, were supremely confident heading into Game 1. They traditionally play well in Madison Square Garden and had reaffirmed the level of their talent, dedication, and resilience against Washington. "I like our chances," Lemieux said. The Rangers had no shortage of confidence — they were convinced the franchise's Stanley Cup drought that began in 1940 was a few weeks from ending — but understood the challenge the Penguins represented. "They're a different hockey club when the playoffs start," Messier said. "Definitely, they play defense better than I've seen them play before."

He saw them play a lot of it during the third period of Game 1, as the Penguins held New York to eight shots while protecting the 4-2 lead that gave them a 1-0 edge in the series. He also saw Lemieux throw himself in front of a James Patrick shot during one flurry, a show of commitment to defense neither team could overlook. "That kind of says where his heart is," Troy Loney said.

The Penguins were able to drop into a defense-oriented style after Loney, Larry Murphy, and Kevin Stevens staked them to a 3-0 advantage during the first 22 minutes. "They got the lead and played well with it," Neilson said. New York whittled the lead to 3-2 on goals by Kris King and Tony Amonte, but Ron Francis restored Pittsburgh's two-goal edge with some deft footwork. He was cutting toward the New York net when he stopped a Stevens pass with his left foot, nudged the puck onto his stick with the right, then flipped a backhander past Vanbiesbrouck. "If you can use your feet well, it can be a plus in certain situations," said Francis, whose experiences as a youth soccer player probably made his goal possible.

With a fairly comfortable lead restored, the Penguins stacked four players at the blue line to disrupt New York's offensive rushes, and had Barrasso shoot the puck out of the defensive zone whenever he was able to get his stick on it. It was an efficient, if not entertaining, tactic. "I've never seen them play that way," King said. "It's an effective way to play in the playoffs. We have to find a way to stop it."

Roger Neilson bemoaned the lack of physical play in Game 1 and said, "It was not a hitting game, and we wanted it to be," but a few Penguins finished the evening with fresh scars. Gord Roberts got a three-stitch cut when he was high-sticked in the face by Jan Erixon during the first period, and Bryan Trottier got a gash on the outside corner of his left eye when he was clipped by a stray stick. "Just a little nick," Trottier said. "I was down in the corner one time with a bunch of guys. There was just a little bit of a scrum, and I came out with a souvenir."

And then there was the Really Ugly Incident That Never Happened. During the third period, Barrasso crumpled to the ice in obvious agony after being blasted by Kocur. The catch is, replays showed Kocur had done nothing except make a half-hearted effort to knock the puck from under Barrasso's glove, which was on the ice. Any contact between the two was minimal, even though Barrasso acted as if he had been mortally wounded. "That's part of the playoffs," he said. "Every time I get hit, I'm going down, because the referees are supposed to call it. That's the new rules, and that's just the way it's going to be. You have to try to get every advantage you can."

Their victory in Game 1 gave the Penguins one advantage they had not enjoyed for a long time; it was the first time in six playoff series that they had won the first game. "It's strange, but it's a good strange," Loney said. "I like it." And he smiled. But it would be quite a few days before any of the Penguins would do that again.

The Penguins' chances of winning Game 2 looked to be enhanced about 90 minutes before the opening faceoff when Messier, who had been bothered by back spasms for more than a week, removed himself from New York's lineup. And they looked even better when Stevens gave Pittsburgh a 1-0 lead at 1:29 of the first period.

But at 5:05 of the first period, six seconds after the Penguins went on a power play, Rangers penalty killer Adam Graves made a play that would generate headlines and controversy for weeks. He took a two-handed baseball swing at Lemieux that broke a metacarpal bone in Lemieux's left hand and, most observers believed, shattered Pittsburgh's chances of another championship.

Graves acknowledged targeting Lemieux's hands — videotape of the incident made that painfully obvious — but denied he had any intention of injuring Lemieux. "When you're penalty killing, you try to put pressure on the guy's hands to move the puck, for him to give up the puck so you can shoot it down the ice," he said. "It wasn't an intent to hurt him. In no way would I want to hurt him. I tried to hit him in the gloves, where all the padding is."

The scary thing is, Graves succeeded. His stick struck Lemieux on the padded area on the back of his glove, but the blow was still hard enough to break a bone. Referee Dan Marouelli gave Graves just a two-minute minor penalty for slashing, but Dave Newell, a supervisor of officials who was working the game, decided NHL executive vice president Brian O'Neill should review tapes of the incident to determine if additional punishment was called for. Newell said it was "an incident I feel should be reviewed . . . based on the severity of the slash."

When Lemieux, who was prone for several minutes after the slash, returned to the bench, Scott Bowman noticed that the skin on Lemieux's hand had been broken and that the injured area was already getting perceptibly larger. "He took his glove off so we could have a look as soon as he came off the ice," Bowman said. "And it was badly swollen that soon. I told him to forget (playing in) this one."

Losing Lemieux so violently and suddenly numbed the Penguins, and their body count rose before the first period was over. Joe Mullen's season ended abruptly when, after losing his balance while stepping over the extended leg of New York forward Paul Broten, he absorbed a forearms-high hit from Kris King. By the time Mullen touched the ice, the ligaments in his left knee had been ripped apart, and there was a bout of reconstructive surgery in his immediate future. "The injuries were . . . ridiculous," Loney said. "A lot of things going on out there were totally absurd."

But even as their depth chart disintegrated, the Penguins battled New York evenly and had a 2-1 lead with less than nine minutes to play. But Pittsburgh, denied the services of two of its most important players for the majority of the game, began to wear down, and Jeff Beukeboom tied it 2-2 at 12:36 of the third period. The Rangers exploited another crack in the Penguins' defensive shell a few minutes later, and Kris King beat Barrasso to give New York its first lead of the series. Beukeboom sealed New York's 4-2 victory with an empty-net goal at 19:57.

If the Penguins weren't sufficiently outraged by what had happened to Lemieux, reading Neilson's assessment of the situation the next day surely sent them over the edge. He was quoted as saying, "It's great not having to worry about Lemieux. You have a plan for him, obviously. If you don't need it, you can play a more straightforward game."

Neilson's point might have been that, without the offensive dimension that Lemieux gives the Penguins, the Rangers could focus their attention elsewhere. But his remarks were perceived in some quarters as evidence that Lemieux's injury wasn't entirely accidental, that hurting him somehow, sometime, was an integral part of New York's game plan. Neilson's reputation as a coach who was not reluctant to have his players stray outside the rules to neutralize opponents undoubtedly was a factor in that interpretation.

Reaction to Graves' slash was swift and largely one-sided among the North American media. Columnists suggested that if the Rangers went on to win the Cup, their triumph would be forever tarnished because of the incident. At least one suggested that rather than champagne, the Rangers fill the Cup with blood if they captured the championship.

A notable exception to the anti-Rangers outcry was Mike Lupica of the *New York Daily News*, who scoffed at the notion that a Rangers title would be diminished in any way because of what had been done to Lemieux. "If the Rangers win the Cup, it's tainted?" Lupica wrote. "Because a guy got hurt in a hockey game? Give me a break." Perhaps he believed that Lemieux had uttered that very phrase — "Give me a break" — to Graves seconds before the slash that fractured his hand was delivered.

So the Penguins returned home with a split of the games in Manhattan, and a challenge more overwhelming than anything most of them had ever faced in their careers. They had to win three of five games against the winningest team in hockey, and do it without the game's top offensive talent and one of its best two-way wingers. It helped that Tocchet was about ready to return from his shoulder injury, but no player could fully compensate for Lemieux's absence. "We look upon him as probably the best player ever to play this game," Bob Errey said. "Let's face it, I can sit here and honestly say he can do things Wayne Gretzky can't do."

When X-rays verified Lemieux's hand was broken, doctors said it would take 4-6 weeks for the fracture to heal, and that he would be out of the lineup indefintely. The Penguins released few details about the injury, but doctors said patients with similar injuries generally had severe pain for 10-14 days and difficulty gripping for 3-4 weeks. It was obvious that the series, if not the season, was over for Lemieux.

Lemieux's injury dominated off-day conversations between Games 2 and 3. Graves continued to plead his innocence — "I didn't mean to hurt the guy" — and Neilson told New York reporters he had tapes of slashes by Stevens and Errey during Game 2 and intended to share them with league officials. And he reiterated he had not seen the Graves slash, even though it happened directly in front of the team benches.

For their part, the Penguins repeatedly scoffed at the notion Graves was not trying to injure Lemieux. "After I saw the tape, I said, 'This is a joke,'" Phil Bourque said. "It was ridiculous. He wound up like a baseball swing. A two-handed, wallop baseball swing and definitely intended to hurt him." The Penguins also fought the urge to seek vengeance, to retaliate in kind against one of the Rangers' top players. "Obviously, the temptation is there," Errey said. "I can't say it's not. But believe me, if it's a 2-2 hockey game, and I see (Brian) Leetch's ankle, I'm not going to take a whack at it."

The Penguins summoned forwards Jock Callander and Mike Needham from their Muskegon farm team to fill in for Lemieux and Mullen in Game 3. They also summoned an extraordinary effort from within themselves, from the reservoir of character that champions have. They yielded nothing, made the Rangers battle for every square inch of ice they secured. And they lost. Which meant all their efforts, all their resolve, had accomplished nothing.

"We tried as hard as we could, but that doesn't really mean anything," Stevens said. "We're here to win. We're not here to try hard."

When the Rangers' 6-5 overtime victory was final, the toughest thing was deciding which goal that they had given up bothered the Penguins the most. Kris King's game winner from behind the goal line at 1:29 of overtime was a leading candidate. But so was the one Adam Graves scored to give New York a 1-0 lead at 3:45 of the first period.

That Graves was playing while the man he injured was not, let alone that he was able to score a key goal, flustered the Penguins for obvious reasons. "The only thing that could have hurt worse would be if Graves would have scored the winner," Scott Bowman said.

The Penguins threw 50 shots at New York goalie Mike Richter, one shy of the franchise playoff record, but did not have a lead all night. They overcame deficits of 2-0 and 3-1 and, as Bowman said, "played our hearts out to get back in the game after a pretty tough start," but the bottom line was that the Rangers had recaptured the home-ice advantage and had a 2-1 advantage in the series.

New York played Game 3 without Messier and Darren Turcotte, who had a wrist injury, and Neilson theorized that that had offset the absence of Lemieux and Mullen. "As far as guys missing on both teams, Messier to us is like Lemieux to them," he said. "And Turcotte and Mullen are each 30-goal scorers, so they cancel each other out." But Neilson's logic didn't quite add up. The relative values of Messier and Lemieux are conjecture, of course, but Mullen scored 42 goals during the regular season, while Turcotte had 30.

King isn't much of a goal-scorer — he had 10 in 79 regular-season games — but he had been credited with the most important goal in the first three games of the series. Getting the game winner wasn't exactly what he had in mind when he tossed the puck toward the front of the Pittsburgh net, but it struck Barrasso's leg pad as he moved across the crease and skidded over the goal line. "It was a crazy goal," Gord Roberts said. "But they don't ask how, just how many."

It was not only a fluky goal, but a potentially demoralizing one. To have played so hard for so long, then to get so little reward for their trouble, figured to put some serious dents in the Penguins' collective psyche. But Ron Francis, who had gotten two goals and an assist and played an impeccable two-way game, realized the best way to cope with the loss was to forget it. Immediately, if not earlier.

"You let go of it," he said. "It is over now. You can't go back. You can't let it get to you. We knew when we got into this that there would be tough nights and tough losses. This is one of them, but it is time to move on."

Time, meanwhile, was about to run out for Adam Graves. He had a hearing with Brian O'Neill on the morning of May 8 and later that day learned he would serve a four-game suspension for slashing Lemieux. The penalty, coincidentally or otherwise, was guaranteed to keep Graves out of the second round, even if it went to seven games.

Graves, who earned considerable respect with his comportment after the Lemieux incident, accepted the penalty without complaint. "I hurt Mario," he said. "I have my penalty. I have to accept it." Neil Smith, the Rangers' GM, agreed. "A player has been injured, his hand has been broken, and he's going to miss some games," he said. "It's going to hurt the franchise. The league can't let that happen." Craig Patrick released a statement that said the Penguins were "disappointed," but team officials declined additional comment until a press conference the next day.

The Penguins' didn't just react to Graves' suspension at the press conference, however. They unveiled the framework of a plan designed to "fix certain things that are so blatantly wrong in the sport," in the words of team president Howard Baldwin. The proposal, whose points included stiffer penalties for injury-causing incidents deemed to be intentional and the ejection of players who fight during games, was to be submitted to the league for consideration after the season.

"It's that time in history when we have to change our game," Patrick said. "This is a great opportunity to do something for the betterment of the game." Baldwin added that "we've had these problems, as a league, for a long time, and who's kidding whom? If we sit around as owners and management and talk about the same problems and don't do anything about them, then we're the problem. I've talked to a lot of clubs, and they indicate to me that something's got to be done. It's time for us, as a league, to stop it. And we'd better stop it fast, because all we're going to do is screw up the game."

Baldwin declined to say what he thought a fair suspension for Graves would have been, but said, "even if you give him 100 games, it doesn't give us Mario Lemieux back. No amount of games missed by Adam Graves compensates us for the loss of Mario Lemieux."

Lemieux had not spoken publicly since being injured, but his agent, Tom Reich, said speculation in New York that Lemieux was not badly injured, and that his return was imminent was totally inaccurate. "He has a big-league break in his hand," Reich said. "There's no soon time that he's going to be able to move his hand, let alone play. He's out for a good while. This is not to be confused with a career-threatening injury, but it's also not to be confused with something where they'll wrap him up, 'tech him up' a little bit and he'll be out there tomorrow to play."

The Penguins understood they had no chance of getting Lemieux back for this series. There was no way they could have realized, however, that Francis would do such an exceptional job of filling the void. He had played brilliantly in Game 3, but took his game to an even higher level in Game 4. Francis scored three goals, including one at 2:47 of overtime, that gave Pittsburgh a 5-4 victory and a thoroughly improbable 2-2 tie in the series. "This team never quits," Stevens said. "It's got more guts than any team I've ever seen. It seems like we never do anything the easy way, but we always get the job done."

It didn't look like that would happen for most of Game 4. New York had leads of 2-0, 3-1, and 4-2, but an unlikely goal by Francis midway through the third period ignited Pittsburgh's comeback. The Penguins' prospects bordered on hopeless when, trailing 4-2, Gord Roberts received a five-minute penalty at 5:19 of the third for cross-checking New York's Paul Broten.

Pittsburgh survived being shorthanded, however, and eight seconds after Roberts returned, Francis lashed a 65-foot slapshot that caromed off Mike Richter's glove and into the net. The Penguins had no way of knowing that they had just witnessed the pivotal moment in these playoffs.

Troy Loney forced the overtime by swiping a Jaromir Jagr pass behind Richter at 11:52 to make it 4-4, and the Penguins capitalized on a mistake by Messier to get the decisive goal. Messier, clearly hampered by the vast assortment of injuries he had accumulated during the first round, lost the puck to Larry Murphy as he tried to carry it out of the New York zone. Murphy threw it toward the net, and Francis steered it past John Vanbiesbrouck, who had replaced Richter after Loney's goal, to send the series back to New York, 2-2.

"We got some lucky breaks," Murphy said. "We're not kidding anybody. But we took advantage of them. That's the only way we're going to beat this team."

And they had to beat New York two more times, at least once in Madison Square Garden. And do it without Bob Errey, who separated his right shoulder during Game 4 and was out for the series. His spot on the roster went to Dave Michayluk, a minor-league forward who hadn't been in the National Hockey League since the 1982-83 season.

The Penguins' talent level was dropping almost daily, but their work ethic was getting stronger by the shift. "The attitude right now is the best it's ever been," Tocchet said. "It's more of a workman's attitude. Everybody comes to the rink to work. We're kind of playing desperate. There's a feeling like, we have to work with what we have, so let's just go to it."

Perspiration and dedication had kept the Penguins in the series, but it would be talent — raw, unvarnished ability — that would enable them to get through it. And it would come mostly in the form of Jaromir Jagr, the young Czech with the shaggy hair and the silky moves.

Rick Tocchet gave the Penguins a 1-0 lead when he scored on a power play at 1:15 of the first period — his first goal of the postseason — but the spotlight shifted to Jagr shortly thereafter. Referee Terry Gregson awarded Jagr a penalty shot at 7:04 after determining Brian Leetch had tackled him from behind as he cut toward the New York net. Neilson protested the penalty-shot call was "very marginal," but there was nothing questionable about the way Jagr handled it.

He, like many Europeans, has a habit of shifting to his backhand and shooting high when he is near the net, but on the penalty shot Jagr skated down the slot and snapped a medium-height forehand past New York goalie John Vanbiesbrouck. "I changed my move," Jagr said. "I got lucky."

So did the Penguins, because after Darren Turcotte and Mike Gartner scored to tie the game for New York, Jagr singlehandedly shaped the outcome of the game. At 14:27 of the third period, he took a pass from Gord Roberts at the New York blue line and cut down the right side. Jagr then danced around Jeff Beukeboom and slid the puck past Vanbiesbrouck for the deciding goal in Pittsburgh's 3-2 victory. "He's a world-class player," Beukeboom said. "What can you do?"

Nothing, really, except to marvel at the abilities of a player who hasn't begun to approach his potential, but who already has the poise needed to rescue his team in a critical situation. "We were kind of scraping, hanging on," Larry Murphy said. "I thought they really took the game to us, and if it weren't for that big play by Jaromir, it was just a matter of time, I think, before they really took the game ... The only way we were going to win was for somebody to step forward and make a very big play."

Few in these playoffs were bigger than the one Jagr made, but it wasn't entirely coincidental that he emerged as the hero of Game 5. Bowman had begun double-shifting him, hoping Jagr would use the extra ice time to manufacture the go-ahead goal Pittsburgh needed. "You play the percentages," Bowman said. "You don't have to have a lot of offense. You need a goal."

After the game, Jagr spent much time dodging comparisons to Lemieux, and not all of them came from the media. "He's capable of doing those things, just like Mario," Jiri Hrdina said. Jagr dismissed such talk as near-heresy — "I look at him in practice, but I can never be like him" — but there was no denying that he, like Lemieux, had a knack for producing in key situations, which is why the Penguins suddenly had a 3-2 lead in the series. "You go nowhere if your best players don't play great," Bryan Trottier said. "It's been proven in every Stanley Cup."

Jagr didn't just score a couple of big goals in Game 5; he also broke a bit of medical news. When a reporter mentioned Lemieux, Jagr said, "Mario's the best player in the league. He means a lot to us. If we can beat the Rangers, he (will) come back the next series." That was the first indication Lemieux's return to the lineup might be days, not weeks, away.

Down the corridor in Madison Square Garden, the Rangers didn't care much about when Lemieux would be able to play again. Some didn't care to talk about much of anything. "It's best

I don't say much," Mark Messier told a thicket of reporters. "It would not be for the benefit of everybody here . . . You can take it any way you want."

Maybe there really wasn't much the Rangers could say. They had squandered a 2-1 lead in the series and were on the verge of elimination against an opponent missing several key players. Talk of ending the franchise's Stanley Cup jinx went on hold; New York's only concern was forcing a seventh game back at the Garden. "I don't think we're an unconfident team, but we know we're in a battle," James Patrick said. "They're the defending Stanley Cup champions, and they're a good team, but it isn't over yet."

It would be over in some 48 hours, however, as the Penguins completed the most stirring performance in franchise history with a 5-1 victory in Game 6 at the Civic Arena. They got a 33-save performance from Barrasso and two goals by Rick Tocchet, in addition to rookie Shawn McEachern's first goal in the NHL. McEachern had a chance for another when referee Kerry Fraser awarded him a penalty shot, but Vanbiesbrouck rejected the shot.

Not that any of McEachern's teammates minded much. Not after they had stared down some truly staggering odds, and forged a monumentally satisfying triumph out of a predicament that bordered on disastrous. Logic said the Penguins had no business winning this series; they just never bothered believing it. "This team has more guts than brains," Ron Francis said.

That might have been true even if the average IQ was around 150, because few people could look objectively at their lineup after Lemieux and Mullen, to say nothing of Errey, were injured, and believe that the Penguins had a realistic shot at a Wales Conference final rematch with the Boston Bruins. The Rangers looked to be too talented, too tough for the Penguins to beat with the stripped-down lineup they had been forced to use.

"You heard it everywhere you went that we were done," Francis said. "The guys in this (locker) room didn't believe it. Guys like Tocchet and Stevens, they were convinced we weren't finished, and they convinced everybody else in this room we weren't finished."

"They are obviously a pretty gutty team," Rangers right winger Mike Gartner said. "They lose the best player in the world and still come out and play great."

They played well enough that they limited New York to three goals in the final two games, and James Patrick, who had run up 71 points during the regular season, did not have any in the series. Even Lemieux could not have been more impressed by what he witnessed in the four-plus games that followed his injury. "They stuck together and played hard the whole series," he said.

No one played harder — or better — than Francis, who carried Pittsburgh through the middle of the series, who invariably came up with a goal or key defensive play when the Penguins needed it most. "Ronnie was determined to take up the slack in Mario's absence," Bowman said. "He wouldn't let this club be beaten. He stepped forward and had a great series. What a performance he put on for this team."

"I'm not Mario Lemieux and I'm not Joe Mullen," Francis said. "I can't replace them. But I felt I had to do something with them gone." He did. More than anyone could have asked. Or expected. But then, so did nearly all of his teammates. It would have been difficult to imagine a more grueling series than the one Pittsburgh went through against Washington, but the events of the second round made that seven-game run in with the Capitals seem like a church social. "It hasn't been an easy ride," Bowman said.

And it wasn't a pleasant trip back to New York for the Rangers, whose season had ended with the haunting, taunting chant of "1940" spilling down on them from the Civic Arena seats. Their regular-season points championship and the vast promise their personnel held seemed pretty hollow as they jetted toward the offseason. "It's like a poison arrow," Vanbiesbrouck said. "It hits you right in the heart."

As the reality of New York's elimination began to settle in, Neilson told reporters it was not just Jagr and Francis and their teammates who had done in the Rangers. He said Pittsburgh's front office played a major role, too. "Their management played it smart," he said. "They accused Adam Graves of deliberately going after Lemieux, which was not true, and they accused the coaching staff of sending (Graves) out there (to injure Lemieux), which is absurd, and they talked about instituting new rules in the league. They played it for all it was worth, and it worked. It was distracting for us and a rallying point for them."

Messier opted to focus on the future, to talk of the championships New York would chase in coming seasons. "This team is going to win a Stanley Cup, there's no question about that," he said. "It definitely has the desire, it definitely has the talent, and it definitely has the dedication. It's just a matter of when . . . No question about it, I've learned from losses in the past. This is a bitter pill to swallow at this point, but sometimes you need the bitter taste before you can have the sweet taste of victory."

The Penguins knew all about bitter defeats — it had been little more than two years since Uwe Krupp's overtime goal in the final regular-season game prevented them from qualifying for the playoffs — but they had learned a lot about the joys of winning, too. The most important lesson was that teamwork and tenacity count every bit as much as talent, and that there is no such thing as an inevitable defeat.

"I think the Rangers made a tactical error by playing cheap early in the series," Rick Tocchet said. "They underestimated the dedication that made this team champions last year. They underestimated the desire that this team has to win it all one more time."

CHAPTER FOURTEEN

Czech-mate

Jaromir Jagr looked like a standard-issue teenager when he walked out of the customs area at Greater Pittsburgh International Airport on July 21, 1990 after a flight from Frankfurt, Germany. He was wearing blue jeans, a denim jacket and a T-shirt emblazoned with an American flag. A rich mane of brown hair spilled over his collar as he walked into the lobby area with his mother, Anna.

But Jagr hardly was an average 18-year-old. He spoke no English, and knew nothing of the city that was about to become his home. He had a three-year work visa, but wasn't really sure if he would be around long enough to need another. Jagr was, by consensus, the most gifted player available in the 1990 entry draft, but he had serious concerns about whether he could be productive enough to last in the National Hockey League.

He knew the hockey there was different than he had been accustomed to playing in his native Czechoslovakia, and even after the Penguins chose him fifth overall in the draft, he worried about fitting in. On a visit to Pittsburgh a few days after the draft, Jagr made his fears known. "If they picked me first," he said through an interpreter, "I hope they know what they're doing."

The Penguins were fairly certain they did. Jagr had been one of five players grouped together at the top of the prospect ratings, and Craig Patrick confirmed, "We felt all along he was the most talented player in the draft." So when it was the Penguins' turn to select, after Quebec (Owen Nolan), Vancouver (Petr Nedved), Detroit (Keith Primeau), and Philadelphia (Mike Ricci), had made their choices, Patrick's decision was simple. Jaromir Jagr became a Penguin, and in less than two years, Scott Bowman would say, "The bonus for missing the playoffs will never be bigger."

When the Penguins took Jagr, they figured they had gotten a player of considerable ability, one whose skill level was high enough that he could overcome any problems incurred while adapting to the more physical style of play and small rinks in North America. But they didn't dare to dream they had acquired a player who, in a couple of seasons, would become one of the dominant offensive players in the game. "I wasn't aware he was going to be as good as he is," Patrick said in the spring of 1992.

Nonetheless, Jagr's adjustment wasn't always easy. He began taking English classes a few days after arriving in Pittsburgh, but struggled with the language for most of his rookie season and was shy about trying to talk to anyone except his teammates and close friends. He had not gotten an international driver's license, and so commuted to the Civic Arena for practices on a Port Authority Transit bus.

And he didn't always have the best grasp of details, like the time he didn't bother taking his visa along for a trip to Winnipeg. It wasn't until a layover at the Minneapolis airport that assistant coach Rick Paterson, Jagr's caretaker during his rookie season, realized that Jagr had brought no identification except an automated-teller card, which wasn't likely to go over well with Canada Customs officials.

A few months into his rookie season, Jagr was homesick for Czechoslovakia and bewildered by nearly everything about life in North America. "There was one time when he was literally ready to go back home," said George Kirk, the Penguins' director of amateur hockey and Jagr's designated driver for much of his rookie season. "He told me he wanted to leave."

Jagr was baffled by his inability to get much ice time early in his rookie season, but most of his major adjustments had to be made off the ice. Although it took a while to adapt to the NHL style, Jagr showed signs of his superior ability from the early days of training camp, much as Bob Johnson had predicted he would. "I think he'll feel very comfortable being on the ice, because the game is played on ice," Johnson said. "And whether you have great hockey sense as a North American or great hockey sense as a European, it's still the same game."

Jagr played the game well enough during his first season, when he had 27 goals and 30 assists, to earn a place on the all-rookie team. He struggled badly during the early part of the season, but began to put his game together when the Penguins traded Jim Kyte to Calgary for center Jiri Hrdina.

Hrdina was in the twilight of a solid career, but it wasn't just his level of play that interested the Penguins. They wanted to give Jagr a companion, and Hrdina, who had been a highly respected player in Czechoslovakia, was the perfect choice. He embraced the challenge and made Jagr his personal project, became a friend who spoke his language and could explain the ways of life in North America.

Jagr, who teammates said occasionally had been so home-sick that he would weep in the locker room, responded exactly as the Penguins had hoped. He became more confident and asser-tive, and that attitude was reflected in his play. Having Joe Mullen and Mark Recchi on right wing allowed the Penguins to bring Jagr along slowly rather than having to force-feed him into pressure-filled situations. Even so, he scored one of the most important goals of the 1991 playoffs, an overtime winner in Game 2 against New Jersey in the first round.

But it was during his second season in the NHL that the full magnitude of Jagr's ability began to become apparent. He played well enough to be voted the starting right winger on the Wales Conference All-Star team — although the possibility that lovestruck teenaged girls stuffed the ballot boxes cannot be ruled out — and flashed breathtaking skills that prompted some observers to compare him with Lemieux. It was suggested an anagram of his first name — scramble the letters, and you come up with "Mario Jr." — wasn't entirely coincidental.

Jagr also showed that he shares Lemieux's knack for pros-pering under pressure when he scored the game-winning goal in three consecutive playoff games, two against the New York Rangers and one against the Boston Bruins, the latter in overtime. Not that scoring key goals in high-stress situations was some-thing Jagr made a concerted effort to do. He has retained a child's sheer joy of playing the game and seems oblivious to pressure. "I just like to play," he said. "It's the way I was born."

Jagr's almost-innocent approach to his job hasn't gone un-noticed by his teammates. In fact, they believe it might be at least partially responsible for the way he played when the Penguins were trying to get by without Lemieux and Joe Mullen during the Rangers series. "He obviously has done a very admirable job, considering the situation we've been in," Tom Barrasso said. "Obviously, there's more pressure on him, but I don't really feel he's aware of it. I feel as though he's just going out and playing hockey the way he knows how, and I think that's why he's being successful. He's not really letting the outside influences affect his game."

Jagr rarely lets outside influences affect any aspect of his life, for that matter. Rain or shine, sub-zero or tropical temperatures, a contagious grin is almost always plastered across his face. It is as if Bob Johnson had programmed Jagr to carry on his legacy of being perpetually upbeat. Jagr showed his happy-go-lucky side — as if he has any other — the day before he returned from a 10-game suspension for skating into referee Ron Hoggarth during a game in Washington January 26.

He took a brief shift at receptionist Chris Span's desk in the team offices and fielded several phone calls, even briefed one fan on details of the Mark Recchi and Paul Coffey trades that had been completed a few hours earlier. And when transferring calls turned out to be a little too complicated, he asked one caller to try again later, because there was "nobody here except a guy from Czecho."

"He's always happy, always has a smile on his face," Kevin Stevens said. "He's always in a good mood." Well, maybe not always. The only people who might have become more familiar with Jagr than opposing teams during his second season were law-enforcement officials around Pittsburgh. After securing his driver's license, Jagr showed a pronounced disregard for most of the major traffic laws. "He doesn't know there's a speed limit," Stevens said.

But it didn't take him long to discover that there are tickets — and fines — for drivers who ignore the rules of the road. Jagr was sometimes able to get off with a warning — chances of that no doubt increased greatly if the officer who pulled him over was a hockey fan — but Jagr's heavy foot lightened his wallet quite a bit, as his collection of citations reportedly ran well into double figures.

"They know who I am, but they still give me tickets," he said. "Sometimes they stop me and let me go, but I still get lots of tickets." He said three of those came in a span of one week, earning him not only a hefty bill, but also a stern lecture from Craig Patrick.

Jagr's troubles with traffic laws were a serious concern to the organization — there was genuine fear that his proclivity for fast driving could be a threat to his health and safety — and were an indication of his lack of maturity. But in some ways, Jagr's attitude is an important component of his success. The immaturity that causes some problems also makes him immune to many of the pressures and demands of his occupation.

"The kid inside him is the big thing," Rick Tocchet said. "I don't know how long it will last. I'm sure there will be pressure from the media and fans that will get to him at some point, but now it doesn't bother him. I don't think he comprehends it all. Hopefully, he can keep the kid in him."

Jagr's volatile skills appeal to anyone who appreciates the game, but his most devoted fans are teenage girls and young women. That is the segment of the population that responded the most when play-by-play announcer Mike Lange made an off-hand reference during a broadcast to Jagr's passion for Kit-Kat candy bars. Jagr estimated fans shipped more than 1,000 of them to him.

The notion that Jagr attracts young females more than any other type of fan is reinforced every time he accompanies teammates into a bar, where he goes not to drink beer, but to play video games. "There must be 100 young girls lined up to give him quarters," Rick Tocchet said. "When I was his age, I had to get my own quarters. It's pretty scary. Every young girl in Pittsburgh wants to marry him."

His popularity with that age group is responsible for a gig Jagr landed with WDVE-FM, a Pittsburgh rock-and-roll station. He isn't an on-air talent — not yet, anyway — but he is the voice behind "Jaromir Weather," a daily segment in which he gives the day's forecast. Actually, the station taped Jagr giving every conceivable prediction — "Today... rain" — and plays whatever is appropriate. As compensation, Jagr said, he gets "all the CDs I want."

Despite his natural extroversion, Jagr still isn't comfortable in some interview situations, especially with media members he doesn't know. His command of the language, however, has improved significantly since he first arrived in North America. That, Jagr said, is due at least in part to his favorite TV show, "Married With Children," which he watches whenever possible.

But even as he has adapted to life in his new surroundings, Jagr has been forced to make some adjustments. One of the biggest was getting used to the coaching style of Scott Bowman. During his rookie season, Jagr had been perplexed by much that Bob Johnson did, but the two formed a strong bond as the year unfolded. Jagr was distraught when he learned of Johnson's brain cancer and, like most of his teammates, didn't forge much of a personal relationship with Bowman.

Jagr, showing total disdain for locker-room diplomacy, was candid about his preference for Johnson. "He gave me lots of ice time," he said. "Sometimes I play bad, (it was) OK. But when I play bad here with Scotty Bowman, I will play less and less and less. With Bob Johnson, I play the same . . . Scotty Bowman never smile. I don't know why. "

While Bowman will never be mistaken for the Badger, it's not true that he doesn't smile. And it shouldn't be surprising that watching Jagr singlehandedly dissect an opposing defense is one of the things that can coax a warm grin from Bowman. Bowman even likens Jagr to Hall of Famer Frank Mahovlich, whom he coached in Montreal. "They'd both make these swooping rushes," Bowman said. "Get in full gear and they're pretty difficult to stop."

That's a trait he shares with Lemieux, too. Jagr speaks of him in an almost-reverent tone, and still seems amazed that he is a teammate of a player whose poster had adorned a wall of his bedroom in Kladno, Czechoslovakia. "He's like my teacher," Jagr said. "If I don't know something, I just watch him."

Clearly, Jagr is a quick study. He doesn't mimic Lemieux — such creativity cannot be copied — but he, like Lemieux, is constantly adding moves to his repertoire, stretching the bound-aries of puckhandling to the greatest extremes possible. Not every experiment works out, but Jagr has enjoyed some spec-tacular successes. "Every move gets better," Tocchet said.

"He's so strong," Lemieux said. "He's one of the best in the league at holding onto the puck and making the play. He's a great player who is still learning. We have some similarities. I think he's got to learn to move the puck and get it back; sometimes he tries to beat the same guy three times. He's got to learn to shoot it at the same time. That's going to come with experience."

Indeed, Jagr is likely at least a half-decade away from realizing his potential. By then, it's entirely possible he will be recognized as the dominant player in the game. That's the assessment of one guy who knows quite a bit about the subject. "He does things guys in their prime do, and he's not even there yet," Lemieux said. "He's got all the tools to be the best player in the world."

Jagr blushes when such compliments are passed along to him. His respect for Lemieux is overwhelming, and he is quick to dismiss the idea that his game might someday reach the rarified level Lemieux occupies. "I would like that," Jagr said. "But I'm not talented like him."

That might be true, because Lemieux is such a singular talent. It also is likely that Jagr will not develop into the complete package that Lemieux has become, because Jagr has not shown any great interest in honing his defensive work, as Lemieux has done in recent seasons. Still, as an offensive force, Jagr has few peers. He has instincts and reflexes that cannot be taught, and those have combined to produce some breathtaking plays during his young career. "There aren't enough adjectives in the vocabulary to keep describing Jaromir's goals," Tocchet said. "They just keep getting better."

Jagr is still maturing on the ice as well as off of it. He remains, in many ways, a raw talent ready to be molded into an even more imposing player than he is today. "He's got a lot of developing to do, and that's probably the most interesting thing about him," Tom Barrasso said. "He could get better for quite a long time."

That is almost certain to happen. The issue is not whether Jagr will improve, but by how much. He is, for the moment, something of a complementary player because of his age and the exceptional talent pool the Penguins have assembled, but when Lemieux retires, Jagr is the leading candidate to succeed him as the cornerstone of the franchise.

It can safely be assumed that the four teams that passed on him in the 1990 draft have second-guessed themselves repeatedly during the past couple of years, wondering why they let a prospect of such quality get away. Oh, there were some sound reasons for skipping over Jagr at the time — no one was certain when he would be able to leave Czechoslovakia or could predict how he would adjust to North American life and hockey — but none of that logic seems very convincing now. It's all too obvious that he is a rare and natural talent of the sort that doesn't become available very often.

"He was born with it," Tocchet said. "It has to be his parents. It's in his genes. The plays he makes, if I try to do something like that, the puck would be cut up four times. It's not something I'm envious of; it's just that I'm a fan of what some guys can do out there. Like when Paul Coffey takes the puck up the ice, I think, 'Geez, how does he skate like that?'

"It's amazing that he (Jagr) was the fifth pick in the draft. That guy's a No. 1 pick anywhere. He's unbelievable . . . I knew he'd be a great player, but I didn't think he'd be this great, this fast. Everybody knew he'd climb the ladder, but he's taking two steps at a time."

CHAPTER FIFTEEN

A Boston Garden Party

Knocking off the Rangers in six games earned the Penguins a four-day break before the start of their Wales Conference final series against the Boston Bruins, and they were glad to have every second of it. New York's aggressive style had left most of the Penguins covered with bumps and bruises, and getting a little time to nurse them was greatly appreciated. "Four days is perfect," defenseman Larry Murphy said. "It gives guys a chance to feel good going into the first game, heal some bumps and bruises, yet we won't have an excuse for being stale."

The Penguins had some serious physical concerns, like Lemieux's broken hand and Bob Errey's separated shoulder, but there were some worries about their mental outlook, too. During the first two rounds of the playoffs, they had faced the teams with the best and second-best records in the league during the regular season, and had been emotionally taxed while getting through both.

So there was a very real danger they would view the Boston series as a breather, not giving Boston sufficient respect, because the Bruins were a young team with a rebuilt lineup and only a few high-impact players, such as defenseman Raymond Bourque and goalie Andy Moog. The Penguins, though, downplayed the possibility they would take Boston lightly. "There's no way we can't get up for the next series," Ulf Samuelsson said. "This is what it's all about."

Bryan Trottier said that if anything, the grueling series against Washington and New York had given the Penguins even more incentive to play well against the Bruins. "We've done what we wanted to do," he said. "Now we grab that, throw it in our hip pocket and say to ourselves, 'The last thing we do is take these guys lightly, because what we've strived for, we've gained.' You don't just throw that down the drain."

Several of the Penguins had an extra measure of motivation to play well against Boston, because they were Massachusetts natives who had grown up as fans of the Bruins. And some had actually taken up the game because of Boston's successful and entertaining teams of the early 1970s. "That's how I got started playing hockey," Tom Barrasso said. "The growth of hockey (around Boston) is traced directly back to them."

The Penguins would be all business when they went to Boston Garden for Games 3 and 4, but thinking about games there stirred memories of a time when attending a Bruins game was a social highlight for them. "It was a big deal if you got tickets to go to a Bruins game," Phil Bourque said. "When I was real little, I used to have to take a nap in the afternoon so I could go to the game that night and get up for school the next day."

And there was no guarantee the Massachusetts-bred Penguins wouldn't have a flashback or two when they stepped into the Garden. "As much as you want to block it out, you're excited when you go in there because it's where my dad took me to watch hockey games when I was a kid," Paul Stanton said. "That's what I thought pro hockey was."

But as the Penguins grew to adulthood, they learned that what pro hockey was really about was winning, especially winning a Stanley Cup. That reality helped them to shove aside any warm feelings they had toward the Bruins, to view them as nothing more than a hurdle separating Pittsburgh from its dream of a Stanley Cup sequel. "I'm not sentimental in any way toward the Boston Bruins anymore," Bourque said. "They're just another obstacle right now."

And, for that matter, not a particularly recognizable one. Cam Neely, Boston's most formidable forward, was recovering from knee surgery, and the Bruins' lineup had been revamped with an infusion of young talent after the Albertville Olympics. This series would give the Penguins their first look at newcomers such as Joe Juneau, Ted Donato and Gord Hynes.

But even if they weren't familiar with all the names in Boston's lineup, the Penguins had a pretty good idea of what to expect from the Bruins. Boston looked to be faster and more skilled than it had been in the Wales Conference final a year earlier, but there was no reason to believe the Bruins' customary work ethic had suffered during the transition. "The names are different," Barrasso said. "But obviously, the results they're achieving are the same, and that's testimony to (general manager) Harry Sinden's leadership and the tradition of having hard-working teams that get the job done."

The Bruins had done an extremely nice job during the second round, sweeping the Montreal Canadiens in four games, and that alerted the Penguins to the dangers of taking a berth in the Stanley Cup final for granted. "I don't care who you play," Stevens said. "To beat a team four games in a row in the playoffs is something. They are a tough, scrappy team, and they've got a lot of young players who are hungry . . . And when you get a bunch of guys like that, you never know what can happen."

Actually, the Penguins knew exactly what could happen. Knew that if they put too much faith in their decided edge in talent and shifted their intensity into neutral, the series would be far more interesting than it had to be. If they took their role as heavy favorites in the series too seriously, they might self-destruct. If nothing else, the first two series had reaffirmed that things do not always go as most people expect them to. If they did, the Penguins would have been well into their vacations by May 17 instead of preparing for Game 1 against the Bruins.

So the Penguins respected Boston, and it was apparent the Bruins were impressed by what they had seen from Pittsburgh to that point in the playoffs. "We saw how Mario carried that team to the Stanley Cup title last year," Moog said. "But to see them beat the New York Rangers without Lemieux and without Joey Mullen really showed how much heart and soul that team has."

The Penguins, as expected, opened the series without Lemieux, who said he was hoping to return by Game 5. But his absence in Game 1 was offset somewhat by that of Bruins defenseman Raymond Bourque, also the victim of a slashing incident during the second round. The blow by Montreal's Shayne Corson that broke the middle finger on Bourque's right hand was less blatant and celebrated than the one Adam Graves had administered to Lemieux, but Bourque's fracture was no less real.

But the Bruins competed quite nicely in Game 1, even with their captain tucked away in the press box for safekeeping. Bryan Trottier gave the Penguins a 1-0 lead at 3:26 of the first period, but Boston got three of the next four goals and had a 3-2 advantage midway through the third period. Shawn McEachern swept in a shot at 12:27 of the third to tie it, and after both teams survived shorthanded situations during the overtime, the spotlight again settled on Jaromir Jagr.

He took a pass from Kjell Samuelsson at center ice and broke down the right side. He sidestepped Bruins defenseman Matt Hervey, then drifted toward the left circle before snapping a shot that eluded Boston goalie Andy Moog after appearing to deflect off Hervey. That gave Jagr three game-winning goals in a row, and the Penguins a 4-3 victory in a game they easily could have lost.

Bowman said the Penguins "were fortunate to have a player who seems to rise above the rest," but Jagr's teammates were quite accustomed to seeing him fill the role of savior. "If anybody on the ice can score, I think you have to put your money on him," McEachern said.

Bruins Coach Rick Bowness absolved Hervey of any major wrongdoing on the decisive play, opting to praise Jagr for an extraordinary effort. "He's a tremendous individual talent," Bowness said. "He's a threat whenever he's on the ice, and he's obviously a threat when he's got the puck coming at you . . . That particular play he made was a tremendous move. Matt played a very sound game; you can't say that was his fault. Give Jagr credit; he's a great player, and that was a great play."

In truth, Jagr's goal was one of the few great plays the Penguins made during Game 1. For all the talk about avoiding a letdown after the Rangers series, the Penguins appeared to have suffered one. Big-time. Bowness said he felt Boston "played well enough to win the hockey game," and Bowman's analysis was simple: "I thought Boston outplayed us . . . quite a bit."

The Bruins had a 41-31 advantage in shots and, aside from the final score, the Penguins had precious little to be happy about as they looked ahead to Game 2. Kjell Samuelsson said "we can't be satisfied with the way we played," and Bowman suggested that the only thing the Penguins did well was to "have enough charms in our pocket to win the game."

"We definitely stole this game," Rick Tocchet said. "But the thing about it is, good teams steal games once in a while." And that kind of thievery is a lot easier to pull off when you have a player like Jagr on the bench, waiting for a chance to see which laws of physics he can ignore, if not rewrite, during the next shift. "Those (Jagr game winners) are dejá vu all over again," Trottier said.

So was a rather unseemly display a few days later by Mike Milbury, Boston's assistant general manager. A year earlier, while coaching the Bruins, Milbury had labeled Bob Johnson — a man who loved the game in its most pure and beautiful form — a "professor of goonism." When that series ended, Milbury acknowledged that his ugly characterization of Johnson had been mere gamesmanship, an attempt to gain some sort of competitive edge.

This time, his words were even more scorching, but they were directed at referee Denis Morel, who worked Game 2. Unlike his caustic comments about Johnson, which had been delivered directly to reporters, Milbury went after Morel in the relative seclusion of a hallway behind the Bruins' locker room at the Civic Arena. Trouble is, several television cameramen waiting to enter the Boston locker room were in perfect position to record much of Milbury's tirade, with sound from virtually all of the sequence and videotape from much of it.

Milbury was upset by Morel's performance in Game 2, but there were a few other issues that should have concerned the Bruins even more. Like how Lemieux had returned to the lineup nearly a week earlier than anticipated and rang up two goals and an assist in the Penguins' 5-2 victory.

Lemieux said he had decided he would be able to play earlier in the day, although his original plan had been to limit himself to a supporting role on the power play. But that quickly gave way to a stint on the penalty-killing unit and a regular shift at even strength. By the end of the night, Lemieux had gotten a fairly normal evening's worth of ice time.

"After a couple of power plays, the hand felt pretty good, and it's tough to play a little bit when you can play a lot," Bowman said. "I think that what happened was he just decided,

'I want to play this game.' We were very fortunate that we had him. There's a risk for anybody that's coming off an injury. He said it's a bigger risk if we don't win our home game and go in there (Boston Garden with the series tied) 1-1."

Lemieux had almost no semblance of a backhand because of his injury, but said he was "surprised that it went that well." And it turned out that he had used one of his shiftiest moves during the game-day skate, when he wore no pads and misled the media about his intentions for the evening. Such deceit, he said, "is part of the game."

But if Lemieux had been able to trick some members of the media, he had been less successful in keeping his intentions secret from the Bruins. Bowness said Boston "heard rumors" that Lemieux would play during the morning of Game 2, and that he wasn't surprised when Lemieux assumed such a prominent role in the game. "Once he got into the flow of the game, he wanted to play," Bowness said. "Great players want to play, and he's a tremendous competitor."

Lemieux's teammates had a pretty good idea that he would be back for Game 2, but even they were surprised by how much — and how well — he played. "He doesn't practice and he comes out and plays," Kevin Stevens said. "That's not something too many guys can do. That's one of a kind."

But then, Lemieux is a pretty special talent. And while the hockey universe has been aware of his skill level for years, his competititve instincts still do not get much recognition outside the Pittsburgh locker room. "He's got a heart as big as the whole room," Troy Loney said. "I think people tend not to see that all the time, but it's there."

Tom Barrasso, however, wondered aloud about the wisdom of allowing a player with Lemieux's value to the franchise to play when his injury was not healed. "I'm a little overly cautious when it comes to putting people at short-term risk," he said. "You're better off making sure he's ready and allowing him to play, hopefully, in the future. If you don't get to the future, well, that's too bad, I guess. It's better to have him at 100 percent than 70."

Still, Lemieux's mere presence on the bench had a powerful impact on the Penguins and was enough to push their play to another level. "He's the most inspiring player in the league,"

Bryan Trottier said. "Whatever effect any other player has on his team when he returns from an injury, Mario does it ten-fold. I'm not taking anything away from Gretzky, but Mario's inspiration is incredible."

The Bruins had little cause for optimism after losing the first two games of the series, but getting Bourque back in Game 2 provided at least a shred of hope. He has been the NHL's dominant defenseman for much of his career, although even he was unable to jump-start a team that did not manage a shot on Barrasso for one 17-minute stretch during the first period. "When we didn't skate, we didn't get our chances," Bowness said. "We've got to get our skating game going."

At least one facet of the Bruins' game was in peak form: Their storied dislike of Ulf Samuelsson. With just over four minutes left in Game 2, Samuelsson charged toward Boston forward Bob Sweeney at center ice, and Sweeney responded by cross-checking him in the face. Samuelsson received a two-minute penalty, and Sweeney a five-minute major, which choked off any chance of Boston overcoming the 4-2 deficit it faced at that point.

Nonetheless, Sweeney insisted that going after Samuelsson was not part of Boston's strategy. "We're not out for revenge on Ulf Samuelsson," he said. "Why waste time on an idiot like that? That's not what we're here for. We're here to win four games."

But maybe the Bruins should have focused on getting their Ulf-bashing beyond the talking stage, because concentrating on winning one game against Pittsburgh—let alone four—just hasn't worked out for them in the playoffs lately. The Penguins beat them four times in a row during the 1991 Wales Conference final after losing Games 1 and 2 in Boston Garden, and would dump them out of the Wales final in four in 1992.

The Penguins, of course, weren't aware that a sweep was imminent when they headed to Boston Garden for Game 3. If anything, they were a bit unsettled by the idea of having a 2-0 lead in the series, since that had not happened to them since their first-round series against the Rangers in 1989. "That's certainly a change for our team, to be up a couple of games," Lemieux said.

Samuelsson had a bodyguard assigned to look out for him while the Penguins were in Boston, but perhaps the extra protection should have been given to Andy Moog, the Bruins goalie. Kevin Stevens recorded a natural hat trick in less than a six-minute span of the first period in Game 3, then closed out the scoring at 14:31 in the third period of Pittsburgh's 5-1 victory. And, because of some brilliant playmaking by Lemieux and Ron Francis, Stevens was never in danger of overexerting himself on any of the goals. "I was in pretty close on all of them," Stevens said. "I guess they were the easiest four goals I ever scored."

And so it was that what had been the Bruins' fondest wish less than a year earlier — Stevens scoring almost at will while playing in his hometown — had dissolved into a nightmarish evening. "He has a sense of smell to move in for the kill," Bruins defenseman Don Sweeney said. "And obviously, he wants to perform, especially here."

The sheer weight of the Penguins' superior talent was coming to bear on the Bruins, and Boston was collapsing under it. Pittsburgh had been concerned about the Bruins' relentless forechecking, but the Penguins' solid all-around game had knocked Boston out of sync and into a rut. "Right now, they're the better team," Bourque said after Game 3. "But we're not doing much to make it any harder for them."

Defenseman Glen Wesley said the Bruins were "very confused" and "not doing the job we're supposed to do," but he did not seem overly impressed by the Penguins. "We're making them a lot better than they should be," he said. "We believe we can play with this hockey club."

Playing with the Penguins was one thing; beating them was quite another. The Bruins were overmatched against the Penguins, and at times even overwhelmed by them. Pittsburgh was thwarting Boston's fearsome forechecking with diligent work by its forwards, and that work was being reflected on the scoreboard.

Many of the Penguins' centers and wingers sometimes act as if the defensive zone is a minefield during the regular season, but their attitude undergoes a serious adjustment when the playoffs begin, and it shows in the plunge in their goals-against average during the postseason. It also was evidenced by the 3-0 lead they had in the series against Boston. "That's the whole key to it, our forwards coming back and picking up a guy," Kjell Samuelsson said.

Boston had controlled play for much of Game 1 by pressuring the Penguins in their own end, but Pittsburgh took control of the series when its forwards focused on playing a two-way game.

And it was Lemieux who set the pace for his teammates. "When you've got somebody like Mario contributing defensively, that leaves little room for anybody else to find an avenue to escape defensive responsibilities," Barrasso said.

It didn't hurt that Barrasso was performing, in Bryan Trottier's words, "like a sheet of plexiglas." A hot goalie is a necessity for any team trying to contend for a championship, and Barrasso had raised his game back to the world-class level he reached the previous spring. "Tommy is playing unbelievably, and the forwards are paying the price in coming back and helping us," defenseman Ulf Samuelsson said. "Boston's forechecking in the first game was so unbelievable that we couldn't get the puck anywhere. Ever since then, our forwards have done a lot better job of holding them up."

And on those rare occasions when the Bruins breached the Pittsburgh defense, they had to contend with Barrasso. Almost invariably, that meant the Bruins skated away, shaking their heads in disbelief and disgust, after Barrasso kicked his save percentage up another notch. A goalie is probably entitled to hazardous-duty pay when he is forced to play behind the Penguins, at least during the regular season, but Barrasso has learned to accept his teammates' offensive style of play. "I wouldn't trade my job with any other goalie in the league," he said. "I love the team I play on."

It's safe to assume that nothing that transpired during Game 4 at Boston Garden had a negative effect on Barrasso's feelings about playing for the Penguins. The outcome of the series had been virtually assured by the Penguins' victory in Game 3, but they dispatched the Bruins to the offseason in a most emphatic way, running up a 4-0 lead en route to a 5-1 victory.

There's nothing particularly surprising about that, considering Pittsburgh had beaten the Bruins in the previous seven playoff games, but the relative ease of the Penguins' victory did not do much for the mood of the sellout crowd of 14,448. Only the most fervent of Boston fans could have believed the Bruins had any chance to salvage a berth in the Stanley Cup final after losing the first three games, and even those fragile hopes were shattered quickly.

Jaromir Jagr gave Pittsburgh a 1-0 lead at 4:51 of the series, and Mario Lemieux notched the eventual game winner at 13:09. It came while the Penguins were shorthanded, and merits a prominent place on his personal highlight film. It might not have been the most spectacular goal of his career, but it certainly deserves a place in the top 10.

Paul Stanton was serving a holding penalty when Lemieux picked off the puck inside the Pittsburgh blue line. He carried the puck through center ice, then put it between the legs of Raymond Bourque — one of the truly outstanding defensemen in recent NHL history and a guaranteed Hall of Famer — and reclaimed it after going around Bourque. He then broke in alone on Andy Moog and snapped a shot over his glove for a goal that clinched Pittsburgh's spot in the Cup final.

It was a timeless example of Lemieux's artistry on ice, of his ability to make the almost-impossible look downright effortless. He had beaten one of the greatest defensemen ever to play the game without breaking stride. Or a sweat. "I told him that when I write my book, that one gets a chapter," Ron Francis said.

The story of the Bruins' season, conversely, was about to end. Stanton and Lemieux scored to make it 4-0, before Steve Leach spoiled Barrasso's shutout bid with a goal at 5:53 of the third period. Dave Michayluk closed out the scoring with his first NHL playoff goal with 11 seconds to play in the game, and the Penguins were on their way back to the championship round. And they were going there on a roll, with seven consecutive victories since their overtime loss to New York in Game 3 of the second round.

Boston was understandably dismayed by the way it had been manhandled — "I thought we had the capabilities to extend them more than we did," Sinden said — but it was clear the Bruins were overmatched against Pittsburgh. Especially when a quiet sense of invincibility was taking root in the Penguins' locker room. "They're a very confident team," Bruins center Adam Oates said. "They're a hell of a good team. I don't mean to undermine them. I just thought we were better than a sweep."

Perhaps the Bruins were. Certainly, Boston had a legitimate claim that it deserved to get more than an overtime loss out of Game 1. But after that — which, not coincidentally, is when Lemieux returned to the lineup — the Bruins could not begin to approach the level the Penguins played at. And they certainly had no one whose impact and ability rivaled that of Lemieux's.

Maybe it would have been a competitive series if he hadn't been able to return from his fractured hand so quickly. Maybe

Boston might even have been able to steal a few victories, build some confidence, and pull off a staggering upset. But such conjecture became moot the instant Lemieux stepped onto the ice for the first time.

"We did a pretty good job against him (in Game 4) and he gets two goals," Bowness said. "He's in a class by himself, no doubt. When he came back in Game 2, we were up 1-0. But when he came into the game, our focus changed almost instantly. It changed to Mario Lemieux."

CHAPTER SIXTEEN

Stanley Goes Home

The Stanley Cup stands 37 inches high. It has a base 18 inches in diameter, and weighs 35.5 pounds. It is the oldest trophy in North American professional sports, as well as the most famous and revered. And it hadn't made more than a perfunctory stop in Chicago since 1961.

That championship drought might not rival the one the New York Rangers have endured, but it had dragged on a few decades longer than the denizens of Chicago Stadium would have liked. And the Blackhawks knew that if there was to be an evening of chugging champagne from the Cup in their immediate future, they would have to do some significant damage control against Mario Lemieux. "He'll tear us apart if we allow him to run loose," Chicago defenseman Steve Smith said.

That wasn't exactly a revelation to Blackhawks right winger Rob Brown, who had been Lemieux's frequent linemate during his tenure with the Penguins. Brown has offensive instincts and skills that complemented Lemieux's, and had extensive first-hand knowledge of the problems Lemieux could cause. "Mario is more talented than Wayne Gretzky because of his size and because he can do it by himself when he has to," Brown said.

Containing Lemieux was shaping up as the focus of Chicago's strategy in the final series. Blackhawks coach Mike Keenan told reporters that, while he wasn't normally given to shadowing opposing players, he felt that Lemieux might warrant such attention. "These aren't normal times, and he's a pretty good player," said Keenan, who added, "Boston didn't lean on him."

Or, more to the point, beat on him. Chicago figured the best way to hold down Lemieux's production would be to keep him on his back, if not on the bench. Nobody would dare to suggest Lemieux couldn't score while prone — anyone who has watched him enough wouldn't rule out anything — but the Blackhawks thought that might be the key to holding his production down to a more mortal level. And they planned to apply similar tactics to Pittsburgh's other big-point men.

"Boston let him (Lemieux) skate blue line to blue line without being touched," said Jeremy Roenick, Chicago's splendid young center. "We have to hit him. I know if we pop guys like Jaromir Jagr and Kevin Stevens, they'll get frustrated and take penalties they shouldn't. I know Stevens hates to be hit. I don't think Pittsburgh has had a very physical playoff. Jagr likes to be fancy. But he can't be fancy with his face in the glass. Keep on hitting Lemieux, and he'll get frustrated, too."

The Penguins were worried about being matched up with the Blackhawks, but it had nothing to do with a fear of body contact. Hockey is a contact sport, often a violent one, so the Penguins knew they would have to cope with varying degrees of hitting in any playoff series. Their lifetime record against Chicago was 30-55-13, and they were 8-33-9 at Chicago Stadium, where the compact ice surface and raucous crowd conspire to unsettle visiting teams with alarming regularity. "They're a very difficult team to play against," Craig Patrick said. "We always have trouble against them."

It wasn't the Penguins' history against Chicago that troubled them most, however. The previous seven playoff series had eased any thoughts that the Penguins were caught up in their struggles of the past. But they were concerned that the Blackhawks entered the final series with an 11-game winning streak — the longest in playoff history — and that Chicago's lineup was laced with some superb players.

There was Roenick, point man for a generation of young U.S.-born stars. Steve Larmer, a magnificent two-way player whose talent level far exceeded his public profile. Chris Chelios and Steve Smith, a pair of stellar defensemen who could hurt you in every literal and figurative sense. And Ed Belfour, the goalie who had run up a 12-1 record as the Blackhawks overwhelmed St. Louis, Detroit, and Edmonton during the first three rounds of the playoffs.

And the Blackhawks had more than an imposing arena and an impressive lineup going for them. Mike Keenan has legions of critics who decry his unyielding style of coaching, but it has been proven repeatedly that he has a knack for extracting every ounce of effort his players have to give. And, for that matter, will settle for nothing less.

That point was not lost on Rick Tocchet, who had played for Keenan in Philadelphia a few years earlier. Keenan wouldn't be the favorite to win a popularity contest inside his team's locker room — he figured to place about fifth if it were a three-man race — but his emphasis on discipline and conditioning had played a key part in the Blackhawks' run to the Cup final. His teams never played fancy hockey, just a solid, defensive style that, if executed well, could cause considerable problems for the Penguins.

"They're a meat-and-potatoes team, a team that's in great shape and is going to work its hardest," Tocchet said. "Mike takes pride in his team being in shape and they're going to work their behinds off. We're going to have to be prepared to work, because those guys are. I can't stress that word enough because Keenan is going to have those guys ready to go."

Tocchet proved to be prophetic, and for a time it looked as if the Blackhawks were prepared to end Game 1 shortly after it began. The Blackhawks set the early pace, and it was a bruising one. Dirk Graham shouldered Lemieux to the ice in the neutral zone 28 seconds after the opening faceoff. Half a minute later, Steve Smith cross-checked Lemieux repeatedly when he ventured behind the Blackhawks' net. Chicago had Lemieux in its cross-hairs, and was bent on keeping him there.

And while the Blackhawks weren't getting worn down from doing all that hitting, there was a chance the Chicago players would be arm-weary by the end of the evening. That was because the Blackhawks were raising them so often in the early going, usually to celebrate goals.

Chelios scored on a power play at 6:34 of the first period with a blast from above the right faceoff dot. Michel Goulet made it 2-0 at 13:17 after Smith forced Jagr to cough up the puck with a crushing check along the left-wing boards. Graham ran the lead to 3-0 by swiping in a loose puck from the bottom of the left circle at 13:43. Phil Bourque got the Penguins back into the game with a power-play goal at 17:26, but the Penguins — and the Civic Arena crowd — were stunned by Chicago's strong start. "We made mistakes, and they capitalized on them," Tom Barrasso said.

And when Brent Sutter came across another flaw in Pittsburgh's defense at 11:36 of the second period, the Blackhawks had a 4-1 lead, and Pittsburgh was confronted by a monumental challenge. The Penguins had to make up a three-goal deficit against one of hockey's top defensive teams — and do it in less than half a game — or face the distressing reality that their home-ice advantage in the series was gone. Gamblers go broke fast when they try to buck the kind of odds Pittsburgh was facing. Even Rick Tocchet would later concede to reporters that "4-1 is almost impossible to come back from."

Even though defeat seemed unavoidable, the Penguins didn't dwell on how hopeless their situation was. Instead, they focused their energies on how to make it better, and they launched a comeback when Tocchet deflected a Paul Stanton shot behind Belfour at 15:24 of the second. That goal didn't exactly get the Penguins back into the game, but at least it slammed the brakes on Chicago's momentum.

The Penguins realized that, against a team as defensively sound as the Blackhawks, they would need some good breaks to get back into the game. And they got one almost too incredible to believe 59 seconds after Tocchet scored, when Lemieux cut Chicago's lead to 4-3.

Lemieux is one of the most natural goal scorers in hockey history, but even he couldn't have anticipated how the play would unfold. He had the puck behind the Chicago goal line, and some basic scientific principles dictated that there was no way Lemieux could get the puck into the Chicago net from that position. Not without help, anyway. And with none of his teammates available to take a pass, Lemieux looked for assistance elsewhere.

He finally decided to strike a working relationship with Belfour; the fact that they had different employers didn't matter for the moment. What happened next was part magic, part mystery, and much Mario. Lemieux banked a shot off Belfour's leg pads and into the net. He had turned an impossible angle into some instant offense, a pretty neat trick for a player of any caliber.

Belfour was understandably upset about allowing the goal or, more to the point, playing a pivotal role in it. "It was a good shot on his part, but my leg should have been out of the way," he said. He was right, of course. Goaltenders don't last long in the league if they make a habit of helping opponents in distress.

But there was more than dumb luck behind that goal. Sure, Belfour could have played the shot better, but only a player with Lemieux's instincts for the game could have scored on such a play. Or, likely would even have tried to manufacture a scoring opportunity when none seemed to exist. "I've scored a couple of goals like that," he said. "I had no angle; I was behind the net. It was a lucky goal."

Timely, too. If Tocchet and Lemieux hadn't scored in the closing minutes of the second period, the Civic Arena might have emptied during the second intermission. Wiping out any lead that the Blackhawks build up is difficult, regardless of how much time is left, and even an offensive strike force like the Penguins would have little hope of making up a three-goal deficit in 20 minutes.

But getting one goal in the third, the one they needed to force an overtime, was hardly out of the realm of possibility. It wouldn't be easy, but at least the odds weren't stacked overwhelmingly against them anymore. "We got those two quick goals," Bowman said. "That got us right back in the game. There was a lot of time left. When you have fellows like Jagr and Lemieux, there's always time left."

But there was precious little of it remaining when Jagr made an indelible impression on the game, the series, and the Blackhawks by scoring a goal that almost defies description. A goal that prompted Mike Keenan to label Lemieux and Jagr "1-A and 1-B" among goal-scoring threats in the hockey world.

Never did the "Mario Jr." anagram fit so well as it did at 15:05 of the third period, when Jagr, in a singular flash of brilliance, tied the game 4-4. Jagr slipped past Chicago's Stephane Matteau just inside the Blackhawks' blue line, and eluded Brent Sutter and Dirk Graham. He then began moving across the ice, from the left circle toward the slot, and weaved past Chicago defenseman Frantisek Kucera. At that point, Shawn McEachern set a pick on the other defenseman, Igor Kravchuk, and Jagr threw a low shot past Belfour.

No less an authority than Lemieux called it, "probably the greatest goal I've ever seen," and even Bowman, who has coached some of the most dynamic players in hockey during the past 25 years, had to grope for words to describe what he had witnessed. "I've seen a lot of goals, but I haven't seen one like that," he said. "It took a great individual effort. That's exactly what we needed at that time."

Of course, the Penguins were getting accustomed to the idea of Jagr coming through for them in key situations by that time. His decisive goal in Game 5 of the New York series had been huge, and he had knocked in three other game-winners along the way. He had scored more key goals by age 20 than most players can expect to produce in a career.

"Anytime he gets it like that, and he's got an inch, he's going to make something happen," Larry Murphy said. "Look at these playoffs, and look at the type of goals he scored. How many players have ever done that? He's pulled us out of so many jams it's not funny . . . Without players like Jaromir and Mario, we have no chance."

Perhaps the only person, at least outside of the Chicago locker room, who was not overwhelmed by Jagr's goal was the guy who scored it. He was glad he had gotten it, to be sure, but wasn't sure he understood exactly what all the fuss was about. "I just want to play my best hockey, and sometimes things like that happen," he said, "Play hard, and good things happen . . . I think I can beat anybody, and anybody can beat me."

But the Blackhawks weren't beaten just yet. Oh, they were reeling somewhat, wondering what had happened to the 4-1 lead that seemed so secure an hour or so earlier. But if Chicago got the next goal, there was a pretty good chance Pittsburgh's inspired comeback would be forgotten, written off as a footnote in the Blackhawks' victory. Whichever team got a 5-4 lead figured to be in for a pretty enjoyable evening. "After Jaromir got that goal, it's just like you're in overtime," Bowman said.

That's precisely where the game seemed to be headed, at least until referee Andy van Hellemond called Larry Murphy for hooking Chicago's Mike Hudson with 2:21 left. That meant the Blackhawks, who had scored on their first power play of the game, would have an extra man until just 21 seconds were left in regulation, unless Chicago scored earlier. And if that happened, the outcome would be all but official the instant the puck crossed the goal line.

"If they score on that power play at some time, the game is theoretically over," Tom Barrasso said. "Your odds of scoring with 20 seconds left aren't real good, so it was important to make that kill."

The Penguins survived Chicago's power play and, with 18 seconds left in the period, the momentum swung sharply in their favor. Lemieux carried the puck into the Chicago end and, as he went toward the net, Steve Smith impeded his progress with his stick. Lemieux went down, Van Hellemond's arm went up, and Smith trudged to the penalty box to serve a hooking penalty. "At the last second, he got his stick on me," Lemieux said. "I actually didn't dive that time."

The Blackhawks had a decidedly different perspective on the play but, because Van Hellemond's opinion was the only one of consequence, the Penguins had a power play for the final 18 seconds of regulation and, if needed, the first 1:42 of overtime.

Suddenly, Pittsburgh was positioned to win a game that seemed totally out of its reach just a short time earlier, and was fully intent on using the man-advantage to end the game early in overtime. "My plan was to get into the dressing room at the end of the third period and have fresh ice for the rest of the power play," Bowman said.

So much for strategy. Bowman and his players were about to head for the locker room, just as he planned, but they wouldn't have to come back out on this night. For with 12.6 seconds left, Lemieux gave his teammates a 5-4 victory and the fans of Pittsburgh a goal that will endure in their memories forever.

The play began with a faceoff to the right of the Chicago net. Ron Francis and Brent Sutter battled to control the puck, and Francis eventually nudged it to Larry Murphy at the right point. Murphy threw a shot toward the net and Belfour kicked it toward the left side of the ice. And right onto Lemieux's stick. A millisecond later, the puck was in the net and the game, save for a last-second flurry by the Blackhawks, was over. The improbable comeback was complete, capped off by one final sweep of the magic wand that is Lemieux's hockey stick.

"I just tried to read the play as well as I could and go to the net," Lemieux said. "It wasn't a set play. Murph just got it on the net and the rebound was there. I went to the net and nobody (from the Blackhawks) was there. Everybody was covered except me."

That was quite an oversight by the Blackhawks. A penalty-killing unit can't always cover everyone from the other team because it is playing with fewer men — that's pretty much the idea behind being penalized — but leaving such a lethal goal scorer unchecked in a situation like the one that produced Lemieux's goal was a ghastly breakdown. And Steve Larmer, one of hockey's finest penalty killers, later took full responsibility for the mistake.

"I got caught drifting," he said. "I was trying to get myself in position so that if Murphy came in and got the puck, he wouldn't be able to pass it to Mario."

Keenan didn't mention Larmer by name after the game, and didn't confine his sharp criticisms to any one player. Instead, he issued a fairly broad indictment of the way his team had handled the entire play. "We gave up a power-play goal in the last minute when our forwards (didn't cover) the most dangerous player in the league," he said. "He was left uncontested to go to the net, and the goaltender deflected the puck on an easy shot out in front of the net."

Their four-goal outburst in the final 25 minutes of regulation allowed the Penguins to become just the second team in Stanley Cup finals history to win a game after trailing 4-1. Montreal managed that feat against the Blackhawks in 1944.

Keenan called it an "atypical exposure of our club to relinquish a three-goal lead" and said that "to give it up was inexcusable." That sentiment was heard a lot in the Chicago locker room, although many of the players showered and left the arena quickly in an effort to duck the mass of media. "We beat ourselves," Belfour said. "When we have a lead like that, we have to play a lot smarter."

The Blackhawks also bemoaned their inability to show a killer instinct, to put the game completely out of Pittsburgh's reach after running up that 4-1 lead. "I suppose if we had gotten a fifth goal, it might have killed them," Brent Sutter said. "It's all hindsight now. It's a tough way to lose, but we have to rebound.

It's only one game; it's not the end of the world. It's going to be a long, hard series."

And the Penguins knew it would be longer and harder than they cared to go through if they continued to spot Chicago big leads. They had dodged a bullet — no, a cruise missile — in Game 1, but understood the folly of expecting to do that with any sort of regularity. "You don't want to give a team like Chicago a two- or three-goal lead," Lemieux said. "You're not going to win too many games. I think we got lucky ... We have to change a few things, that's for sure. We were down three goals, and we feel like we stole that one."

It's true that their victory in Game 1 was viewed in some quarters as grand larceny, but it also was testimony to the Penguins' resilience and will to win. Had they accepted what seemed like an obvious truth — that there was no way to overcome Chicago's 4-1 lead with so little time left — the Blackhawks would have been guaranteed the early advantage in the series. "We never quit," Lemieux said. "We showed that last year. That's why we won the Cup."

Game 1 had given the Penguins a look at the rugged, gritty style they could expect from Chicago throughout the series, but it also reaffirmed that Pittsburgh had a pronounced edge in talent over its opponent. "They check hard, but we have better forwards and better players," Jagr said. "Can score more goals."

Indeed, Chicago relied on a handful of players, particularly Jeremy Roenick and Larmer, to generate much of its offense, and neither had been much of a factor in Game 1. After the game, Keenan spelled out his disappointment in Roenick's performance. "Jeremy didn't play very well," he said. "He wasn't prepared for this game. Hopefully, he'll learn from the experience."

Some observers, apparently not aware of Keenan's brutal candor — he sometimes comes across as an honors graduate of the slash-and-burn school of public relations — were taken aback by his harsh assessment of Roenick's play. But in case anyone doubted him, Keenan repeated his evaluation the next day, albeit not until he had labeled Roenick "the best young player in the game."

"I just told the truth," Keenan said. "Jeremy Roenick played an awful hockey game. Because he didn't have this (Cup finals) experience before, he was uptight and nervous ... It took him about 30 minutes to get going, and you can't have your best player not be at his best for 30 minutes of a playoff game."

Roenick, who entered the series with a team-high 20 points in 14 playoff games, had long since become accustomed to Keenan's caustic outbursts and did not seem especially troubled by this one. Perhaps because he shared his coach's opinion, at least to a degree. "I'd be stupid and selfish to argue with him," Roenick said. "He has to give me a kick in the butt once in a while."

Not surprisingly, Roenick wasn't the only Blackhawk who took a verbal beating from Keenan between Games 1 and 2. Ed Belfour, who had been burned for several soft goals, took an unhealthy share of heat, too. Keenan said Belfour "had a real bad night" in the series-opener, and that Game 2 represented a "big opportunity" for redemption. "Lots of goaltenders have played well in the playoffs, but they've never had that big, big game," Keenan said. "Now, he has to respond."

Belfour offered no excuses for his play in Game 1, nor did he ask that anyone provide one. He agreed that he had performed below expectations and seemed resolved to compensate for any mistakes he had made. "I have to stop more pucks," Belfour said. "This is the playoffs and you have to play your best. They made some good shots (in Game 1), but I also didn't play them as well as I should have."

But the best shots from the early part of the series came from Keenan who, like Scott Bowman, his mentor, has a track record for prodding players with negative reinforcement. In Keenan's case, that often translates to a blistering public analysis of a player's failings. But if the Blackhawks were bothered by the verbal bashings they were subjected to from time to time, it didn't show.

"We'll be fine," Brent Sutter said. "The guys have been through enough to know how Mike reacts (to a loss). Mike's an intense man; every game is a do-or-die situation. He wants to win. There's nothing wrong with that."

"We react better to getting kicked in the rear than we do to being patted on the back," Roenick said. "We respond better to adversity than praise."

And it might be that Keenan's proclivity for fierce criticism is contagious. Steve Larmer, whose blown assignment had made

Lemieux's game-winning goal possible, lambasted his own work in Game 1 with nary an assist from his coach.

"I definitely didn't play with any jump," Larmer said. "It was the anxiety of it, about playing in the finals. For a lot of us, it was our first time. There were a lot of nervous people out there. Some people play a long time and never get a chance to play for the Stanley Cup. A lot of us are looking at it as this might be our only chance."

And it should be mentioned that Keenan can be an equal-opportunity destroyer. While carving up some of his own players for the benefit of the media, Keenan took a broadside blast at Lemieux, accusing him of "diving" to draw the penalty that led to the decisive goal in Game 1. He called Lemieux "an embarrassment to himself, to the game, and to the players he's playing with."

Now, there's never been much evidence that Lemieux's teammates are embarrassed to be associated with him — if so, they have strange ways of showing it — and Keenan's allegation about diving was likely aimed at the officials as much as Lemieux, but there was a measure of risk in assailing Lemieux's integrity at that point in the series. Giving the best player in the world extra, highly personal motivation isn't necessarily a master stroke of strategy.

Lemieux, however, didn't seem interested in contributing to an off-day controversy. When asked how he felt about Keenan's charge, Lemieux said simply, "No comment." After a pause, he smiled and said, "At this point."

One night later, it was the Blackhawks who didn't have much to say. At least not if the subject under discussion was their offense. Chicago managed only 19 shots on goal, just eight in the final two periods, and the Penguins seized a 2-0 lead in the series with a 3-1 victory.

Bob Errey gave Pittsburgh a 1-0 lead with a shorthanded goal at 9:52 of the first period and, shortly after Bryan Marchment tied the game for Chicago midway through the second period, Lemieux threw two pucks behind Belfour. And the Penguins then proved they could withstand the pressure exerted by Chicago's formidable forechecking, as they wrapped Tom Barrasso in a cocoon of sound team defense.

"I give full credit to the Pittsburgh players," Keenan said. "They played exceptional defensively. They never gave us any room after they acquired the lead."

If they were to survive in the series, or even extend it, the Blackhawks knew they had to make some fundamental strategical adjustments. They had been trying to set up their offense by shooting the puck into the Pittsburgh end, then trying to reclaim it, a tactic known as "dump and chase." Trouble is, Barrasso was getting to the puck before the Blackhawks, and it was usually on its way out of the zone before the Chicago players had made their way into it. "We have to play smarter," Blackhawks forward Brian Noonan said.

That much was obvious, but more than a few observers felt the same criticism could rightly be directed at Keenan. Even though the Chicago offense was sputtering in Game 2, he sat his two top scorers, Roenick and Larmer, on the bench for much of the evening, and gave their ice time to tough-guys Mike Peluso and Stu (The Grim Reaper) Grimson.

"Our offensive players gave us very little offensive thrust," Keenan said. "We were trying to wear them (the Penguins) down a little bit, take the body a little more than our skilled players had."

So Keenan, in what was almost universally regarded as a tactical gaffe, effectively neutralized his most menacing scorers. As gifted as Larmer and Roenick are, neither is much of a threat to do serious damage from the far end of the bench. Pittsburgh was baffled by Keenan's move, as were the players most directly affected by it.

"He had his reasons, but I don't know what those reasons are," Roenick told reporters. "I'm not the coach. I'm not going to argue with him . . . I can't say I'm surprised. Nothing he does surprises me anymore . . . It was very frustrating. I knew the position we were in. I feel I was working hard. I was getting good hits. He sat me out three or four shifts, the last eight minutes of the game. But I can't worry about what he's going to do. This is something I have to work through. When you're out there, you have to do the job."

The job of holding down their goals-against average was infinitely easier for the Penguins when they didn't have to contend with Roenick and Larmer. Those two are renowned for their hands, Peluso and Grimson for their fists. Peluso and Grimson might beat you up, but Roenick and Larmer can flat-out beat you. Consequently, it was surprising the Penguins didn't dispatch someone to the Chicago bench to open the gate every time Keenan was preparing to send his enforcers out for another shift.

"We really didn't see that much of Roenick and Larmer," Tocchet said. "Mike was putting Grimson and Peluso out there. I respect those guys; they're tough guys. But a lot of times, they're talking to you, pushing you at the faceoff circle. I mean, you're not going to intimidate guys in the Stanley Cup finals . . . you're not going to intimidate Mario Lemieux . . . Every time we play a team, they say they're going to run the (expletive) out of us. It looks easy from upstairs, but on the ice, it's tough to hit guys like Lemieux and Jagr."

Whether Keenan thought there was a chance the Penguins could be intimidated by a show of muscle isn't clear, but it had long since been apparent that Pittsburgh wouldn't be rattled by physical play. They withstood countless hits, hacks, and high sticks during the New York series, for example, but never showed any signs of being flustered.

"I don't know if they (the Blackhawks) watched the Washington series or the New York series, but it's not going to work," Kevin Stevens said. "They'll probably try to do it more in Chicago, but the more they have those guys (Peluso and Grimson) out there, the more Roenick and Larmer are going to sit, and that's a bonus for us."

While the Blackhawks' top offensive players had been non-factors in the first two games, the Penguins' dominant point producer was scoring at a prolific rate. Lemieux's game-winning goal in Game 2 was his fifth of the playoffs, tying the NHL record shared by Mike Bossy (Islanders, 1983), Jari Kurri (Edmonton, 1987), and Bobby Smith (Minnesota, 1991).

No one expected Lemieux to singlehandedly beat Chicago, but the Blackhawks were in very real jeopardy of being hustled out of the series unless they elevated their level of play. Keenan said Roenick, "as well as the rest of our club, has to get better if we want to be successful in the next game. If we have to rely entirely on Roenick and Larmer, then we're not going to win this series."

Chicago officials added a measure of intrigue to the series when, after returning home, they had Roenick appear at a press briefing with a bulky cast on his right arm. The problem, Roenick said, was a thumb injury caused by slashes from Kevin Stevens and Rick Tocchet during Game 2.

Some skeptics openly questioned whether the severity of Roenick's injury was being overstated, but Keenan was emphatic that the injury was legitimate and that discussing it publicly — hardly a common practice in hockey, where information on even minor injuries is often treated as top-secret stuff — was not a ploy to gain some sort of psychological edge. "Jeremy Roenick is hurt," Keenan said. "He was slashed on the hand. Are you questioning the integrity of our medical staff?"

Chicago seemed to be feeling the pressure of its precarious situation, while the Penguins were justifiably relaxed as they prepared for Game 3 at Chicago Stadium. The worst-case scenario for them would be to lose both games on the road, in which case the series would become a best-of-three, and two of those games would be at the Civic Arena. But they also recognized the dangers of giving the Blackhawks life, of allowing them to claw back into the series.

They also realized they would have to contend with more than just 20 opposing players in Game 3, because of the enormous home-ice advantage provided by Chicago Stadium. The crowd noise has no peer, and the Blackhawks' high-pressure style is designed to get maximum mileage from the rink's undersized ice surface.

The logical approach, the Penguins figured, would be to play a classic road game. That is defense-oriented, blasé hockey, a style that bores all but the most rabid purists into a near-coma. It is the antithesis of the game Pittsburgh prefers, but nobody was worried about personal statistics or satisfaction at this point. Not with the possibility that a second Stanley Cup was only 120 minutes away.

Still, the Penguins allowed Chicago to generate more offense than they would have liked in the first period of Game 3, when the Blackhawks threw 13 shots at Tom Barrasso. Chicago began pressuring him on the first shift of the game and rarely relented until the intermission. "Tommy saved our tails in the first period," Tocchet said.

"We had talked about the quick start they would have," Scott Bowman said. "And that start wasn't what we wanted. We were playing in our own end too much." But the Penguins spent a lot less time there during the final two periods, as they clamped down on the Chicago attack and held it to six shots in the second period, eight in the third. And then there was the most important statistic of the evening: Of the 27 shots Chicago took, none got behind Barrasso.

All of which meant Barrasso had his second career playoff shutout with the Penguins; the first had come in the Cup-clinching game in Minnesota a year earlier. "When he's on top of his game, he's tough to beat," Keenan said, and few would deny Barrasso was at his peak on this night.

"It's pretty easy to play the angles (in Chicago Stadium) because you don't have to move a lot," Barrasso said. "I was able to find the puck for the most part." And to stop all that he saw, and a couple that he didn't.

Barrasso's work no doubt contributed to the Blackhawks' growing frustration — they were watching a dreamy run through the playoffs dissolve into an ordeal of defeat and despair — and it was Penguins defenseman Larry Murphy who paid the most painful price for it.

With 31 seconds left in the third period of Game 3, Chris Chelios turned on Murphy in the Pittsburgh zone and began to pummel him. Chelios didn't do much damage to Murphy, who wisely opted to protect himself instead of fighting back, but he did effectively kill any hopes the Blackhawks had of getting the tying goal.

Referee Don Koharski gave Chelios a five-minute fighting major and 10-minute misconduct — Murphy was not penalized, even though the Blackhawks contended he had initiated the entire incident with a cross-check — and that assured Chicago of being a man short for the rest of regulation. Later, Chelios would say he had assaulted Murphy to bring about a stoppage in play, because he feared Pittsburgh was about to score into the net Belfour had vacated in favor of an extra attacker. He got a whistle, all right, but his team had paid a terrible price for it.

So the Blackhawks had turned in what Keenan called "our best game of the series," but their 1-0 loss had shoved them to the verge of elimination, while Pittsburgh had moved to within 48 hours of another championship.

But the Penguins didn't move so close to a second Cup without the benefit of a considerable measure of luck. They got the only goal of the game at 15:26 of the first period, when a Jim Paek shot caromed off several bodies before hitting Kevin Stevens and skidding past Belfour. "Paek was shooting and I wasn't even looking at it," Stevens said. "It hit my skate and trickled past him (Belfour). It would have gone 10 feet wide otherwise."

The goal was, to be sure, a break of enormous magnitude, but the Penguins insisted it wasn't just an inexplicable stroke of good fortune, some type of cosmic compensation for the decades of bad luck the franchise had been subjected to before 1991. "Luck is where hard work meets opportunity," Barrasso said simply.

No one could accuse the Blackhawks of giving their sweat glands the night off, either. The difference is, Chicago had nothing to show for its efforts except soiled uniforms and second-guesses. "You could say we were a little snakebit," Keenan said. "It's hard to explain how a game could unfold as this one did. There was great, stingy defense by both clubs."

That is to be expected from the Blackhawks, because Keenan-coached teams always have played well in their own end. But it still surprises some to see such outstanding defensive work by the Penguins, who usually end up in the headlines and highlights because of their peerless goal-scoring. "We're not used to that, winning games 1-0," Lemieux said. "But playing good defense is how you win Stanley Cups."

The Penguins prefer run-and-gun hockey during the regular season — that style is tailored to their talent and besides, it's the best way to earn some big bonus money — but they've proven repeatedly they can adjust their game in any way needed. Dump-and-chase, bump-and-grind, whatever, the Penguins have the personnel to pull it off. "It doesn't make a difference to us," Stevens said. "We'll play any way they want to. If they want to run, we'll run. But we can play just as well defensively as any team in hockey."

With security born of the knowledge that the 1942 Toronto Maple Leafs are the only team in NHL history to rally from a 3-0 deficit to win a Stanley Cup final, the Penguins slipped into a laid-back mode during the day between Games 3 and 4. Some players spent the afternoon at Wrigley Field and others went golfing before they got together for a team meal in the early evening.

During a brief session with the media early in the day, the players recited the standard playoff litany about the fourth victory being the most difficult to get, about how Chicago was a quality opponent fully capable of coming back in the series. And Bowman put the situation in mathematical perspective — "We know we have to win four games" — just in case anyone was having trouble working out the championship equation.

The Penguins were still calm and confident when they arrived at the Stadium late in the morning of June 1 for their game-day skate. Any pressure they were feeling was strictly self-imposed, because the burden of extending the series for even two more days fell squarely on Chicago.

And the game began in a chilling manner for the Blackhawks, as Jaromir Jagr beat Belfour from above the right faceoff dot just 1:37 into the first period. But Chicago refused to fold, and Dirk Graham knocked his own rebound behind Barrasso at 6:21 to trigger a furious exchange of goals.

Kevin Stevens made it 2-1 at 6:33 on Pittsburgh's fourth shot of the game, at which point Keenan replaced Belfour with Dominik Hasek, who had not seen game action since April 22. Graham promptly countered at 6:51 with the third goal in a 30-second span. And, after Lemieux gave Pittsburgh a 3-2 lead with a power-play goal at 10:13, Graham became the fifth player in league history to get three goals in one period of a Cup finals game by tucking in a shot at 16:18.

The tight checking of Game 3 had given way to an offensive free for all, and the Penguins were immersed in the type of shootout that is their forte. From Chicago's perspective, it had to be like getting into a border skirmish with a superpower, although the Blackhawks never backed down. Rick Tocchet restored Pittsburgh's lead with a goal 58 seconds into the second period, but Roenick finally snapped his scoring slump at 15:40 by swatting a pass out of midair and past Barrasso to tie the game again.

So there were 20 minutes of regulation time left when the teams headed to their locker rooms for the second intermission. The Penguins believed they were one strong period away from their second Cup, while the Blackhawks understood that nothing less than their season was at stake. The third period, it seemed, would be as much a test of wills as skills.

Lemieux had a chance to put Pittsburgh back in front when Tocchet sent him in on a breakaway at 3:49, but Hasek would not be beaten. Not then, anyway. But at 4:51, Larry Murphy threw a shot past him high on the stick side to make it 5-4. And at 7:59, Ron Francis gave the Penguins their first two-goal advantage of the game when he scored from inside the left faceoff dot during a 2-on-1 break.

The killer instinct had kicked in, and the end of this most grueling season was in sight. Roenick injected a measure of suspense when he picked up another goal at 11:18, but the Blackhawks would not get another puck past Barrasso. And so, after Bryan Trottier blocked a Chris Chelios shot in the waning seconds, the series was over. The Cup was going back to Pittsburgh.

When the game ended, the Penguins players and coaches poured over the boards for an extended round of hugs and handshakes. They had waited a long time for this celebration — there had been plenty of times when it appeared it would never happen — and they wanted to savor what they had accomplished. To remember all that they had overcome to make this moment possible.

The Stadium crowd stood to salute the Blackhawks, who had gathered at their end of the ice. And even after the traditional handshake between the teams was over, and the Blackhawks had gone to their locker room for the final time, the fans stayed. They showed a keen sense of hockey tradition — and no small measure of class — by hanging around to applaud the Penguins as they received the Stanley Cup from NHL President John Ziegler and paraded their trophy around the arena.

Finally, after posing for an informal team picture that nearly had been forgotten, the Penguins headed for their dressing quarters, which was jammed with players, family members, hangers-on, and media. Nearly all of whom were doused with champagne and beer within seconds of entering the room.

The post-game interviews weren't very insightful — hearing a player say, "This is really unbelievable," loses its impact after the 50th or 60th time — but perhaps they weren't supposed to be. This was a time to celebrate, not to be scholarly or analytical. The post-mortems could wait until the party was over, and it was just starting to rock.

The Penguins had become the 16th team to sweep a Cup final series, even though the outcome of nearly every game had been in doubt until the final horn. Three of the four had been decided by one goal, and Chicago's Brent Sutter insisted that "the only game we didn't deserve to win was Game 2." Graham told reporters that "When you don't win when you play your hearts out, all that's left is to give the other team credit."

Keenan said the series "was closer than it looked," but added that Pittsburgh was "more prepared for the ultimate level." And while the Blackhawks were gracious in defeat, some were haunted by demons of doubt, by a feeling that they could have done more to get ready for the most important series many of them ever will play.

"There is a difference (between) expecting something and being fully prepared for it," Stu Grimson said. "I think we expected it (the Cup final) to be as hyped as it was and as stressful as it was. But were we totally prepared for it? Obviously not."

Chicago center Mike Hudson suggested the Blackhawks' confidence was swollen — then shattered — by the events of Game 1, when Pittsburgh had fallen behind by three goals before rallying for a 5-4 victory. "The first game, we jumped out to that (4-1) lead, and we got too complacent," Hudson said. "We said, 'Geez, this is easy. What's going on here? This is going to be a cake walk.' "

Instead, it turned out to be an exploding cake, and it blew up in the Blackhawks' faces. Pittsburgh had entered the series with a big advantage in skill, and that edge was magnified when the Penguins' best players — and quite a few of their lesser luminaries — outplayed their Chicago counterparts by a wide margin.

Predictably, no one played better than Lemieux, who reinforced the increasingly popular idea that he is hockey's premier player. Along with the belief that his memory is almost as impressive as his puckhandling. For even as he was enjoying the Penguins' victory, Lemieux reflected on Keenan's charge that he was an "embarrassment" for diving to draw a penalty in the final minute of Game 1. "I'm just going to go in the locker room and try to dive in the Cup now," Lemieux said, smiling.

Lemieux was voted the Most Valuable Player in the playoffs for the second year in a row. He joined Bernie Parent, goaltender for the Philadelphia Flyers' back-to-back champions of the mid-

1970s, as the only players in history to win the Conn Smythe in consecutive years.

It was difficult to argue with the selection. Lemieux led the playoffs in scoring, despite sitting out six-plus games with a separated shoulder and a broken hand, and he more than doubled the production of Chicago's No. 1 line during the final by himself. Lemieux had five goals and two assists; the Goulet-Roenick-Larmer unit combined for two goals and one assist.

Lemieux was an almost-consensus choice as MVP, but only because he didn't have a vote. If he had been given a chance to fill out a Smythe ballot — a chore given to a panel of Professional Hockey Writers Association members — Lemieux would have penciled in Tom Barrasso as his choice.

"I thought it was Tommy all the way," he said. "I missed six games, and Tommy was superb the last three games against Washington, against the Rangers he was unbelievable, and the same against Boston and in this series. This (Smythe) should have gone to him."

Maybe it was modesty that made Lemieux say that. Maybe he just didn't grasp the magnitude of his own contributions. Or maybe he understood that without the exceptional goaltending Barrasso provided, especially in games when the pressure and stakes were at their highest, this second championship would not have become a reality. "You've got to pick Mario, because he's the best," Rick Tocchet said. "But Tommy Barrasso was right on his heels."

Ron Francis probably got no more than token support, if that, in the Smythe balloting, but that is more testimony to the talents of his teammates than any shortcoming on Francis' part. And it was entirely fitting that Francis scored the Cup-clinching goal, because there probably would have been no championship for Pittsburgh if Francis had not risen to the challenge so brilliantly when Lemieux's hand was broken.

What's more, Francis played the final months of the season on a knee that cried out to be surgically repaired. He injured it February 20 against Quebec and an examination revealed torn cartilage in his right knee, but Francis refused to leave the lineup. The Penguins were fighting the Islanders for a playoff berth at the time, and Francis was too much of a competitor to watch the race for fourth place from the press box.

"We were in a battle with the Islanders, so we said, 'Let's just go ahead and play with it and hopefully it will be all right,' " Francis said. "It was funny, because some nights I didn't notice it at all, and some nights it was popping all the time. I guess it just depended on where that piece of cartilage was inside the knee."

Francis wasn't always sure he would be able to get through the playoffs, but still managed to score more points (27) than anyone except Lemieux and Stevens, and to lead the playoffs in assists, with 19.

"I didn't think it (the knee) was going to make it through the Washington series," Francis said. "It started off all right, then seemed to go downhill. Then it seemed to get better, and the last couple of series it was a struggle every night. But when you're winning hockey games, you don't feel it as much. And when you see the finish line ahead of you, it gives you the incentive to just play through."

But Francis was just one of many players who deserved at least a piece of the Smythe. Guys like Jagr, Stevens, and Barrasso were obvious candidates, but virtually everyone in Pittsburgh's lineup made a significant contribution to the second Cup.

There was Bryan Trottier, who did so many of the little things well that his game added up to a major plus. Ulf Samuelsson who, after running up 35 minutes in penalties during the first four games against Washington, regained his discipline and limited himself to two minor penalties during the rest of the playoffs. Shawn McEachern, the rookie who developed into a force as the playoffs unfolded. Troy Loney, whose sound defensive work was complemented by a handful of timely goals. The complete list of heroes is pretty much synonymous with the Pittsburgh roster.

And for the second time in as many years, a measure of the credit belonged to Craig Patrick. Maybe the Penguins would have been able to win another Cup if he hadn't made the deals that brought Tocchet, Kjell Samuelsson, Ken Wregget, and Jeff Chychrun to Pittsburgh, but it was hard to argue with the results after those trades were made. Tocchet, in particular, had a major impact, playing on the No. 1 line, and adding a physical dimension that had been missing from Pittsburgh's game.

"When we added Tocchet, we became a team that could play more ways," Scott Bowman said. "We gained a tough guy, a top corner man, and a scorer, all at once." Patrick said, "We felt

Tocchet could give us a lot of the offense that we might be giving up (with Mark Recchi and Paul Coffey). He could also give us a physical presence on the ice and better defense."

Which is to say, play the all-around game that is Tocchet's forte. But which, because of circumstances far beyond his control, he wasn't always able to do during his time in Philadelphia. "In Philly, I had to score, or a couple of guys had to score, or we wouldn't win," he said. "Here, they want me to score, but they also want me to play defense, and they want me for leadership, so I'm much more of an all-around player for Pittsburgh. You always hear nightmares about guys getting traded (how) they have to move and it takes them a while to adjust, but it was probably the easiest thing for me. I just fit right in with the guys. That takes a lot of pressure off, when you don't have to worry about outside things."

Another thing the Penguins didn't have to dwell on during the playoffs was their relationship with Bowman. He never got close to his players — no one expected him to — but Bowman was brilliant during the postseason, and the strain that had been apparent during his dealings with players for most of the regular season was gone.

"Scotty had to learn us, and we had to learn Scotty," Trottier said. "He's a lot more open-minded than he was early on. He had a pretty firm mindset when he first came in. Then he realized, and we realized, how we could kind of meet him in the middle."

Maybe all concerned really did reach an acceptable compromise. Or perhaps they just put their differences aside so it wouldn't impede their pursuit of a common objective. Bowman's name was conspicuous by its absence when many players spoke of the people responsible for this championship, but it would be folly to downplay his contribution. Pittsburgh might have less need for a coach than most teams — so many players do so much that simply cannot be taught — but no team can function effectively without quality leadership.

Bowman has won six Stanley Cups, the second-highest total in history, and joined Tom Johnson as the only men to coach a Cup-winner after being inducted to the Hall of Fame. And winning two Cups in as many springs earned the Penguins several other distinctions.

Pittsburgh became the eighth franchise to capture the Cup in consecutive years during the NHL's first 75 years of existence, and the Penguins were the first team to win back-to-back Cups with different coaches since the Montreal Canadiens in 1968-69. Trottier joined Frank Mahovlich, Red Kelly, and Dick Duff as the only players in league history to win multiple Cups with two teams.

Individual honors and another ring were not all that the Penguins had to show for their second championship. They also earned respect and, in some cases, admiration from around the league. They were praised by opponents who had bullied them so frequently just a few years before. Put on a pedestal by the very teams that had tried so hard to knock them off it.

"They've got a collection of great players," Keenan said. "Once they won one championship, they were hungry for another. We were just beaten by a better club. They have youth, experience, and the greatest player in the world."

CHAPTER SEVENTEEN

Dawn of a Dynasty?

June 4, 1992 was a rainy, overcast day in western Pennsylvania. A good day to stay indoors. Or, from the perspective of about 40,000 area residents, a terrific day to troupe to Three Rivers Stadium. Not to watch the teams that call that facility home, the Pirates and the Steelers, but to express their appreciation to the Penguins. One incredible year later, it was another hockey day in Pittsburgh.

The setting for the celebration was different than it had been in 1991, but the emotions were largely the same. Oh, the sense of wonderment the fans had a year earlier might have been missing — the feelings spawned by that first Cup will never be duplicated — but they poured affection over the players as they were driven around the inside perimeter of the Three Rivers seating area. The most raucous applause, predictably, was reserved for Mario Lemieux and Jaromir Jagr.

It was, again, a largely forgettable program, although a few moments stand out. Like Larry Murphy asking the crowd to pose for a group photo, just as he had done in 1991. The difference was, this time he asked them to hold up two fingers. But Bryan Trottier made it a memorable afternoon when, with the strains of Queen's "We Are The Champions" — the anthem of title-winning sports teams — echoing around the stadium, he grabbed the Cup and sprinted across one of the tarpaulins covering the infield. Then slid on his back. Twice.

It was a show of unbridled enthusiasm, of the zeal for the game — and for winning — that allowed Trottier to be a productive and valuable player long after he had passed the normal retirement age for hockey players.

Trottier had been an integral part of the New York Islanders' dynasty, and there was growing talk in the hockey world that he might have been around for the birth of another in Pittsburgh. Two consecutive championships are not enough to earn a team a spot among the game's immortals, but the second was pretty compelling evidence that No. 1 had not been a fluke.

"Last year, everybody looked at us and said, 'Ah, they kind of got lucky.' All the good clubs were upset," Ron Francis said. "We wanted to prove we were a talented hockey club and deserving champions. I don't think anybody can question that this year; we beat some great hockey clubs on the way to the Cup." Kevin Stevens added that "If you win two Stanley Cups in a row, you should go down in history a little bit. It's not an easy thing to do."

Obviously not, since only Philadelphia, Montreal, the New York Islanders and Edmonton have managed it in the past couple of decades. But the Canadiens and Islanders each won four Cups in a row, and the Oilers grabbed five championships in seven years, so it is premature to suggest that the Penguins have reached the level of dominance those teams showed.

"We've got a long way to go before you can include us with the Islanders and the Canadiens and the Oilers, but there's such parity in the National Hockey League that for us to have done this two years in a row — and under the circumstances we've done it — speaks volumes for our players and our commitment to winning," Barrasso said.

Indeed, the scope of what the Penguins accomplished during the 1992 playoffs cannot be appreciated unless it is viewed in the context of what the team endured, dating back to the summer of 1991. "We had a very trying year for a lot of reasons," Craig Patrick said. Almost too many to remember, actually. Bob Johnson's tragic illness. The drawn-out contract disputes with Stevens, Recchi, and Francis. The sale of the franchise, and all the speculation that surrounded it.

"There was more stuff going on than we knew what to do with," Stevens said. And it was the type of stuff, Tom Barrasso said, "that throws a team right down the gutter."

The Penguins never sank quite that far, but there were times when it seemed their season was unraveling. In retrospect, the bleakest point of the season — on the ice, anyway — was probably their 8-4 loss to Hartford at home in late February, when the New York Islanders were poised to take fourth place away from them. Still, while the confidence of nearly everyone in the organization was badly shaken, it was not shattered.

The fact that anyone associated with the Penguins was able to retain even a shred of faith in those dark days of late winter was testimony to the confidence built during their heady run to the Cup in 1991. "I never really thought that everything was coming apart," Bowman said. "I know a team that has won it before has a better chance than one that hasn't."

And it's entirely possible that the adversity that threatened to undermine the Penguins' season actually was a critical component in their ultimate triumph. The Penguins learned to not only deal with tough times, but to react to them in a positive way. They understand that it's more productive to focus on solving a problem than to dwell on the troubles it can create. "Everything we went through earlier this year . . . are all factors that force different individuals to step forward every night," Barrasso said.

And make no mistake, the Penguins have more individuals who can step forward than any other team in the league. No franchise boasts a nucleus of talent more impressive than the one Pittsburgh has with the likes of Lemieux, Stevens, Jagr, Tocchet, and Barrasso. So while parity is rampant in the National Hockey League, and particularly the Patrick Division — the Penguins entered the 1992-93 season justifiably concerned about simply qualifying for the playoffs — Pittsburgh has personnel that should keep it on the short list of championship contenders for at least several more seasons.

"When you look at the great teams, you say, 'Their third line looks as potent as their first line,' and 'They're pretty scary,' " Francis said. "But then you see Mario Lemieux, probably the greatest player in the world, and Kevin Stevens, a super power forward, and Tocchet, and Trottier, with all his experience, and Jagr with all the talent he has, and Mullen and Murphy and Samuelsson . . . you say, 'Yeah, we really do have a heck of a hockey club.' I don't see any reason why we can't continue. A lot of this hockey club is still very young. We feel good about ourselves, we feel confident, and the talent level is there."

The attitude produced by winning two Cups is an asset that is often overlooked, but whose value cannot be overstated. For years, the Penguins' organization was permeated by the belief that no matter how promising a situation appeared to be, it was doomed to turn sour. And almost invariably, it did.

Their outlook has taken a 180-degree turn during the past two years, however. The Penguins have become convinced that no matter how bleak things appear to be, no matter how formidable a hurdle before them might be, they will find a way to overcome it. That confidence was a critical factor when they came back from a 3-1 deficit against Washington during the first round, and played a significant part in their second-round success against the Rangers.

"The biggest thing we have now is the mindset," Troy Loney said. "That's something that only comes with winning." Stevens said that, "We feel like we can win any game, anywhere," that "when we put that equipment on, we feel like we're going to win."

You can't blame the Penguins for being so supremely confident; that attitude has its roots in some pretty impressive numbers. Pittsburgh won its final 11 playoff games, a streak dating to Game 4 of the New York series and tying a single-season record set by Chicago — immediately before the Blackhawks were swept by the Penguins. And the Penguins had a killer instinct too finely honed to ignore: During their championship runs, they were 8-0 in games in which they could eliminate their opponents from the series. When the Penguins got you down, there was no getting back up.

Not, of course, that bygone accomplishments automatically translate to future successes. There are too many volatile variables in sports, too much risk of untimely injuries, too much potential for bad breaks and bounces that can influence the outcome of a season or a series. No team, regardless of its talent and intangibles, ever orders rings until its championship is safely stashed away.

"You have to wait for things to happen, to fall into place," Trottier said. "There are a lot of things that can happen that are beyond this team's control . . . bad calls, bad bounces, injuries. There's always something that can come along and throw a monkey wrench into the whole thing. Fate might give this team a different road to follow."

So might finances. There is no shortage of fervent and free-spending fans in Pittsburgh, but the economic realities of the NHL — where salaries have been soaring and broadcast revenues for most franchises are modest — dictate that teams in smaller markets are going to be faced with the grim prospect of struggling to survive, let alone contending for a championship.

The Penguins can count on drawing a capacity crowd almost every time the Civic Arena doors swing open, but their payroll has been among the highest in the league for several years. And it isn't likely to get any lower in the foreseeable future. In the months following their second Cup, the Penguins were negotiating a contract that would keep Lemieux in Pittsburgh through the end of his playing days. They also signed Barrasso to a five-year deal reportedly worth $6.5 million and were negotiating a seven-figure contract with Jagr.

So while it's no secret that the price of success is high — money emerged as the major snag in talks to convince Scott Bowman to return as coach for the 1992-93 season — management was discovering just how much it would cost to keep the players who had been responsible for the back-to-back championships happy. "We have a high payroll," Howard Baldwin said, "But we have a great team."

Baldwin spoke about the need to minimize the impact of soaring salaries by negotiating "creative" contracts for big-money players, while players near the bottom of the depth chart were being sacrificed to free money that was needed to pay those at the top. Craig Patrick said the Penguins did not intend to keep 50 players under contract — the maximum number allowed by NHL rules — and long-time minor-leaguers such as Jock Callander and Dave Michayluk were not offered contracts, even though they performed commendably during the 1992 playoffs. Decisions on whether to re-sign free agents Joe Mullen, Phil Bourque, Bryan Trottier, and Jay Caufield were difficult and, in some cases, gut-wrenching.

"I seriously hope our owners have the financial means to keep us together to make a legitimate defense of our Cup for the second time," Barrasso said.

At least there seemed to be no short-term danger that the Penguins' nucleus would have to be torn apart for financial reasons, and such a move might prove to be counterproductive, anyway.

With parity rampant in the NHL, the Penguins and every other team needed any competitive edge they could secure. Had Pittsburgh made some money-saving personnel moves around the March 10 trading deadline, for example, the Penguins might not have had the personnel they needed to survive the first round, and that would have cost the owners millions in lost revenues.

"If they can keep our team together, I feel we can win for a long time," Stevens said. "You need luck to win Stanley Cups, but I believe we can win some more."

If the Penguins are to do that, it will be with a lineup at least slightly different than the one they used in 1992. A few weeks after the playoffs, defenseman Gord Roberts signed with Boston as a free agent, and defenseman Peter Taglianetti and goalie Wendell Young were lost to the Tampa Bay Lightning in the expansion draft. Bourque signed with the New York Rangers, and Trottier moved into a front-office job with the New York Islanders. "The potential (for major personnel changes) is definitely there," Troy Loney said. "You can see where something like that might happen."

Still, history has shown that roster changes are not necessarily a precursor to imminent disaster. Few, if any, teams keep their lineup intact from one season to the next. "To be successful as a franchise, you have to keep moving a certain amount of players all the time," Loney said. "Someday, it's going to be me who's going out the door. That's just the way it is. You have to have a certain amount of turnover in order to be competitive."

That shouldn't be a problem in Pittsburgh, at least not in the short term. The days when victories — and respect — were in precious short supply for the Penguins are over. It doesn't look like any 38-point seasons, like the one they had in 1983-84, are imminent. And it will probably be a while before anyone again refers to them as the "Pen-guns," as a Washington-area bus driver identified the team to a Capital Centre security guard a few years back.

No, this team earned a niche in hockey annals during the springs of 1991 and 1992. Its place in hockey history is secure; the only uncertainty is just how large it will be. Winning back-to-back championships is an exceptional feat, but the Penguins are convinced that there might be a couple more Cups in their immediate future.

" 'Dynasty' is a pretty strong word," Lemieux said. "But I like our chances for the next few years." Stevens was even more blunt. "The dynasty," he said, "is here in Pittsburgh."

And so, for two years running, were the Best in the Game.

EPILOGUE

I realized just what the Penguins mean to the people of Pittsburgh, and how great an impact this team has had on the area, when I went to a shopping mall about a week after they won their first Stanley Cup. Little old ladies were coming up to me — I mean, women who were 75 or 80 years old — and these people, who you never dreamed would be involved with hockey, knew everything about it. There had been so much interest generated that it really shocked me. These were the last people in the world you would expect to be so interested, because they had never been around hockey.

But I had realized when I came to Pittsburgh in 1974 that this was a good hockey town, that the people would support it if the team played well. That was apparent during my first season broadcasting Penguins games, 1974-75, which, except for the two Cup years, was probably the most exciting one the franchise has had.

That team still has the franchise record for most points in a season, 89, and it had nine guys who scored over 20 goals. It was Pierre Larouche's rookie season, and the Penguins had "Battleship" Kelly and Steve Durbano; they were tough. It was a good hockey club. Every game was sold out, and I was just overwhelmed by the response, how people got crazy about the Penguins.

But that was the year when the Penguins lost their playoff series to the New York Islanders after winning the first three games, and it wasn't long after that that the team went bankrupt. The owners just pulled the rug. Jack Button, who was the GM in those days, walked in and said, "Effective today, nobody has a job. That's it. You're done." That was after the Internal Revenue Service had padlocked the doors.

I went to San Diego and ended up broadcasting for a soccer team, the San Diego Jaws, then came back to Pittsburgh for the 1976-77 season. But after the owners had gone bankrupt, I just sensed that they were just putting the operation together on a shoestring, and history bears that out. They were trying to win to keep people interested in hockey, and they ended up giving away their future.

The Penguins had mediocre teams in those days. They didn't have great teams, and they didn't have bad ones, but the disappointing thing was that you knew they weren't going anywhere. Even if they upset somebody in the first round of the playoffs, you knew they didn't have enough talent to go all the way. They finally realized they had to change that aspect of it.

And you have to remember that in the late 1970s, they were competing with the Steelers, one of the greatest teams in the history of the game, for the attention of the public. Plus, the Pirates were one of the best baseball teams of the 70s, so the Penguins were definitely down the ladder.

The darkest hours during my time in Pittsburgh came during the 1983-84 season. Not because the team had the worst record in the league, but because it came so close to being sold and moved to Hamilton or wherever. Every day there was talk about where they were going to go and what was going to happen.

But you knew what might be coming if they could survive times like those. Nobody realized how great Mario Lemieux was going to be, of course, but you had to figure things would get better if management stuck to its new plan of building for the future.

Some people think that drafting Lemieux was the turning point for the franchise, but I think it actually came about two years earlier, when the front office decided it wasn't going to mortgage the future for short-term gains anymore. Mario certainly has had a lot to do with the success of the franchise, but I think the decision to look beyond tomorrow, which was made before Mario was drafted, was the key to everything.

Craig Patrick deserves much of the credit for what the Penguins have been able to do. He has provided stability and leadership at the top of the organization, and has pushed the right buttons on some important personnel moves. And people should also remember that Bob Johnson played a huge part in everything the Penguins have accomplished. He was able to win, and do it in a class manner. That carried over to his players, and they learned to hold their heads high and handle things with class, no matter what type of adversity they were facing. The Badger earned a place alongside the other sports legends in this city.

I think the interest in the Penguins that exists in Pittsburgh today has exceeded almost everybody's expectations. Still, I don't think it's quite reached the level the Steelers attained during their glory days, when it seemed like everybody knew everything about each of the players on that team. In their glory days, the Steelers just dominated everything.

The Penguins are probably the most popular team in the city now, but that may be because people like to see winners, and to be associated with champions. I think the same thing would happen with the Steelers if they began contending for championships again.

But I also believe that in 10 or 12 or 15 years, people will talk about guys like Mario Lemieux, Kevin Stevens, and Tom Barrasso the same way they now speak of Terry Bradshaw, Franco Harris, Lynn Swann, and the other great players from the Steelers, and legends such as Roberto Clemente, Bill Mazeroski, and Honus Wagner of the Pirates. These guys have established themselves on that level, and Mario just might be the greatest athlete ever to play in Pittsburgh in any sport.

It's always difficult to predict how a season, or even a playoff series, will go, because so many different things can happen. Even so, I always figured that if I lived long enough, I might see something great happen with this franchise.

No one can ever take away what these players have accomplished during the past two years, no matter what happens in the future. I'm sure they'll tell you that those Stanley Cup rings they've earned are sacred to them, that they mean more than all the money in the world.

With the parity in the league and all the great players and teams in the Patrick Division, the fans in Pittsburgh are going to see some unbelievable hockey for at least the next five or six years. What people have to realize is that for this team to win another Cup, they're going to have to deal with some very tough challenges to accomplish that. You can lose a seven-game playoff series very easily.

That's why people should savor what the Penguins have done. They might win another Cup in 1993, or it might be 20 or 30 years before it happens again. Who knows?

But I also think that the people of Pittsburgh have a lot to do with the success of sports teams here. I believe they're a big part of the reason that no Pittsburgh team has lost a major pro championship since 1927. You see the way the people get involved, the way they put signs in their cars and windows, even the way office workers do things to their buildings to show support, and that's something no other city does. Everybody pulls together, and I'm convinced that has a lot to do with why those teams win.

Seeing the way people who have followed the team for so many years react to what has happened the past couple of seasons is probably the most enjoyable part of these two championships for me. There are a lot of people who spent a lot of dollars to watch the Penguins. They paid their dues, and they've finally been rewarded for it. So "Scratch my back with a Hacksaw!!" I'm just proud to have been a part of it all.

—Mike Lange

KEY DATES IN THE 1991-92 SEASON

1991

August 29 — Bob Johnson, who led the Penguins to the first Stanley Cup in franchise history during his only season as coach, is rushed to Mercy Hospital in Pittsburgh after suffering an apparent stroke while eating dinner. Subsequent tests show Johnson's ailment was caused by brain tumors, which prove to be malignant.

September 6 — Training camp opens at the Civic Arena, but Mark Recchi, Kevin Stevens, and Ron Francis head a list of players who do not report because of contract problems.

September 18 — Recchi, who had been courted heavily by the Philadelphia Flyers, elects to stay in Pittsburgh and signs a four-year deal worth $3.6 million.

September 19 — The Boston Bruins sign Stevens, a Massachusetts native, to an offer sheet that will pay him $5.375 million over five years. The package reportedly includes a hefty signing bonus — $1 million, to be paid in two installments of $500,000 each — designed to discourage Pittsburgh from matching the offer.

September 25 — The Penguins retain Stevens by matching Boston's offer, but general manager Craig Patrick hints the Penguins will consider the possibility of trading Stevens because of his salary.

October 1 — Scott Bowman, the winningest coach in NHL history and Pittsburgh's director of player development and recruitment since 1990, is named to replace Johnson on an interim basis.

October 4 — The Penguins open defense of their Patrick Division championship with a 5-4, come-from-behind victory in Buffalo in the first game of the 1991-92 regular season.

October 6 — The Penguins tie Philadelphia, 2-2, in their home opener, but do not raise their championship banners because Johnson, who has returned to his home in Colorado Springs, is not well enough to attend the game.

October 19 — Banners commemorating the Penguins' Patrick Division, Wales Conference, and Stanley Cup championships are hoisted to the Civic Arena ceiling, but the New York Rangers put a damper on the festivities by beating Pittsburgh, 5-4.

October 25 — Francis, who has missed the first nine games because of contract negotiations, accepts a five-year $4.1 million deal and rejoins the team.

October 29 — Washington crushes the Penguins, 8-0, at the Civic Arena as Capitals goalie Don Beaupre, making his first start of the season after a lengthy contract dispute, stops 26 Pittsburgh shots.

October 31 — The Penguins rebound from their dismal showing against the Capitals with an 8-1 victory against Minnesota in their first meeting since the 1991 Stanley Cup final. The only drawback is that defenseman Paul Stanton suffers ligament damage in his right knee, an injury that forces him from the lineup for 16 games.

November 4 — Several media outlets report that a letter sent by Howard Baldwin, who heads a group negotiating to purchase the franchise from Edward J. DeBartolo, to Paul Martha, the team's general counsel, refers to financing part of the deal by selling some of the team's "assets" — to wit, players — for $7 million. The letter is several months old, and Baldwin insists he has arranged no deals to sell or trade high-priced talent, but the reaction among players, fans and the press is overwhelmingly negative.

November 6 — The NHL Board of Governors tables action on the proposed sale of the franchise, citing concerns about the structure of the deal and saying more time is needed to study it.

November 18 — The governors approve the purchase by Baldwin and his partners, with DeBartolo staying on in a limited role. Details of the Board's vote are not released, but league by-laws require a three-quarters majority to approve such sales.

November 26 — Bob Johnson dies in Colorado Springs, less than three months after being stricken with brain cancer.

November 27 — Johnson is honored in a moving pregame ceremony before the Penguins' 8-4 victory against New Jersey at the Civic Arena.

November 29 — Kevin Stevens has the first four-goal game of his career as the Penguins beat Philadelphia in the Spectrum, 9-3.

December 2 — Pittsburgh players and staff attend a memorial service for Johnson in Colorado Springs. The plane that takes the party to Colorado Springs drops the team off in Edmonton late that evening before returning the office workers to Pittsburgh, where they arrive shortly before 5 a.m. the next day.

December 3 — Right winger Jay Caufield receives an automatic 10-game suspension after leaving the bench and becoming involved in an altercation during a 5-3 loss in Edmonton.

December 12 — Defenseman Ulf Samuelsson undergoes surgery to remove bone chips from his right elbow.

December 23 — Joe Mullen, who got his 800th career point six days earlier, scores four goals during a 6-3 victory on Long Island.

December 26 — Mullen becomes the first player in franchise history to get four goals in consecutive games as the Penguins beat Toronto, 12-1, at the Civic Arena. Pittsburgh ties franchise records for most goals in a game and the largest margin of victory. Larry Murphy joins nine other defensemen in NHL history who have reached the 700-point level in their careers.

December 31 — The Penguins close out the calendar year with a disturbing 7-4 loss to New Jersey on home ice.

1992

January 4 — Mario Lemieux sits out a 3-2 victory against Winnipeg because of back spasms, the start of a streak during which he will miss 10 of 15 games.

January 21 — Team USA forward Shawn McEachern, in Pittsburgh as part of a pre-Olympics tour, signs a multi-year contract with the Penguins.

January 23 — Defenseman Jim Paek undergoes surgery to repair tendon damage in a finger on his left hand, an injury that causes him to sit out 14 games.

January 26 — Jaromir Jagr skates into referee Ron Hoggarth near the Pittsburgh net in the final minute of a 6-4 loss in Washington. After reviewing the incident, league officials suspend Jagr for 10 games. They would be the first games he had missed during his NHL career.

February 5 — Bryan Trottier, the sixth-leading scorer in NHL history, earns his 1,400th career point during a 4-3 loss in Madison Square Garden.

February 19 — The Penguins, staggering through an extended slump, pull the trigger on two major trades. Paul Coffey is sent to Los Angeles for defensemen Jeff Chychrun and Brian Benning, and a first-round draft choice. The Penguins then send Mark Recchi and LA's first-rounder to Philadelphia for right winger Rick Tocchet, defenseman Kjell Samuelsson, goalie Ken Wregget, and a draft choice. Craig Patrick says the trades were made primarily to fortify the Penguins' team defense. Reaction to the deals is mixed in the Penguins' locker room, with some players endorsing the changes, and others saying they might not have been necessary.

February 27 — The Hartford Whalers embarrass the Penguins, 8-4, at the Civic Arena, as Pittsburgh's lead over the fifth-place New York Islanders shrinks to one point.

March 2 — Craig Patrick summons the players to his hotel room in Calgary for a no-holds-barred discussion of why the team has been struggling. The players are told to avoid discussing the session with reporters, but several say Scott Bowman was the main topic of conversation and was the subject of scathing criticism for the way he has been running the team.

March 10 — Patrick makes two trades intended to help the team at some point in the future. Defenseman Bryan Fogarty, once a highly regarded prospect whose development has been retarded by alcohol abuse, is acquired from Quebec for the rights to winger Scott Young, who spent the season in Italy and playing for Team USA, and goalie Frank Pietrangelo is traded to Hartford for a conditional draft choice.

March 14 — Mario Lemieux picks up his 400th career goal, but the Penguins lose in Toronto, 6-3.

March 15 — Rick Tocchet, playing despite having his jaw broken by a Lemieux pass earlier in the game, scores two third-period goals to help the Penguins pull out a 4-3 victory in Chicago.

March 17 — Joe Mullen becomes the first American-born player to score 400 career goals as he beats Edmonton's Bill Ranford in the third period of a 6-5 Penguins victory at the Civic Arena.

March 22 — Lemieux records his 1,000th career point during a 4-3 loss in Detroit. It comes in his 513th NHL game, which means Lemieux has reached that plateau faster than anyone in NHL history except Wayne Gretzky. The historic point is an assist on Kevin Stevens' 50th goal of the season, making it a unique dual achievement.

March 26 — Lemieux reaches yet another milestone, ringing up his 600th career assist during a 7-3 victory over Vancouver.

March 31 — The Penguins run their home-ice winning streak to eight games with a 6-5 victory against Philadelphia. Kevin Stevens sets a record for points by an NHL left winger by chalking up his 122nd, one more than Michel Goulet had in 1983-84.

April 1 — The NHL Players Association, which has been operating without a collective bargaining agreement since September 15, calls the first strike in league history.

April 3 — Defenseman Peter Taglianetti undergoes back surgery to remove the herniated portion of a disc, and does not return to the lineup.

April 10 — The strike ends, as the league and NHLPA agree on a CBA that runs through the 1992-93 season. Pittsburgh personnel, particularly Howard Baldwin, Paul Martha, and Bryan Trottier play a prominent role in the settlement.

April 16 — The Penguins close out the regular season with a 7-1 loss to the New York Rangers at Madison Square Garden. They finish behind New York and Washington in the Patrick Division, despite having a 39-32-6 record that ties them for sixth place in the overall standings. Mario Lemieux sits out the game because of a shoulder injury, but still clinches his third NHL scoring title with 131 points in 64 games.

April 19 — The Penguins open post-season play with a 3-1 loss to Washington at the Capital Centre. Lemieux, still recovering from the shoulder injury he suffered in New Jersey April 13, does not play.

April 23 — Lemieux, who returned to the lineup for Pittsburgh's 6-2 loss in Game 2, gets three goals and three assists to lead the Penguins to a 6-4 victory that slices Washington's advantage in the series to 2-1.

April 25 — Dino Ciccarelli scores four goals as Washington humiliates the Penguins, 7-2, at the Civic Arena and moves to within one victory of a berth in the Patrick Division final.

April 27 — Pittsburgh, seemingly inspired by widespread talk among the press and public that its season is about to end, staves off elimination with a 5-2 victory at the Capital Centre in Game 5.

April 29 — The Penguins fall behind, 4-2, with less than four minutes gone in the second period, but reel off four unanswered goals on home ice to beat Washington, 6-4, and send the series back to the Capital Centre for a decisive seventh game.

May 1 — Pittsburgh becomes the 11th team in playoff history to win a series after trailing 3-1, by limiting the Capitals to 19 shots on goal en route to a 3-1 triumph. Washington Coach Terry Murray singles out Lemieux, who had 17 points in the six games he was healthy enough to play, as the main reason his team was beaten in the series, but Pittsburgh's emphasis on sound defense in the final three games was also a key.

May 5 — The Penguins, holding a 1-0 lead in their second-round series against the New York Rangers, absorb two devastating injuries during the first period of a 4-2 loss at Madison Square Garden. Lemieux has his left hand broken by an Adam Graves slash, and Joe Mullen's left knee is torn apart on a tag-team hit by two New York forwards. Team officials say Lemieux and Mullen, both on the short list of Pittsburgh's most valuable and versatile players, are sidelined indefinitely.

May 7 — New York, now regarded as a prohibitive favorite to capture the series, takes a 2-1 advantage when Kris King scores at 1:29 of overtime for a 6-5 victory at the Civic Arena.

May 9 — Ron Francis completes a hat trick by deflecting a Larry Murphy shot past New York goalie John Vanbiesbrouck at 2:47 of overtime to give Pittsburgh a 5-4 victory in Game 4 and even the series.

May 11 — Jaromir Jagr's goal on a breathtaking individual effort at 14:27 of the third period enables the Penguins to steal a 3-2 victory in Madison Square Garden.

May 13 — Pittsburgh finishes another stunning comeback with a 5-1 victory at the Civic Arena, as Tom Barrasso stops 33 of 34 shots, and Rick Tocchet scores two goals to knock the Rangers out of the playoffs.

May 17 — Jagr salvages a 4-3 victory for the Penguins in Game 1 of their Wales Conference final matchup with Boston by beating Bruins goalie Andy Moog at 9:44 of overtime for his third consecutive game-winning goal.

May 19 — Lemieux, who had missed five-plus games because of his broken hand, returns about a week earlier than expected and has two goals and an assist in Pittsburgh's 5-2 win in Game 2.

May 21 — Kevin Stevens gets four goals, including a natural hat trick in the first period, as Pittsburgh takes total command of the series with a 5-1 victory at Boston Garden.

May 23 — The Penguins advance to the Stanley Cup final against the Chicago Blackhawks by completing their four-game sweep of the Bruins with another 5-1 win in Boston. Dave Michayluk, a career minor-leaguer who had not been in the NHL since the 1982-83 season, closes out the scoring with the first playoff goal of his career.

May 26 — Pittsburgh rallies from a 4-1 deficit midway through Game 1 of the final, as Jagr ties the game at 15:05 of the third period and Lemieux racks up the game-winner on a power play with less than 13 seconds to play in a 5-4 win at the Civic Arena.

May 28 — The Penguins limit Chicago to 19 shots on Barrasso, just four in each of the final two periods, and Lemieux scores two goals en route to a 3-1 victory.

May 30 — Barrasso stops 27 shots for his second career playoff shutout with the Penguins and a Jim Paek shot caroms off Stevens and past Blackhawks goalie Ed Belfour for the only goal Pittsburgh would need in a 1-0 victory at Chicago Stadium.

June 1 — The Stanley Cup heads back to Pittsburgh after the Penguins run off their 11th victory in a row, tying the playoff record set by Chicago during the first three rounds. Ron Francis scores the Cup-clinching goal in Pittsburgh's 6-5 victory at 7:59 of the third period and Mario Lemieux receives the Conn Smythe Trophy as the playoff MVP for the second year in a row, joining ex-Philadelphia goalie Bernie Parent as the only players in league history to manage that feat.

June 4 — The site and the weather are quite different from 1991, but the sentiment is the same. The Penguins' civic celebration is held at Three Rivers Stadium instead of Point State Park and rain, not sunshine, pours from the skies, but a crowd of about 40,000 turns out to honor the Penguins and revel in their latest championship.

KEY DATES FROM THE FRANCHISE'S FIRST QUARTER-CENTURY

June 5, 1967 — Pittsburgh is awarded a National Hockey League expansion franchise. Teams from Los Angeles, St. Louis, Philadelphia, Minnesota, and Oakland, California enter the league at the same time.

October 11, 1967 — The Penguins played their first game, a 2-1 loss to Montreal at the Civic Arena before a crowd of 9,307. Andy Bathgate scores the first goal in franchise history.

October 13, 1967 — Pittsburgh claims its first NHL win, a 3-1 decision in St. Louis.

February 3, 1968 — The Penguins attract the first sellout crowd in their history, as 12,563 fans turn out to watch them play Toronto.

April 1, 1970 — The Penguins lock up a playoff berth for the first time with a 4-1 victory against Chicago that clinches second place in the Western Division.

May 15, 1970 — Michel Briere, coming off a superb rookie season, is fatally injured in an auto accident in his home province of Quebec. He died on April 13, 1971.

Jan 30, 1973 — Left winger Greg Polis becomes the first Penguin to be named MVP of an All-Star Game as he scores two goals for the West Division at Madison Square Garden.

January 22, 1975 — Syl Apps earns MVP honors at the All-Star Game in Montreal.

February 22, 1975 — The Penguins extend their team-record unbeaten streak on home ice to 20 games with a 3-2 win against St. Louis.

April 26, 1975 — The New York Islanders win Game 7 of a second-round playoff series, 1-0, at the Civic Arena to become the second team in NHL history to rally from a 3-0 deficit and win the series.

June 13, 1975 — The Penguins declare bankruptcy. Team offices at the Civic Arena subsequently are padlocked by the Internal Revenue Service.

July 11, 1975 — Wren Blair, Al Savill, and Otto Frenzel buy the franchise.

March 24, 1976 — Jean Pronovost becomes the first player in team history to score 50 goals in a season on the same night Pierre Larouche becomes the first Penguin to hit the 100-point plateau.

April 5, 1978 — Edward J. DeBartolo assumes control of the franchise after having assumed a one-third interest the previous year.

January 3, 1980 — The Penguins move into first place for the first time in history, as a 4-3 victory against the Islanders boosts them into the top spot in the Norris Division.

January 30, 1980 — The Penguins wear black-and-gold uniforms for the first time.

July 1, 1981 — Edward DeBartolo takes control of the Civic Arena.

February 21, 1982 — The Penguins defeat the Islanders, 4-3, to end New York's 15-game winning streak, an NHL record.

March 15, 1983 — General manager Baz Bastien is killed in an auto accident. Coach Ed Johnston is named to succeed him.

June 9, 1984 — Pittsburgh selects Laval Voisins center Mario Lemieux with the first choice in the NHL entry draft.

February 12, 1985 — Lemieux is named MVP in his first All-Star Game after racking up two goals and one assist during the game in Calgary.

April 7, 1985 — Lemieux joins Dale Hawerchuk and Peter Stastny as the only players to get 100 points during their rookie seasons in the NHL.

June 12, 1985 — Lemieux receives the Calder Trophy as the NHL's Rookie of the Year for the 1984-85 season.

February 15, 1986 — Lemieux becomes the first player in franchise history to record 100 or more points in two consecutive seasons.

May 26, 1986 — Lemieux receives the Lester B. Pearson award, which goes to the league's MVP as chosen by members of the NHL Players Association.

February 9, 1988 — Lemieux earns his second All-Star Game MVP award by getting three goals, including the game-winner in overtime, and three assists at the game in St. Louis.

April 14, 1988 — Tony Esposito is named to replace Eddie Johnston as general manager.

June 8, 1988 — Lemieux receives the Hart Trophy as the NHL's Most Valuable Player, making him the first Pittsburgh player to win that award.

April 25, 1989 — Lemieux tied NHL playoff records by getting five goals and eight points in a 10-7 victory.

December 5, 1989 — Craig Patrick is named general manager and coach, replacing Tony Esposito and Gene Ubriaco, respectively.

January 21, 1990 — Lemieux scores four goals and is named MVP of the All-Star Game, played for the first time at the Civic Arena.

February 14, 1990 — Lemieux's 46-game scoring streak, second-longest in NHL history, ends when back problems force him out of a game at Madison Square Garden.

June 12, 1990 — Bob Johnson is named coach, and Scott Bowman is hired as director of player recruitment and development.

July 11, 1990 — Lemieux undergoes surgery to repair a herniated disk in his back, and the procedure is deemed a success. However, an infection later develops and prevents Lemieux from playing for nearly the first four months of the 1990-91 season.

March 26, 1991 — Penguins wrap up the first division championship in franchise history with a 7-4 victory at Detroit.

April 25, 1991 — Penguins earn their first Patrick Division playoff title by winning a best-of-seven series against Washington in five games.

May 11, 1991 — Penguins clinch their first Wales Conference championship by beating Boston in six games.

May 25, 1991 — Penguins claim their first Stanley Cup with an 8-0 victory in Minnesota in Game 6 of the finals.

October 1, 1991 — Scott Bowman is named interim coach to fill in for Bob Johnson, who has brain cancer.

November 18, 1991 — Howard Baldwin, Morris Belzberg, and Thomas V. Ruta purchase franchise from Edward J. DeBartolo.

June 1, 1992 — Penguins complete successful defense of their Stanley Cup by sweeping Chicago in four games, including a 6-5 victory in Game 4 at Chicago Stadium.